BRAZILIAN JIU JITSU MASTERS

Jose M. Fraguas

EMPIRE BOOKS/AWP LLC
Los Angeles, California

BRAZILIAN JIU JITSU MASTERS
JOSE M. FRAGUAS

EMPIRE BOOKS
Los Angeles, California

Disclaimer
Please note that the author and publisher of this book are NOT RESPONSIBLE in any manner whatsoever for any injury that may result from practicing the techniques and/or following the instructions given within. Since the physical activities described herein may be too strenuous in nature for some readers to engage in safely, it is essential that a physician be consulted prior to training.

Published in 2021 by Empire Books/AWP LLC.
Copyright (c) 2021 by Jose M. Fraguas.

All rights reserved. No part of this publication may be reproduced or utilized in any form or by any means, electronic or mechanical, including photocopying, recording, or by any information storage and retrieval system, without prior written permission from Empire Books/AWP LLC.

Library of Congress Cataloging-in-Publication Data

Names: Fraguas, Jose M., author.
Title: Brazilian Jiu Jitsu Masters/ by Jose M. Fraguas.
Description: Los Angeles, California: Empire Books, 2021. | Description based on print version record and CIP data provided by publisher; resource not viewed.
ISBN: 978-1-949753-36-3 (pbk.: alk. paper)

1. Jiu jitsu-brazil-Masters I. Fraguas, Jose M. II. Title GV1114.M339 2020
796.815 '2' 0899103-dc22

2224012553

"Supreme excellence consists of breaking the enemy's resistance without fighting."

- Sun Tzu

Dedication

To the memory of Grandmaster Carlos Gracie, the first member of the Gracie family who trained in the art of Jiu-Jitsu.

To the memory of Grandmaster Helio Gracie, a true pioneer who broke barriers and put himself to test in behalf of his beloved art. His study and sacrifice paved the road for all future generations.

Acknowledgments

Special thanks to the members of the Gracie and Machado family, whose permission to quote and peruse from personal notes has given this text its core and to all the instructors appearing in this work from granting me access to interviewing them.

I want to thank all the students and practitioners around the world whose support and dedication to the art has tremendously helped to promote and popularize the art of Brazilian Jiu-Jitsu.

— Jose M. Fraguas

About the Author

Jose M. Fraguas had his first contact with the martial arts (the grappling art of Judo) at the age of nine. Practicing as a child under Sensei Lee in Madrid, Spain, Fraguas progressed rapidly until he decided to pursue a different but related martial art style. The seeds of contact grappling arts, however, had been planted.

Recognized as an international authority on the martial arts and author of many books on the subject, he began his career as a writer at age 16 by serving as a regular contributor to martial arts magazines in Great Britain, France, Spain, Italy, Germany, Portugal, Holland and Australia. Having hands-on experience and training allowed him to better reflect the physical side of the martial arts in his writing. He started his training in Brazilian Jiu-Jitsu in the late 1980s with several members of the Gracie family.

"I would love to mention the members of the Gracie family and the Machado brothers who spent so many hours in private and group classes sharing their knowledge with me, but I am afraid that crediting them with being responsible for my Jiu-Jitsu skills would make them feel more pain than pride," Fraguas says laughing.

His desire to promote both ancient philosophy and modern thinking provided the motivation for writing this book. "I want to write books so I can learn as well as share." Fraguas continues, "The martial arts are like life itself. Both are filled with experiences that seem quite ordinary at the time and assume a fabled stature only with the passage of the years. I hope this work will be appreciated by future practitioners of the art of Brazilian Jiu-Jitsu."

He currently lives in Los Angeles, California.

Introduction

I've been both lucky and fortunate. Some of my best days were spent interviewing and meeting the jiu-jitsu masters appearing in this book. There is little I enjoy more than "gnawing" on a great interview while time slows and sometimes even seems to stop. Having the opportunity to meet and interview the most relevant and prestigious martial artists of the past four decades is something that every martial artist doesn't have the chance to do. Hopefully, in some small way, this will help make up for that.

Meeting the masters and having long conversations with them that were published in magazines around the world allowed me to do more than simply "scratch the surface" of the technical aspects of their respective styles, but to also research and analyze the human beings behind the teachers. Some of the dialogues and interviews began by simply commenting about the superficial techniques of fighting, and ended up turning into a very uncommon spiritual conversation about the philosophical aspects of the martial arts.

Although they are all very different, considering their respective styles and backgrounds, they all share a common thread of the traditional values such as discipline, respect, positive attitude, dedication, and etiquette.

For more than 35 years I've faced the long odds of interviewing these fighters and martial arts masters, one-on-one, face-to-face, and with no place to run if I asked a stupid question. Many times, it was a real challenge to not just make contact with them, but also how to make the interview interesting enough to bring out the knowledge that resided inside them. In every interview I tried to absorb as much knowledge as I could, ranging from their training methods, to their fighting methods, and to their philosophies about life itself.

Their different origins and cultural backgrounds heavily influenced them but never prevented them from analyzing, researching, or modifying anything that they considered appropriate. They always kept an open mind to improving both their arts and themselves. From a formal philosophical point of view many of them follow the wisdom of Zen and Taoism-others just use common sense.

They devoted themselves to their arts, often in solitude, sometimes to the exclusion of other pursuits most of us take for granted. They worked themselves into extraordinary physical condition and stayed there. They ignored distractions and diversions and brought to their training a great deal of concentration. The best of them got as good as they could possibly get at performing and teaching their chosen art, and the rest of us watched them and, leading our "balanced lives," wondered how good we might have gotten at something had we devoted ourselves to whatever we did as ferociously as these masters embraced their arts. In that respect they bear our dreams.

It would be wonderful to find a single martial artist who combined all the great qualities of these jiujitsu masters and fighters - but that's impossible. That, however, was one of the things that inspired me to write this book. I wanted to preserve some things that were said a long time ago, of which not many people today are aware.

If you read carefully between the lines, you'll see that these men either trained hard to personify their personal idea of what it means to be "the best fighter in the world," or dedicated time and knowledge to create the most devastating martial arts system known to man. Interestingly enough, at the same time they also focused on how to use the martial arts to become better human beings. There are many links that once discovered open a wide spectrum of possibilities, not only to martial arts, but to a better existence as individuals.

The interviews often lasted as long as three or four hours of non-stop talking. I would begin at their school and finish the conversation at a restaurant or coffee shop. A lot of information in these interviews had been never published before and some had to be trimmed either at the master's request or edited to avoid creating senseless misunderstandings later on. It is not the questions that make an interview. An interview is either good or bad depending on the answers given. Considering the masters in this book, I had an easy job. My goal was to make these masters comfortable talking about their life and training-especially those who trained under the founders of original systems. In modern time, there are not many who have had the privilege of living and learning under the legendary founders.

"The masters are gone," many like to say. But as long as we keep their teachings in our heart, they will live forever. To understand the martial arts properly it is necessary to take into account the philosophical and psychological methods as well as the physical techniques. There is a deep distinction between a fighting system and a martial art, and a general feeling in the martial arts community is that the roots of the martial arts have been de-emphasized, neglected, or totally abandoned. Martial arts are not a sport - they are very different. Someone who chooses to devote themselves to a sport such as basketball, tennis, soccer, or football, which is based on youth, strength, and speed chooses to die twice. When you can no longer do a certain sport, due to the lack of any one of those attributes, waking up in the morning without the activity and purpose that has been the center of your day for twenty-five years is spooky. Martial arts can and should be practiced for life. They are not sports, they are a "way of life."

A true martial arts practitioner-like an artist of any other kind-be this a musician, a painter, a writer or an actor, is expressing and leaving part of himself in every piece of his craft. The need for self-inspection and self-realization of "who" he is becomes the reason for a journey in search of that perfect technique, that great melody, that inspiring poetry, that amazing painting or that Academy Award performance. It is this motivation to reach that "impossible dream," that allows a simple individual to become an exceptional "artist" and "master" of his craft.

Many of the greatest teachers of the fighting arts share a commonly misunderstood teaching methodology. They know the words that could be used to pass their personal experience to their students have little or no meaning. They know that to try "self-discovery" in quantitative or empirical terms is a useless task. A great deal of knowledge and wisdom (the ability to use knowledge in a proper and correct way) comes from what is called the "oral traditions," which martial arts, like every other cultural aspect, has. These oral traditions have been always reserved for a certain kind of student and have been considered "secrets." I believe these secrets are such because only few very special students, perspicacious and with a keen sense of introspection, have the minds to attain them. As Alexandra David-Neel wrote: "It is not on the master that the secret depends but on the hearer. Truth learned from others is of no value, the only truth which is effective and of value is self-discovered...the teacher can only guide to the point of discovery." In the end "The only secret is that there is no secret," or as Kato Tokuro, probably the greatest potter of the last century, a great art scholar, and the teacher of Spanish painter and sculptor Pablo Picasso (1881-1973) said: "The sole cause of secrets in craftsmanship is the student's inability to learn!"

As human beings, we are always tempted to follow straight-line logic towards ultimate self-improvement-but the truth is that there are no absolute truths that apply to all. You have to find your own way in life whether it be in the martial arts, in business, or in cherry picking. Whatever path you pursue, you have to distill your personal truths to what is right for you, according to your own life. The quest for perfection is actually quite imperfect and is not in tune with either human nature or human experience. To

have any hope of attaining even a single perfection, you have to concentrate on a single pursuit and direct all your energies towards it. In this sense, perfection comes from appreciating your endeavors for their own sake-not to impress anyone-but for your own inner satisfaction and sense of accomplishment.

Martial arts are a large part of my life and I draw inspiration from them, both spiritually and philosophically. I really don't know the "how" or the "why" of their affect on me, but I feel their influence in even my most mundane activities. It's not a complex thing where I have to look deep into myself to find their influence. All human beings have sources or principles that keep them grounded, and martial arts is mine. I believe that is when the term "way of life" becomes real. In bushido, the self-discipline required to pursue mastery is more important than mastery itself-the struggle is more important than the reward. A common thread throughout the lives of all the masters is their constant struggle towards self-mastery. They realized that life is an ongoing process, and once you achieve all your goals you are as good as dead. But this process is not all driven by action. Often the greatest action is inaction, and the hardest voice to hear is the sound of your inner voice. You need to sit alone and collect your thoughts, free from all forms of technology and distraction, and just think. It is perhaps the only way to achieve mental and spiritual clarity.

I don't believe that great books are meant to be read fast. I've always thought that really good writing is timeless, and that time spent reading doesn't detract anything from your life, but rather adds to it. So take your time. Approach the reading of this book with either the Zen "beginner's mind" or "empty cup" mentality and let the words of these great jiu-jitsu teachers help you to grow not only as a martial artist but as a human being as well.

Contents

ANTONIO SCHEMBRI 1

CARLOS "CAIQUE" ELIAS 9

CARLEY GRACIE 17

CARLOS GRACIE JR. 25

CARLSON GRACIE 35

CLEBER LUCIANO 41

FABIO GURGEL 47

FABIO SANTOS 55

HELIO GRACIE 61

HELIO "SONECA" MOREIRA 73

JEAN JACQUES MACHADO 83

LEO VIEIRA 91

LUIS HEREDIA 101

MARCIO FEITOSA 109

NELSON MONTEIRO 115

PAULO GILLOBEL 123

RALEK GRACIE 129

RELSON GRACIE 135

RENATO MAGNO 141

RICKSON GRACIE 149

RIGAN MACHADO 163

RODRIGO MEDEIROS 171

ROYCE GRACIE 179

RORION GRACIE 193

ROYLER GRACIE 203

VITOR BELFORT 211

WALLID ISMAEL 221

WANDER BRAGA 229

GERSON SANGINITTO 237

PEDRO SAUER 243

CARLOS VALENTE 249

ANDRE GALVAO 257

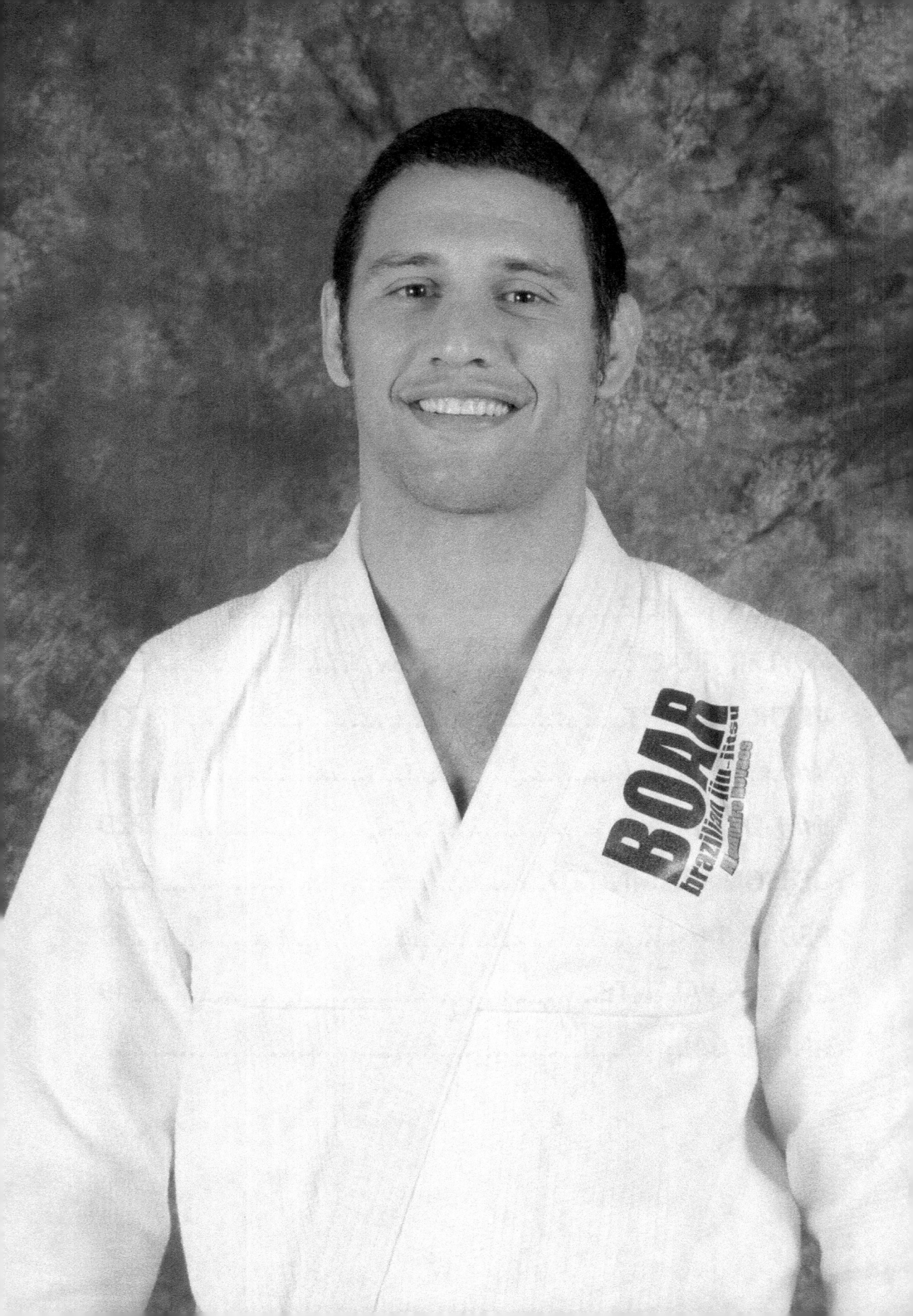

Antonio "Nino" Schembri

The One and Only

IT'S AUGUST 16, 2000, AND NINO "ELVIS" SCHEMBRI IS ON A PLANE TO THE U.S. TO ATTEND RICKSON GRACIE'S SECOND INTERNATIONAL TOURNAMENT. AS THE PLANE STREAKS THROUGH THE SKY, HALFWAY ACROSS SOUTH AMERICA, WITH NEARLY EVERYONE ONBOARD SLUMBERING, NINO PROWLS THE AISLES, FINALLY STOPPING BESIDE THE SEAT WHERE MARTIAL ARTS WRITER KID PELIGRO SLEEPS. HOLDING A GLASS OF CHABLIS IN ONE HAND, NINO PRODS PELIGRO WITH THE OTHER. KID AWAKES GROGGILY AND LOOKS UP. "I JUST WANTED TO LET YOU KNOW THAT TODAY IS THURSDAY," NINO SAYS QUIETLY, RAISING HIS UNTOUCHED GLASS OF WINE IN A TOAST. "ELVIS PRESLEY DIED 23 YEARS AGO ON THIS VERY DAY. I JUST THOUGHT IT WAS IMPORTANT THAT YOU KNOW." WITHOUT ANOTHER WORD, NINO WALKS SOMBERLY AWAY.

A RIDDLE WRAPPED IN A MYSTERY INSIDE AN ENIGMA, NINO SCHEMBRI WALKS TO BEAT OF A DIFFERENT DRUMMER. WITH HIS EVER-PRESENT SIDEBURNS, WHICH HE WEARS AS A TRIBUTE TO "THE KING OF ROCK AND ROLL," SCHEMBRI IS ONE OF MIXED MARTIAL ARTS MOST EASILY RECOGNIZABLE FIGURES. NINO'S EVERYDAY PATH IN LIFE IS THE ROAD LESS TRAVELED, AND EVERY FORK HE TAKES IS USUALLY A DIRECTION NOT CHOSEN BY ANYONE ELSE.

BUT NINO'S GOOD-NATURED ORIGINALITY DOESN'T OBSCURE THAT FACT THAT HE IS ONE OF THE TOP SPORT JIU-JITSU COMPETITORS IN THE WORLD WHO IS ALSO 3-0 IN MIXED MARTIAL ARTS. HE ESTABLISHED HIMSELF AS AN INTERNATIONAL STAR WITH A KO WIN OVER JAPANESE SUPERSTAR KAZUSHI SAKURABA IN PRIDE. BUT TO NINO, JIU-JITSU IS NOT ONLY ABOUT FIGHTING, IT IS FAR MORE THAN THAT. IT IS PHILOSOPHY, PRINCIPLE, POWER AND STRENGTH – IT IS HISTORY AND ART – IT IS LIFE ITSELF.

Q: How long have you been practicing jiu-jitsu?

A: I started with Sylvio Behring when I was 6 years old, and I trained for one year under his supervision. I came back at 13 to train with Jorge Pereira, who was the instructor at my condominium in Nova Ipanema at Barra da Tijuca. When I was 17 years old and a blue belt, I went to Gracie Barra to train with Carlos Gracie Jr. and Renzo Gracie. It was then my career in sport jiu-jitsu really started. I have been very fortunate to have received instruction from excellent teachers who were great human beings, too. All together, I've been training for a long time.

Besides Brazilian jiu-jitsu I have also been training in boxing, karate, and muay Thai. These are very good fighting systems and I think they complement jiu-jitsu very well. I never felt that adding them to my fighting arsenal would take anything away from my jiu-jitsu. Definitely my main art is jiu-jitsu and everything else I do revolves around it. Unfortunately, I have seen great jiu-jitsu fighters train kickboxing for a few years and then go into a fight and forget all about jiu-jitsu and just punch and kick! It is hard for me to believe that. If your base if jiu-jitsu then learn other arts to complement what you have, but don't be so naïve as to try and beat an experienced kickboxer when you have only trained stand-up for a few years. If you're a grappler, then stick to what you know best and make everything else work around it.

Q: Were you aggressive as a child?

A: Not so much. When I was 7 and only a yellow belt, Sylvio and Marcelo Behring took me and my brother to fight in our first tournament. When we got there, I got extremely nervous and would not leave my parent's side for a second. My brother fought and won, but that wasn't enough to give me the courage to fight. While waiting for them to call my name, I grew even more nervous and started clinging to my father's legs. I was so frightened that my father just couldn't bring himself to force me to fight. I still remember how relieved I was when I ended-up not having to fight. Who would have thought that eventually I would become one of the most active jiu-jitsu sports competitors and compete in mixed martial arts as well.

The lesson this taught me is that we all have fear and insecurities, but it is up to us to overcome that fear and try our best. I was frozen with fear and after that day I had to learn to deal with my fear and insecurities on the jiu-jitsu mat. Long hours of hard training brought me confidence and self-esteem, and I used those qualities to go forward in my competition career. The only thing that can beat fear is the confidence gained from experience.

Q: Were you a natural at jiu-jitsu?

A: I think I can honestly say that jiu-jitsu was a very good physical fit for me, since my natural ability lies in my flexibility and strength. Of course,

I have also worked very hard to achieve, maintain, and create effective techniques. You can have all the natural talent in the world but if you don't cultivate them then they are worthless. I have studied and still do all the basic jiu-jitsu positions, trying to adapt them and find new ways of moving from one position to another. I try to be creative and the only way I can do that is by keeping an open mind. I love to look at other competitors and grapplers and study what they do. The knowledge is out there for all of us to take. I do think that my exceptional flexibility helps my game flow more naturally. I have better control and awareness of my overall body mechanics with less effort than many other fighters.

To develop your own game you have to find what really works for you based on your physical characteristics. I have great flexibility and I use it to get the most possible benefits from certain techniques. Other people shouldn't necessarily try to copy my same exact movements because there are movements that one person can do and others can't. Find out how your own body moves – what your strong and weak points are – and then develop a game that works specifically for you.

Q: Is your jiu-jitsu game constantly evolving?

A: Nowadays, my personal game has more power and subtle techniques than in the past. I constantly create new techniques in order to always surprise my opponents. But don't misunderstand my words – I'm not saying that everybody should go out and create their own advanced techniques. That's stupid. You need many years of hard training and experience in the basics before you can really understand what works for you. It takes years to find that out. Sometimes you may think that a certain technique doesn't work for you and not work hard to learn it, but all what you are doing is justifying your own mental limitations – your mind is limiting your body. You need to work hard for many years before you can truly say that a certain technique is not good for you. At that point you'll have the understanding to develop and create your own movements. My personal game is a reflection of Brazilian jiu-jitsu in general – it is always growing and always being perfected.

Q: What is the most important quality for a new jiu-jitsu student to have?

A: My main advice is to have discipline and to follow the advice of the experienced teachers. There are experienced martial artists with a great deal of knowledge and it is up to new students to listen and learn from them. That way they save time and avoid making the same mistakes their teachers made. The young always think they know everything, but 20 years later they will realize that they simply didn't know anything when they started! I know because I've been there myself! For instance, new students always want to learn several new techniques every single day. They don't want to spend endless hours repeating the basic techniques because that's boring. In a few years, though, they'll realize that working hard on the basics is the secret to becoming a true champion and a great instructor.

Q: Is it necessary to fight MMA matches to achieve good self-defense skills?

A: I don't think a martial artist should ever use street fights to train themselves. Use martial arts for your own well-being and personal advancement. The satisfaction of overcoming your own weaknesses and expanding your physical ability will be enough to lead to confidence in the ring and self-defense skills on the street. I don't agree with the idea of going out to bars and parties and looking for fights. If you do that the only thing you show is your stupidity. Many people get into fights because they are insecure and deep down inside need to prove something to themselves. They have some kind of issues going on. A professional fighter does fight – but he does it in the ring with proper rules and respect for his opponent, not in the street. Martial artists who need to fight in the street only degrade their technical ability and show their immaturity.

Q: What motivated you to train for so many years?

A: My motivation comes from the fact that I need to keep learning because I think that no one knows it all – not even Professor Helio Gracie, the creator of Brazilian jiu-jitsu. Look at him, he still trains and is still learning in his 90s! The person who practices jiu-jitsu or any other martial art needs to be humble enough to keep learning. Professor Helio is an example of a true martial artist – he is humble, he keeps teaching and training, and is always open to evaluate and analyze any new movement or technique.

Q: How do you prepare yourself before a fight?

A: To get myself ready mentally, I listen to Elvis Presley backstage. He was a pioneer and broke many barriers in the music world. He set the pace and opened the doors for what Rock and Roll is today. One of the most important things a man can achieve is to leave a legacy and create or write something that in 200 years people will still talk about. That's why musicians, writers, artists and filmmakers are truly the building blocks of all cultures and societies. That is why I have so much respect for Elvis Presley and why I get so much inspiration from him.

On the physical side, I try to loosen up by doing a lot of stretching exercises. Those two things keep me at peace inside and prepare me to deal with the outside world. We all need to find those things that bring us peace and tranquility. Only then can we face the challenges of daily life. It is that way with martial arts. Jiu-jitsu is not something that you can leave at the academy – you need to take it hone with you, feel it, and then go back to the school to make it grow inside of you.

Q: Who has been you biggest inspirations?

A: Elvis Presley and Renzo Gracie are both great inspirations to me. I never met the King of Rock and Roll, but I was fortunate enough to meet Renzo Gracie and learn many things from him. These two men have been examples and inspirations to me.

Q: What are the most important qualities of a successful fighter?

A: I think that it is the sum of many things, however, discipline and humility are fundamental. If a fighter thinks that all he has to do is train, he is definitely wrong. He needs to keep an open mind and be aware that he doesn't know everything and needs to keep learning. Some fighters keep repeating what they know and they don't realize that the fighting game has changed and new techniques are being developed. You can get caught in a new technique simply because you think that you know everything there is to know. I have seen this to happen many times in sport jiu-jitsu competitions; someone develops a new choking technique, for instance, and chokes several of his opponents with it. Of course, the only way to prevent this from happening again is to study the new technique and find efficient ways to avoid and counter it.

A jiu-jitsu champion thoroughly knows the rules of the competition. He has a lot of genuine competitive experience, is in excellent physical condition, demonstrates superior attitude and character, is an expert at controlling his opponent's tempo and timing, and can change his game relative to the strengths and weakness of his adversary. All these qualities are developed through a dedicated training program that requires years of sacrifice and work. Championship performance comes only from the champion himself. A thousand perfect lessons cannot guarantee improvement. Winning is not found by who you learn from in the academy, but rather in the heart of the fighter who brings dedication and intelligence to a realistic and complete program.

> **"Cross-training is necessary if you want to become a professional fighter. Look at the sport today – athletes are bigger, stronger and better conditioned than ever."**

Q: Do you think fighters should cross-train or just do jiu-jitsu?

A: Cross-training is necessary if you want to become a professional fighter. Look at the sport today – athletes are bigger, stronger and better conditioned than ever. In the past, martial arts techniques were the only thing we really cared about, but today you need to have technical skill, good nutrition, proper rest, solid cardiovascular endurance, a regular weight training program, and a stretching routine specifically designed for mixed martial arts. You need to supplement and support your pure jiu-jitsu training with any other aspects that will make you better and stronger. In sport jiu-jitsu there are various weight classes that in some ways limit the differences between the fighters. But the classes are fairly broad and sometimes you can be at the bottom range of your weight class and your opponent at the top. You also might be fighting up a class. So you need that extra edge. Then you need to combine your fight training with nutritional habits and enough hours of rest. You body needs these two as much as it needs the hard physical training.

Q: You have developed a personal training system, would you describe it?

A: First of all, I am a very disciplined athlete and I maintain a rigorous training routine. My daily practice is comprised of Brazilian jiu-jitsu, muay Thai and boxing. I also supplement my technical workout with strength exercises done with elastic rubbers, which effectively prevents the injuries usually related to weight training. I also spend time maintaining my flexibility, which for me is a very important aspect of my jiu-jitsu game.

Q: How can a fighter control fear and nervousness in the ring?

A: When someone starts to feel too much fear in training or competition, that means that they are not controlling themselves mentally. To reach the mental level required for successful competition you have to learn to rely on your mind to defeat that weakening fear. Fear is not a bad thing if you know how to use it to your benefit. You need to use it as a spark to start the fire inside. Unfortunately, many people get frozen, as I did when I was a kid, and can't get out there and perform. In the very end, defeating that fear inside of you is a reflection of what you are going to do in the other aspects of your daily life.

> **"The true meaning of the practice of jiu-jitsu is having respect for yourself and others. Respect for your training partners creates the friendly and unique environment in the world of Brazilian jiu-jitsu that everyone loves."**

As human beings we have many fears about a lot of different things in life and we have to learn how to not be frozen by it. Defeating fear is a result of facing that fear head-on, again and again, as you do on the jiu-jitsu mat every day. If you run away from fear or give into it, then you will always be a slave to it. So don't run. Stand tall. Even if it is hard for you. You might not conquer it the first time or even the fiftieth time, but the important thing is to mentally resist and struggle against it. Over a period of time, if you resist your fear again and again, you will finally get used to it and then eventually conquer it. That is how the human brain works. The main thing is to face it.

Q: You beat Kazushi Sakuraba in Pride 25 in a very tough fight. How do you remember that?

A: Before the fight some people said, "Sakuraba was not that good anymore. He is not the same fighter he once was." Well, I didn't believe that. He has had some injuries lately but he is still a great fighter and he turned out to be one of the toughest opponents I have ever faced. His kickboxing skills are first rate, even compared to K-1 kickboxers. And when you go to the ground he has a really good defense. He is not that good in submissions, but he knows how to defend against them. He is a very calm and strategic fighter and doesn't lose his head in the ring. Of course, once in a while he does crazy things and the audience goes wild. That's why people love to see him fight, because of the excitement he produces. But when you do crazy things, instead of focusing on your opponent and finishing a fight, you run the risk of eventually getting caught – and that's what happened in our fight. He landed a really good hand to my face and broke my nose. I started bleeding but that didn't bring me down. But then he relaxed and that gave me an opening. I came back up and landed a hard knee to his face and knocked him down. He was caught totally by surprise. Sakuraba didn't know that Elvis was a karate black belt. He thought that because I had a broken nose everything was over. But he was wrong.

Q: What are your plans for the future?

A: Keep doing more of the same – teaching and competing in jiu-jitsu, and fighting in MMA events whenever I get a good offer. I try to stay calm and relaxed and to balance all my opportunities in life. I don't want rush into anything, because when you rush you always end up crashing.

Q: What does jiu-jitsu mean to you?

A: The true meaning of the practice of jiu-jitsu is having respect for yourself and others. Respect for your training partners creates the friendly and unique environment in the world of Brazilian jiu-jitsu that everyone loves. The practice of jiu-jitsu in our daily lives and gives us energy and also fresh approach to things. I truly believe that by incorporating a physical discipline such as jiu-jitsu into our lives, we can balance and improve our overall existence.

CARLOS "CAIQUE" ELIAS

The Possible Dream

RELATIVELY LITTLE HAS BEEN WRITTEN ABOUT THIS MAN KNOWN SIMPLY AS "CAIQUE"- BUT ANYONE WHO SPENDS ANY AMOUNT OF TIME RESEARCHING THE GRAPPLING ARTS KNOWS THAT HE IS ONE OF THE TOP BRAZILIAN JIU-JITSU INSTRUCTORS IN THE UNITED STATES.

A DIRECT STUDENT OF RELSON AND RICKSON GRACIE, CARLOS "CAIQUE" ELIAS' EXPERTISE AND KNOWLEDGE OF THE TECHNICAL ASPECTS OF JIU-JITSU ARE SECOND TO NONE. MANY YEARS OF HARD TRAINING AND COMPETITION AGAINST THE WORLD'S ELITE HAVE PROVIDED HIM WITH AN IMMENSE UNDERSTANDING OF THE COMPLETE GROUND GAME. WHEN HE MOVES, IT IS WITH PRECISION AND DIRECTION; ALL HIS ENERGY FOCUSED TOWARD THE END RESULT - TO SUBMIT HIS OPPONENT USING THE "GENTLE" PERSUASION OF JIU-JITSU.

BUT JIU-JITSU TO CAIQUE ISN'T ALL ABOUT CHOKES AND LOCKS; IT IS ABOUT RELATIONSHIPS, FRIENDSHIPS AND STRONG BONDS WITH HIS STUDENTS. OUT OF ALL THE MARTIAL ARTS INSTRUCTORS IN NORTH AMERICA, CAIQUE IS ONE OF THE MOST REVERED AND RESPECTED BY THOSE HE TEACHES. HOLDING NOTHING BACK, CAIQUE HAS NO "HIDDEN" OR "SECRET" TECHNIQUES-WHEN A STUDENT IS READY TO LEARN, HE TEACHES. AND THIS TEACHING EXTENDS TO LIFE AS WELL AS TO THE DEVASTATING ART OF JIU-JITSU. CURRENTLY LIVING AND TEACHING IN SOUTHERN CALIFORNIA, CAIQUE TEACHES HIS STUDENTS WITH THE SAME PATIENCE AND DEDICATION THAT HE USED TO BECOME A CHAMPION IN HIS NATIVE BRAZIL.

"THE KEY," SAYS CAIQUE, "IS TO BALANCE EVERY SINGLE ELEMENT IN YOUR TRAINING SO THAT ONE ASPECT WILL HELP THE OTHERS. YOU DON'T WANT TO BE UNBALANCED IN JIU-JITSU. REMEMBER THAT THE SECRET IS BALANCE, NOT ONLY IN MARTIAL ARTS BUT IN LIFE AS WELL. TO BE SUCCESSFUL YOU HAVE TO HAVE GOALS AND WORK IN THAT DIRECTION. YOU HAVE TO TRAIN HARD AND SMART - OTHERWISE EVERYTHING YOU WANT WILL JUST BE A DREAM. A GOAL IS AN IMPOSSIBLE DREAM IF YOU DON'T TAKE THE NECESSARY STEPS TO MAKE IT HAPPEN."

Q: How did you begin your martial arts training?

A: I began my training in judo. My teacher taught the art in a very street-fighting oriented format. It was not sport judo but a self-defense approach. He really emphasized the street element. Then I started jiu-jitsu with Relson Gracie and also trained extensively with Rickson Gracie. They are the two people I should mention here. They not only gave me an extensive amount of technical knowledge but also spent a lot of time educating me in the different aspects of jiu-jitsu. The training was tough. It was not as easy as these days but I remember the atmosphere. One of the most important things that you take with you in the martial arts journey is the atmosphere of the places where you train. In the long run, the techniques are important, but the environment and the memories of the other students stay with you forever. I have many memories that have stayed with me. I remember once, a very famous black belt came to the school and he sparred with me-I was a purple belt at that time. He literally run over me; it wasn't him making me tap, not at all, he ran over me. Grandmaster Helio Gracie was there and in the end he called Rickson. Rickson talked to his father and said, "This is the last time he does that to you. From now on you are going to make him tap every single time." Under his tutelage I made that guy tap every single time after that night. I became one of Rickson's top students for many years.

Q: Is it important to specialize in a few techniques or have a wide repertoire?

A: Everybody boils down to what you are looking for in your martial arts training. If you decide to compete then you need to have a wide understanding of many techniques, although not necessarily to use them all. You need to know them and understand the way they work so you can counter them with your specialties-that is the key. You may have five or six special moves, but it doesn't mean these five or six techniques are the only thing you know. However, you must know many different ways of using your special moves or pretty soon all your opponents will know how to stop you before you even think about trying. You need to have a variety of ways to apply your submission techniques and keep your opponent guessing what's going to be next. You must have a complete game and develop an understanding of the advantageous positions and how to get into them-because regardless of the instructor's approach, the principles and concepts involved in maintaining and escaping from each of the main positions are universal.

Q: Why do you think people are attracted to jiu-jitsu?

A: It is very interesting to see how the interest of the so-called "gentle" art has emerged. I think that we can look at this from two different points of view. First, jiu-jitsu has always been a self-defense system, not a sport. As a self-defense method the practitioner has to rely on those techniques that do not require a lot of strength and physical power to be effective. The overall idea is to allow the student to train as hard as possible without getting injured, while still maintaining the effectiveness necessary to defend himself on the street. But that's not the reason why people today are training in Brazilian jiu-jitsu. People today are interested in jiu-jitsu because of the UFC and the need to complete their martial arts training with knowledge about how to deal with aggression on the ground. That's the main reason.

Today jiu-jitsu is both a self-defense art and a sport. Brazilian jiu-jitsu meets both those requirements. It is not a martial arts system that hides behind a veil of mysticism, but instead deals with the realities of combat with no exaggerated claims. A lot of martial artist from other styles realized that their arts were lacking ground strategies and techniques that could be very valuable in a real situation. Therefore, they came to Brazilian jiu-jitsu to get this knowledge. I think is great when people have no fear in learning something that is valuable and can make them better.

> "It's important to understand that the main self-defense methods are very dangerous. This is not only applies to jiu-jitsu but to other arts such as karate or kung-fu."

Q: How does jiu-jitsu apply to MMA?

A: MMA is a completely different game than a real fight. In an MMA fight, weight counts for a lot and the environment is totally different. MMA is a sport and not a real fight-you use different kinds of techniques because of the nature of the sport and concern for the safety for the fighters. It's about winning a trophy and not about self-defense. You have to train specifically for that because the individual in front of you knows how to fight, how to counter your movements, and how to create an opening to apply his techniques. This creates a completely different situation. You have to prepare for this kind of event in a very specific way.

Q: How different from MMA is sport jiu-jitsu?

A: It's important to understand that the main self-defense methods are very dangerous. This is not only applies to jiu-jitsu but to other arts such as karate or kung-fu. People do not always get involved in martial arts because of self-defense. Even if self-defense was the main reason for them to initially train, one day they will enjoy just doing it just for the fun and satisfaction, and not because of the self-preservation aspect. Then the sport element becomes more relevant. People like to train and compete in a more relaxed atmosphere than is encountered in a real streetfight. The simple fact that the training makes them feel at peace with themselves is what really counts at the end of the day. Historically speaking, the original self-defense techniques of jiu-jitsu were extremely dangerous and could not be executed during normal training sessions. So in times of peace the sport aspects took over from the self-defense methods needed during times of war.

Q: How effective, then, is modern Brazilian jiu-jitsu for self-defense?

A: For self-defense purposes you have to evaluate what is really happening in a streetfight, and then choose the style or method that will deal with the circumstances. Jiu-jitsu is expressed in the way the techniques are executed, not in the effect these techniques have upon the opponent. You may decide to control the aggressor by neutralizing him, or you might decide to take it a step further and immobilize him, or even put him into submission hold. It's up to you to decide the degree of pain you'll inflict on the opponent. For instance, you can throw your opponent to the ground and he will be hurt. Or you can decide to control the throw and immobilize him with an arm lock on the floor after the throw has been applied. You may even decide to apply more pressure and break the arm. There are different degrees of execution. In contrast to jiu-jitsu, if you strike to your opponent's body-such as a kick to the groin-that's going to hurt regardless of the power behind the technique. If you attack the eyes, it will hurt the same whether it is done soft or hard. It's almost impossible to calculate the damage with punches and kicks, especially under the stress of a real fight. And legally you can be accountable for that. I have seen a lot of people mixing different styles of martial arts-but that is very difficult. It is one thing to take elements from other methods to make what you are already doing better, and it is another thing to mix styles thinking that you are going to become better. My opinion is that mixing styles confuses the student and puts them in a very difficult situation if they face a real self-defense situation.

Q: Why are there so many similarities between Japanese judo and Brazilian jiu-jitsu?

A: Just do a little research into the history of both arts and you'll find out. Nobody can deny the historical facts. Judo is a direct descendent of the traditional Japanese jiu-jitsu systems, so there are bound to be some similarities. Personally, I believe the changes that Jigoro Kano made to jiu-jitsu, when he turned it into judo, left judo with only a surface similarity to the original art. Judo became a sport and its inclusion into the Olympic Games definitely pushed the art in a new direction. Today judo is not Japanese anymore, but belongs to the world. Soccer, for example, was created by the British but today is an international sport. We don't call it "British soccer," but simply "soccer."

Today, "Brazilian jiu-jitsu" is the term used to describe a certain style of jiu-jitsu that is not Japanese-and I think this is good because not all the jiu-jitsu styles are the same. Like in karate, you have different styles such as shito-ryu, shotokan, goju-ryu, and more. So it's important to know what kind of karate or jiu-jitsu you are practicing. It's like being knowledgeable about your family tree - you'd better know what your last name is.

Q: Do you think the rules used in sport competition condition the way the instructors teach Brazilian jiu-jitsu?

A: I would like to say no, but the truth is that due to the emphasis on sport competition, the real answer is yes. For instance, if you know that a certain technique only gives you one point and another will score three, it's logical that you'll place more emphasis on those techniques that will result in a bigger amount of points. That's the game and you have to play it. As an instructor, though, I recommend training in every single aspect equally. Keep balance in your training. As a competitor, there is nothing wrong with focusing on a few chosen techniques as long as you know how to switch and react under other circumstances with the appropriate technique. By that, I mean that if you have to protect yourself in a real encounter don't try to use the techniques that you use in a competition-they may not work and might put you in a very difficult situation. There is nothing wrong with the sport aspect of jiu-jitsu; just keep in mind that it is only a sport and not a real self-defense situation. If you do that, you'll be perfectly fine.

> **"If your main goal is just to protect yourself, then develop a very strong base with the fundamental techniques and don't go crazy trying to learn 1,000 different techniques."**

Q: Do you think it is important to continually evolve jiu-jitsu techniques?

A: I think evolution is important in everything in life, not only in jiu-jitsu. If you only train a little bit for self-defense then there are hundreds of movements that you don't need to know - basically because you only need a very direct and simple approach for self-protection. But if you are training and competing in sport jiu-jitsu, that's another story. Competition is what raises the level of any sport - be it basketball, jiu-jitsu, karate, or football. The need to get better and improve is what makes athletes look for new techniques and approaches. This raises the bar of any sportive activity. NBA basketball is not the same as it was 20 years ago, and it will definitely be different 20 years from now. The same is true with jiu-jitsu; if you win a world champion and don't compete for three or four years you can bet that you won't win. Why? Because the evolution of the sport has created a totally new environment, and the techniques that were current years ago will be obsolete now, All Brazilian jiu-jitsu practitioners are developing new techniques all the time, and if you are not aware of this then you won't be winning. It's that simple. If your main goal is just to protect yourself, then develop a very strong base with the fundamental techniques and don't go crazy trying to learn 1,000 different techniques. Stick to the basics because is out of the basic techniques that any new maneuver will come.

Q: So for self-defense, simpler is better?

A: Yes. I see many practitioners that spend a great amount of time and energy trying to learn the latest techniques developed by the top fighters and don't pay attention to the basics. The only reason why these top fighters can pull off these new moves is because of the great technical foundation they have already. Every practitioner needs to evaluate their training and know where they are going and what they really need to work on. There are many important elements that a practitioner has to develop before they get into a more complex technical approach.

Q: What are the most important basic elements of jiu-jitsu?

A: There are many: body position, leverage, body feel, the ability to read the opponent's intent at the very early stages of the physical movement, breath control while executing the technique, and more. All these elements are basics you need to have before taking your game to a higher level. If you are not aware of these things, and you try to play the advanced games, then you are just wasting your time. Sorry to say that, but that's the truth. Unfortunately, there are many practitioners these days who pay too much attention to the advanced techniques when they should be working on the basics.

Q: What kind of supplementary physical training do you recommend?

A: Jiu-jitsu is jiu-jitsu. What I mean by that is that if you have a limited amount of time to train, then put as much time as you can into developing your technique. Forget about anything else. Jiu-jitsu should be your main goal. Then after you have a reached a certain level of technical skill you can do some other activities to supplement your jiu-jitsu. I recommend running, swimming, yoga and some kind of resistance and strength training. If you get involved in weight training just do it as a supplementary activity and don't get make the mistake of developing huge muscles. The more muscle you have, the more limited your joint range-of-motion is. Try to strike a balance between muscle mass and the flexibility needed to perform jiu-jitsu techniques. For a martial artist, a supple body is more important than a bodybuilder physique. Try to stretch every day. The key is to balance every single element in your training so that one aspect will help the others. You don't want to be unbalanced in jiu-jitsu. Remember that the secret is balance, not only in martial arts but in life as well. To be successful you have to have goals and work in that direction. You have to train hard and smart-otherwise everything you want will just be a dream. A goal is an impossible dream if you don't take the necessary steps to make it happen.

> "The truth is that if you are happy practicing a particular style, then that is the best style for you"

Q: Is any style better than the rest?

A: The truth is that if you are happy practicing a particular style, then that is the best style for you. Period. We should respect the fact that people train martial arts for different reasons and in the end it is the person who makes the style work. Respect for other styles is very important-even if you don't agree with their approach to combat you should respect them and not criticize them. Without respect there is nothing. Respect is a problem we all face in our lives. Instructors of all styles and systems should strive to preserve the ethics and traditions that the martial arts were based on.

Q: Is anything today's martial arts lack?

A: I would like to see more respect between practitioners. In the Japanese arts you have the "do" element which his brings philosophy, ethics, morality, and honesty into the practitioner's life. In Brazilian jiu-jitsu we don't have that aspect. Unfortunately, people just stick to the physical training and forget all the other important elements such as respect, courtesy, and proper attitude. Whether you win or lose, you have to control your emotions and act in a decent way. You don't have to bow, but it doesn't mean you shouldn't respect you opponent or that you don't have to graciously acknowledge his superiority if you lose. Behave yourself in a proper way at all times, regardless of the situation. I think that all the practitioners of the more combat-oriented systems should look deep into the philosophy of the more classical martial arts and adopt their moral aspects. These elements will only make us a more well-rounded individuals. The "art" within the martial arts means the ability to practice self-control and to think within yourself. No matter how difficult a situation is, or how bad it may appear to be, you have the power to control yourself. Martial arts is not only about winning a championship or beating someone up, but rather about making friends and developing good relationships with everybody. That's the real meaning of the martial arts.

Q: What do you think is necessary to take Brazilian jiu-jitsu to the next level?

A: I believe we need to be more organized. We need to get together because the number of practitioners is very large, but for some reason we are all divided. It would be great to see a unity between European, American, Japanese and Brazilian organizations. That unity would change the direction of the sport. I guess it is very difficult, but if we really want to take the sport to the next level, that's the only way it will occur. I hope it will happen someday because it would be great for everybody in the art.

CARLEY GRACIE

The Brazilian Lion

ARLEY GRACIE, A MEMBER OF THE FAMOUS BRAZILIAN JIU-JITSU FAMILY, KNOWS SOMETHING ABOUT THE REALITIES OF UNRESTRAINED PHYSICAL COMBAT. CARLEY IS THE ELEVENTH CHILD OF BRAZILIAN JIU-JITSU LEGEND CARLOS GRACIE, AND WAS BORN AND REARED IN THE FAMILY TRADITION OF DEDICATED JIU-JITSU TRAINING AND CHALLENGE MATCHES. CARLEY WAS THE FIRST PROFESSIONAL NATIONAL CHAMPION IN BRAZIL AFTER THE JIU-JITSU FEDERATION WAS ORGANIZED IN RIO DE JANEIRO, REIGNING FOR FOUR YEARS (1969 THROUGH 1972) BEFORE COMING TO THE UNITED STATES TO TEACH THE UNIQUE GRACIE STYLE OF JIU-JITSU TO U.S. MARINES. HE WAS THE LAST GRACIE FIGHTER WHO ACTUALLY LEARNED FROM AND WAS PERSONALLY COACHED BY HIS LEGENDARY FATHER CARLOS..

BRAZILIAN JIU JITSU MASTERS

Q: Carley, there have been somewhat varying accounts on the origins of the Gracie family art of jiu-jitsu. Could you give us your insight on how it all began?

A: Everyone admits that our system started with my father, Carlos Gracie, in Brazil. My father originally learned jiu-jitsu from Conte Maeda Koma, a former Japanese and world champion who was visiting Brazil to help settle Japanese immigrants in the north. My father was only 17 years old when he first began studying under Conte Koma, and he opened his first Academy in Belèm (Northern Brazil) approximately four years later. The stories about my uncle Helio Gracie being the founder of our style are simply not correct; my uncle Helio was only about nine years old when my father started teaching jiu-jitsu.

My grandfather Gastão Gracie had nine children: five sons and four daughters. My father Carlos was the oldest. After my father opened his first Academy, he began teaching jiu-jitsu to his brothers Jorge, Osvaldo, and Gastão. Later he also taught my uncle Helio, who was the youngest brother and last to learn.

During this same time period, my father Carlos also established an open challenge. He used these fights to refine traditional jiu-jitsu techniques and develop the Gracie style. My father quickly became famous because of his small physical stature and the fact that he could overpower opponents of much greater size. My father and his brothers spread this powerful martial art all over Brazil and it's been proven since that time. Today our Gracie style is still undefeated against other martial arts.

My father Carlos was the first great fighter of the Gracie family. In addition to jiu-jitsu, he enjoyed boxing and was the Brazilian boxing champion. In the 1920's and 1930's he fought both Brazilians and foreigners. One of the most famous fights was against the Japanese jiu-jitsu champion, Giomori. The fact that my father was able to tie with Giomori, even though Giomori was much larger and heavier than my father, brought tremendous recognition to the Gracie style of fighting.

After my father retired from the ring, he continued the family tradition in his role as patriarch, brain and leader of the Gracie family. My father arranged all the fights and decided which of his brothers would fight against which challenger. Nobody fought without my father's permission. My father also acted as trainer and coach for his four brothers, constantly developing refinements and new techniques to make the system better and guiding each of his brothers as to which techniques would be most effective against each opponent. My father Carlos was constantly concerned with maintaining the good reputation of the family and the Gracie system of fighting in Brazil.

Q: Can you describe your own background and training in the arts?

A: I was born into a family of fighters. We were raised in a enormous house with 28 bedrooms and there were always many brother, cousins and students of the family around, practicing their jiu-jitsu, so I naturally learned how to approach a "fight" early. My father had 21 children and every one of them (even the girls) was trained in the Gracie style of jiu-jitsu. Even before any formal training started, the boys started to fight and practice with one another at home. The atmosphere was friendly but very competitive; if you didn't want to get beaten constantly, you had to learn how to fight well and defend yourself. It was the family way.

In formal jiu-jitsu training, my background is different than my brothers and cousins. My father began saying I would be a champion when I was very young, but because of my love for horses, I chose to stay at our country home (in the mountains above Rio) as long as possible. I did not begin my formal jiu-jitsu training until much later than the rest of the family.

> "When I began my fighting career, the champion was determined by consensus and acknowledgment, based on matches that were conducted by the martial arts schools."

By the time I came to Rio for my formal jiu-jitsu training, my father was coaching only my brother Carlson, who was at that time the champion of Brazil; teaching at the Academy was done by students that my father had trained over the years. However, unlike my cousins and the other brothers of my age group, I never studied under my Uncle Helio; I received my training directly from my father, Carlos Gracie, and my oldest brother, Carlson, who was also Brazilian champion for many years. Carlson's school has always been known for producing the toughest fighters in Brazil.

I am known to be one of the most technical fighters in the family. This is partly because of my personality and dedication to jiu-jitsu, and partly because of the many hours I spent with my father and Carlson when they worked on fight techniques while Carlson was national champion.

Q: You mentioned earlier that you were Brazilian professional national champion from 1969 to 1972. When you say "national champion," how was that determined?

A: When I began my fighting career, the champion was determined by consensus and acknowledgment, based on matches that were conducted by the martial arts schools. There were championship fights that received coverage in the newspapers, magazines and TV throughout the country. During my time, these championship matches were held approximately every three months. Yes, it was many years ago in the mountains of Rio where my father had a country home where the entire family got together on weekends and holiday times. My father made a competition between people from the city and the people of the local town. I remember that I won that first competition – although that's just about as far back as I can remember. There was never any doubt about who was the champion when I was competing because no one could defeat me. I was still the reigning champion in 1972 when I came to the United States.

Q: Do you fear anyone in competition?

A: When it comes to a fight, there is no opponent whom I fear. My whole training has been to prepare me for the ring or the streets. Even though I have something of a disadvantage with my age and I no longer compete or train for competition, my extensive knowledge and the techniques that are now instinctive give me a tremendous advantage and the confidence that come with knowing I have the advantage.

Q: How did they go about selecting fighters for the championships?

A: The Gracies were always leaders in the martial arts, but every school sent their best representative to these matches. Originally, the Gracies got together with other schools to organize the matches and select the names of the fighters who wanted to compete. Later, after the Jiu-Jitsu Federation of Rio was formed in 1967, the Federation took an active role in organizing these matches.

Q: What rules were these championships fought under?

A: We fought two ways: with the kimono on and with the kimono off. When we wore the gi, we were not allowed to punch and kick. In some of the championship matches, we took off the gi tops, and then we were allowed to punch and kick in full-contact fighting. I fought and was champion under both conditions.

Q: How did you win most of your fights?

A: Usually on the ground, but it depends on the style of the opponent and the type of fight (with or without the kimono). For example, there are chokes you can use at the same time someone is trying to throw you; with judo practitioners, I could often finish the fight standing up by completing my choke before my opponent could throw me. But most of the time we went to the ground and I finished the fight there, especially if my opponent was a tough fighter.

Q: Are there any fighters you can remember who particularly gave you trouble?

A: Actually, the fighters who challenged me the most were two of my own brothers. Outside of my family, the toughest fighter I encountered was named Sergio Ines. He was originally trained by Barradas (who had been one of my father's top students). Barradas sent Sergio to fight me because he was the best in his area at that time. Later, Sergio continued to train and fight under my brother Carlson. Of course, there were many other fighters who trained hoping to overpower me, but none ever succeeded.

When a person holds the title of national champion, all the schools send someone to try and defeat him. It's just like in the old West; when a man is fast with the gun, all the young men want to challenge him. There were also matches with other family members. Fights within the family were private, and were usually held on Sundays, when the Academy was closed. I remember one of my relatives who were constantly training in the hopes of beating me. Each time he lost, he would go back and train for another six or eight months and then try again. This went on for years, but he never even came close.

Q: Did you fight against opponents of other styles in open competition?

A: Yes I did. I have sparred and fought matches with men who were very tough fighters or champions in their own styles, but their options are limited when they come up against the Gracie style. Once I close the distance and get them in a clinch, I simply put them on the ground and finish the fight.

Q: The Gracie system is often perceived to be principally a ground fighting art. Do you agree?

A: No. What's happened is that most of the other styles are weak in ground fighting techniques, so that's what students coming from other styles are most interested in learning. As a result, some of the Gracie members teaching in the United States have been focusing mostly on ground techniques. However, the style developed by my father, Carlos Gracie, actually places equal emphasis on standing techniques because we feel it's very important for a fighter to be well-rounded. While it's true that most fights wind up on the ground, they don't have to. As I mentioned earlier, the Gracie system has chokes and arm-locks that can be used to finish a fight in a standing position. There is no reason to go to the ground if you can finish the fight standing up. This is particularly important in street fighting and self-defense, because you are less vulnerable to a second attacker and can leave the scene much more quickly if you are already on your feet.

Q: Why do you think your father's system of jiu-jitsu has become so effective?

A: I think it's because of the development which my father made from the art he was taught. He constantly sought out matches against people trained in other styles of martial arts, and used that experience to help him to adapt and modify the classical techniques he learned so that they became more effective. Efficiency was also important, because my father was small in stature and looked ore like a scholar than a fighter. We use leverage and balance to overcome physically stronger opponents and our style make a point to deal with differences in size, weight and build. When I train, I like to take on people who are much heavier or stronger than I am, or who are skilled in other styles, but I have years of experience and training to use against them.

Q: The Gracie challenge has been the subject of some controversy. How did it get started?

A: The Gracie challenge started with my father Carlos Gracie in the early 1920's. When my father first started teaching jiu-jitsu, people questioned his ability as a fighter because he was small and not very muscular. There were fighters from other styles, such as Greco-Roman wrestlers, who looked much more powerful. My father fought with these other stylists to prove the superiority of his style of jiu-jitsu. He was so successful as a fighter that he began to have trouble finding opponents; no one wanted to lose. That's where the challenge came in. Eventually, my father put an advertisement in a newspaper that went something like this: "If you want to get your face beaten and well-smashed, and if you want broken arms, look for me at this address." It was an open challenge to all fighters and tough guys to test our system of fighting.

Q: What do you think was his motivation for issuing that kind of open challenge?

A: It was partly to promote my father's style of jiu-jitsu by showing its superiority as a fighting style, and partly to continue the process of improving the system. You see, once my father had learned traditional jiu-jitsu, from the Japanese point of view, he adapted it to a more practical style for street fighting. The advertisement was part of the method that he used to find out what worked and what didn't; as he practiced his art against new competitors, some of the traditional Japanese moves were completely eliminated, new ones were added, and others were modified in order to make the system more efficient. For a smaller person, like my father and many of his students, it was important to use energy efficiently; the beauty of our system is that technique compensates for differences in size and weight, and allows the smaller person using the Gracie style to overpower a larger, stronger opponent from another style.

> "The purpose of our style of jiu-jitsu is to prepare students to defend themselves in the streets as well as in the ring."

Q: Some observers have put forth the idea that the Gracie Challenge is not budo-like, that it does not fit with the spirit of the martial arts, and you shouldn't go around challenging people. What are your thoughts on this?

A: Well, I'm not really in favor of public challenge when it is used to humiliate other people and styles. However, I think the reason the challenge goes on here is that some martial artists live in a fantasy world. Some people go to school for years and when they get attacked in the street or the ring, they don't know how to defend themselves. The challenges wake these people up to reality. I believe that the martial arts are about fighting, not fantasy. The purpose of our style of jiu-jitsu is to prepare students to defend themselves in the streets as well as in the ring. The challenge is important to show the differences between the various martial arts styles, and also for the world to know the superiority of the Gracie style of jiu-jitsu.

Q: Are you, in fact, the first Gracie family member to teach your system in the United States?

A: Yes. I came to the United States and began teaching jiu-jitsu in 1972. I was actually invited here to teach by American marines. This happened because when I was in Brazil during my time as national champion, I was teaching a group of American marines who were in charge of security of the American consulate in Rio. After those marines returned to the United States, they continued to practice martial arts, and it turned out that the fighters I trained in Brazil were beating men returning from other countries. When the officers learned where my students had been trained, they contacted me to come to America to teach the Gracie system. Since 1972, I have taught the Gracie style of jiu-jitsu in Virginia, Connecticut, Maryland, Florida and California, where I have lived and taught jiu-jitsu since 1979.

Q: Do you have a personal philosophy regarding martial arts training?

A: Yes. I believe it's better to learn three things well than to know a little bit about a lot of things. One well-executed move can finish a fight, but many poorly-done moves will get you nowhere. As an example, I remember being on the second floor of a high school in Brazil overlooking a recreation yard when I saw a smaller boy with thick glasses being punched and kicked by a bigger boy. The smaller boy kept backing up and everybody was screaming for him to fight back. Finally, the smaller boy put one hand on the larger boy's collar and with the other hand, grabbed the opposite collar. Soon, the aggressor stopped punching and fell to his knees. The boy who was strangling was crying as he held on and all of a sudden, it became very quiet. I ran down the stairs and pulled the boys apart, because no one else seemed to realize what was happening. The strangle was so effective that the larger boy passed out and lost control of his bodily functions. That choke was the only thing the smaller boy knew; it wasn't very well put together, but even so, if you hold it long enough, it will be an effective defense. I tell my students this story because I want them to master each move I teach them, and this story illustrates the importance of doing so.

Q: Finally, what do you think is your role now as a teacher in jiu-jitsu?

A: I have to explain clearly the principles of techniques of the art in a way that people can understand. I enjoy training professional fighters and teaching people how to defend themselves on the streets. I am also developing instructors who can pass on the knowledge correctly even if they are not black belts with many years of experience. I see teaching as an art within an art! You have something inside you, which you know, and your goal is to get another person to know what you know and do what you do. For me this is an art!

CARLOS GRACIE JR

Heir to the Throne

CARLOS GRACIE JR. IS THE PRESIDENT OF THE BRAZILIAN CONFEDERATION OF JIU-JITSU, AND IS THE PRIME MOVER BEHIND THE GROWING WORLDWIDE MOVEMENT TO ORGANIZE OF THE ART.

FOR DECADES, PEOPLE FROM ALL AROUND THE WORLD HAVE BEEN ENCHANTED WITH BRAZIL-A LAND FAMOUS FOR BEAUTIFUL BEACHES, THE STRING BIKINI, AND UNCONTROLLABLE PASSION FOR "FUTEBOL" (SOCCER). BUT THOSE THING ARE ALL SECONDARY TO THE WORLD'S MARTIAL ARTISTS-THEY NOW TRAVEL TO BRAZIL TO TRAIN IN THE METHOD OF FIGHTING AND SELF-DEFENSE CREATED BY CARLOS GRACIE, KNOWN THROUGHOUT THE WORLD AS BRAZILIAN JIU-JITSU. AND WHO BETTER TO LEARN FROM THAN THE SON OF THE FOUNDER?

CARLOS GRACIE JR., KNOWN TO ALL IN THE JIU-JITSU WORLD AS "CARLINOS," IS A WORTHY NAMESAKE OF THE MAN WHO STARTED IT ALL. HE CONDUCTS HIMSELF THE SAME WAY THAT HE PERFORMS THE TECHNIQUES DEVELOPED BY HIS FATHER-WITH FLEXIBILITY AND ADAPTABILITY, ALWAYS HAVING A FIRM GOAL IN MIND. A RELAXED AND THOUGHTFUL MAN WHO ALWAYS ORGANIZES HIS THOUGHTS BEFORE SPEAKING, CARLOS GRACIE JR. LIVES IN A VERY HECTIC WORLD AND APPRECIATES THE INFREQUENT "QUIET TIME" HE GETS.

"BECAUSE OF MY DUTIES IN THE CONFEDERATION, I HAVE A VERY FAST-PACE LIFE," CARLINHOS ADMITS, "BUT TO CREATE AND DEVELOP NEW AND IMPORTANT THINGS YOU NEED ISOLATION TO CALM YOUR MIND DOWN. AFTER ALL, THE MIND IS LIKE A LAKE, YOU CAN ONLY SEE THE BEAUTY THE LAKE IF IT IS CALM. GOOD IDEAS ONLY COME WHEN YOUR MIND IS RELAXED. ONLY THEN CAN YOU FIND THOSE THREE OR FOUR THINGS THAT WILL REALLY CHANGE YOUR LIFE. BECAUSE AFTER ALL, THAT'S WHAT LIFE IS ALL ABOUT: THREE OR FOUR DEFINING MOMENTS THAT WILL CHANGE EVERYTHING FOREVER."

Q: How did you get started in jiu-jitsu?

A: Jiu-jitsu training was a very natural thing at my home. Practicing jiu-jitsu was like eating, brushing my teeth, or sleeping. No more, no less-something natural and logical to be done on a daily basis. I didn't have a true appreciation of what the art was all about until I was around 14 or 15 years old. That's when I became more interested in technical development, competition, and in improving my game.

Before that it was simply a physical activity and a chore, because I had no understanding or purpose. My father made sure I was training, but for me it just wasn't that important. When you are a child you do what you're told without really understanding why-like going to school. But when I reached my teens my whole perception of jiu-jitsu changed. I became aware of the responsibility of carrying the Gracie name and of the many things expected of me.

Q: How did your father, Carlos Gracie, come to lean jiu-jitsu?

A: The jiu-jitsu method my father learned was very Japanese in nature, but definitely not the modern Japanese jiu-jitsu you can see today. It was the old method that influenced the judo techniques later on. My father learned that method and modified certain aspects of what was taught to him; but it was his brother, my uncle Helio, who made great improvements in the defensive aspects of the art. The jiu-jitsu learned by my father had all the necessary attacking components. The offensive techniques were really strong and barely needed any improvement. The old jiu-jitsu was strong on attacking techniques, but weak on defense. Due to his physical limitations, Helio, who was very small and light in stature, came up with new ways of controlling the opponent and developed new strategies for the defensive aspects of jiu-jitsu. How to control a bigger and stronger opponent became the main point of the defensive maneuvers. This completely new defensive approach took the art to a higher level. Helio proved through all his vale tudo fights that the jiu-jitsu developed by the Gracie family had the tools to control and defeat bigger opponents, wearing them down and putting them into submission. My father was much older than his younger brother Helio, so it was Helio who went out and fought against anyone who doubted the effectiveness of Brazilian jiu-jitsu.

Q: How did Helio defeat bigger and stronger opponents?

A: If you match two people with the same technical knowledge and training experience, and one of them is bigger than the other, for sure the bigger and heavier man will win. But if the bigger man does not know

> **"The jiu-jitsu method my father Carlos Gracie learned was very Japanese in nature, but definitely not the modern Japanese jiu-jitsu you can see today."**

how to handle an opponent on the ground and the smaller man takes him down to the ground, the bigger man will lose because the weight difference that is so relevant when standing up will became nullified once they are on the ground. This is because there is no body weight to put behind punches and kicks. Of course, if both men are knowledgeable in jiu-jitsu and the have the same technical level then weight will be a factor. That's the reason we have weight divisions in sport jiu-jitsu. Practitioners are athletes and they have extensive technical knowledge, so we do the right thing and put them in a fair competition environment. A small jiu-jitsu man will defeat a bigger opponent who doesn't have the same jiu-jitsu knowledge, but if the bigger man is also good at jiu-jitsu then that's another story.

Q: What was the reason for starting vale tudo fights?

A: Vale tudo was created by my father, Carlos Gracie. The only reason he did it was to prove to everybody that the art of the Gracie family was an effective system of fighting. At that time, the people's perception of hand-to-hand combat was two men standing. Ground fighting and grappling was something people didn't understood, let alone accept as an effective fighting method. My father realized that the only way to prove jiu-jitsu was effective was to make vale tudo fights. That's the reason vale tudo was created. Once everybody in Brazil accepted what jiu-jitsu was about, it became unnecessary to keep challenging people. The point was proven. My uncle Helio did many of these fights and became a national hero in Brazil.

> "Vale Tudo was created by my father, Carlos Gracie. The only reason he did it was to prove to everybody that the art of the Gracie family was an effective system of fighting."

A similar thing happened here in the United States. Royce Gracie, through the UFC, proved to everybody that the jiu-jitsu method developed by the Gracie family was effective in no-hold-barred fights, and that having knowledge of grappling was not just advisable but necessary. After that point was proved and accepted by all martial artists in America, all vale tudo fighting afterwards became solely motivated by business factors. When my father created vale tudo he was not making money. When my uncle Helio was fighting bigger and stronger opponents it was not for money. The reason they put themselves on the line was more important than money to them-it was prestige and recognition of their art. Nowadays, vale tudo events around the world are just a good way for fighters to make money. It has become a show and a business-and the goal is different.

Jiu-jitsu practitioners don't need to fight anymore to prove that Brazilian jiu-jitsu is an effective self-defense and fighting method. Everybody knows it is. I remember my father sitting and telling me that once jiu-jitsu was accepted, there was no reason to keep doing challenges and vale tudo matches anymore. They did it for respect and recognition, not for money or fame.

Q: Is jiu-jitsu harder or easier to learn now, than in the old days?

A: Methods of teaching and training have to be continually improved so students can learn as quickly and easily as possible. The beginning students should be patient and hang in there until they get good results, otherwise they will not succeed in jiu-jitsu. If quit early in your training, you are apt to be discouraged and developed a negative attitude towards yourself. Throughout your life, the tendency to give up prematurely will stifle the development of the self-confidence which comes from accomplishment. Anyone who undertakes jiu-jitsu training must be determined to stay, otherwise they will lose something very important-the opportunity to know themselves, their potential, and their personal abilities.

Q: Is there anything missing in Brazilian jiu-jitsu today?

A: Today Brazilian jiu-jitsu is well known and everybody is aware of how effective the fighting method is. But when I look at the technical state of the art I see something very important is missing. I see thousand of great athletes who are capable of showing hundreds of technical variations and modifications, but who lack maturity in the basic and fundamental movements of jiu-jitsu. For instance, in the past we had ten different "raspadas" (sweeps), and now there are 100 modifications because the sport has greatly evolved during the last two decades.

> **"I see champions who are able to display a great amount of technique, but who lack high technical skill and understanding of the basics."**

I see champions who are able to display a great amount of technique, but who lack high technical skill and understanding of the basics. In the basic techniques, you have the necessary tools that will open doors for a more evolved technical game. But if you spend less and less time on the basics because you need to catch up on all the new modifications, you'll end up with many weak positions and few strong one. You'll be able to perform your personal specialties very well - maybe four or five movements, but you'll lack the necessary basic structure to improve and grow in the art as you get older. This is simply because you don't have the right knowledge of the foundations of the art.

My advice to students is to spend more time on the basic techniques instead of diversifying your training into an endless number of techniques that will bring you momentary recognition. You'll be able to display more techniques than other practitioners of your same rank, but the consequence after years of training will be that you become incapable of developing a more mature and stronger jiu-jitsu game, simply because you never spent the necessary time developing the basics. No basics, no nothing. It's that simple.

Q: Has competition affected the way the art is evolving?

A: Competition has affected the way many practitioners train jiu-jitsu, and the perception of the outside world is that jiu-jitsu is simply competition due to the way most instructors teach it. The sportive aspects are an important part of the whole art-a part where the best compete against the best and raise the technical level of the art. My advice to those who teach Brazilian jiu-jitsu, however, is that they should incorporate more classes for those people who are not athletes. There are many people out there who don't have the physical attributes of these athletes-people who are normal citizens, who go to work, have family lives and who would like to learn the art for fun and exercise. Teachers should incorporate more classes into their academies where the training is more relaxed and more natural-where the emphasis relies on learning proper basic techniques and the physical demands are not like those for people who are going to compete.

Jiu-jitsu has to be accessible to the regular individual, and progressively bring these people into a more demanding kind of training. The classes should be separated. You cannot have in the same people who will compete in the national championships, training with people who simply want to learn jiu-jitsu for personal fun and enjoyment. I would like to see more classes where the true essence of jiu-jitsu is being taught. This is what will allow jiu-jitsu to attract the general public. Otherwise, the sport will die out and fewer and fewer students will come to train.

Competition classes and training for athletes who are going to compete should be addressed outside the normal classes. It is something specifically for those individual who spend a lot of time in jiu-jitsu. These people should be trained differently. Not everybody should receive competition training. Many people are not interested in competition, but they are interested in receiving the benefits that Brazilian jiu-jitsu can bring into their lives.

Q: What are the benefits?

A: Ultimately, the greatest benefit of all martial arts training, not only jiu-jitsu, is self-understanding. Many of the people training jiu-jitsu never try to understand their own condition or limitations. It is through jiu-jitsu training that they can get a clearer picture not only of their own physical abilities, but also of their mental limitations. They will find out by themselves what these are, what they are capable of accomplishing if they put their mind to it, and will want to continue their training. Jiu-jitsu training is very similar to life itself. To receive the most out of your training you have to be capable of seeing these similarities.

For instance, when you enter a jiu-jitsu school, everybody makes you "tap." You lose to all the people who have been training there for years. It's normal, you don't know much and you are a beginner. After years of training, it happens that now you are the one making people tap. You are a black belt, and by having an extensive knowledge of the art you are capable of defeating other jiu-jitsu practitioners with less experience. Now you are on the top, but as the time goes by, new and younger athletes come up and you get older. Once again, you see how these newcomers are faster and stronger than you-you come full circle. If you don't accept this simple fact, you'll probably quit jiu-jitsu training all together and won't be capable of reaching the highest levels of the art.

Q: What is that higher level?

A: Once you find yourself in a position where you can't overcome an opponent because he is younger and stronger, that is when the real and authentic jiu-jitsu will come out. This usually only occurs when you can't rely on strength and power because you are not that young anymore. I often train with students of mine who are bigger and stronger than me. What I try to do is to find out how to neutralize their strength and physical power. I need to find out by trial and error what amount of physical energy is necessary to keep the opponent in a position where he is vulnerable. I don't want to use more energy than necessary because he is younger and stronger, so I must conserve my energy and use it in the proper way. This concept involves a very deep understanding of the basic techniques of jiu-jitsu, because that understanding will show you the way to reach that higher level. Only when you have a strong base, and deep understanding of the foundation of the art, can you use certain technical aspects that would be fatal if you didn't have that knowledge.

Q: Some people believe that weight divisions should not exist in Brazilian jiu-jitsu or vale tudo events. What is your opinion?

A: Let me put it this way. The effectiveness of the jiu-jitsu developed by my family is proven. Everybody knows and accepts that fact. Number one, there is no reason to do vale tudo for that purpose and if vale tudo events still exits is it because it is now a business. Number two, everybody who fights in vale tudo knows jiu-jitsu to some extent. They may punch and kick but they know Brazilian jiu-jitsu as well. If you put two skilled jiu-jitsu practitioners in a jiu-jitsu sport event, the heavier one will probably win because weight, when skill is equal, is definitely a factor. If the smaller fighter is better than the heavier one, then the smaller will win-but if they are technically the same, weight is an issue. Sport was developed to compare relative skills on a level playing field. This is the reason why there are weight classes in jiu-jitsu, boxing, karate, taekwondo, judo, et cetera. We do it to level the playing field. From a sportive point of view it is simply logical. It is a combat sport, not a real self-defense situation.

Q: What will it take for the sport of Brazilian jiu-jitsu to grow in the future?

A: We need to organize the overall structure of the sport worldwide. This is what I plan to do, as the main individual responsible for the Brazilian Jiu-Jitsu Confederation. First of all Brazil, and eventually all other countries, will have an official national team, much like in World Cup soccer. In the World Cup, there is only one national Brazilian team. The members of each national team will be chosen by their competition records in city, state, regional, and national tournaments. This way, the corporate sponsors and government agencies who are not interested in spending big amounts of money sponsoring private academies and schools, will be motivated to put up money for the national team.

> **"We need to organize the overall structure of the sport worldwide."**

This is the way other big international sports like basketball and football (soccer) have been successfully organized. Jiu-jitsu needs to do the same. Later on, every country will use the same format to come up with a national team of its own, and a World Brazilian Jiu-Jitsu Federation will control the sport to ensure fairness.

Q: Will this improve sponsorship involvement?

A: Absolutely, because there will be only one national team per country. The sponsors will put their money into that team and the members of the team. This way, the members of the team won't have to work eight or ten hours per day at their daily jobs and go to train in the night to improve their jiu-jitsu. They will have money to become professionals so they can dedicate all their time to training and competition-similar to Olympic athletes. The members of the Olympic team do not work for four years; they simply train. The money for the Olympics comes from the various governments.

Q: Although you live in Rio de Janeiro, Brazil, you keep close contact with family members residing in the United States, particularly the Machado Brothers. What do you think has made them so successful in spreading jiu-jitsu in America?

A: The Machado brothers came to the United States a long time ago, although other members of the Gracie family were already in the country. They have been together all these years and never stopped supporting each other. This simple fact reflects their attitude and personality and how reliable they are as individuals. They were well trained and achieved exceptional recognition as competitors in Brazil. Once they moved to America they kept training, teaching, and competing-and succeeded in all these areas. It is very difficult to teach and compete at the same time. Their students are among the best in the country and nobody can deny their teaching ability and their friendly and accessible personalities. It's no wonder that the top American martial artists and movie stars have come to them for instruction in Brazilian jiu-jitsu.

Q: You started a terrific international program, offering interested practitioners worldwide the chance to compete in something called "Gracie Camp." What exactly is that?

A: The idea of the Gracie Camp came because I was receiving a large amount of solicitations from foreign students wanting to train at my school, Gracie Barra, in Rio de Janeiro. People would come from around the world and stay in hotels way too far from the school, and from the nice beaches and the fun and safe Rio areas. Gracie Camp is not only about learning jiu-jitsu, but also about enjoying and experiencing an entire Brazilian adventure. This encompasses jiu-jitsu training, good restaurants, nice beaches, and a lot of fun. Many people were coming to Rio de Janeiro for training but because they didn't know the city, the transportation and the society, they ended up expending huge amounts of money, staying in hotels at very bad locations, and spending a lot of money and time on transportation and basically having a real nightmare there. My idea was to offer these dedicated practitioners and students, of any skill level from white belt to black belt, a safe opportunity to enjoy jiu-jitsu and the Brazilian culture and lifestyle, with us taking care of them. We pick them up at the airport, take them to hotels located very close to the Gracie Barra Academy, and within walking distance of the famous beaches, nice restaurants, and nightclubs where they can have a great time.

> "All instructors should try to teach the art in the right way, emphasizing the basics and fundamentals that will allow the practitioner to evolve in their future years."

The technical level of the classes is designed to fit any practitioner's skill level. If you are a blue belt you'll have a training program specifically for your rank, plus a lot of additional techniques and training that will increase your skill. The same applies for purple, brown and black belt. There is special training for every person and every rank. Nobody is going to force you to train eight hours a day. If you want to go to the beach in the morning, train in the afternoon, and have fun at night, you'll be able to do it. If you want to train all day long, skip the visit to the beach, and then party at night, you'll be able to do that too. You're the boss of your time.

Knowing how to safely find your way around without problems, especially in a developing country like Brazil, can be tough. So everyone can enjoy all the facilities and personal help we provide at the Gracie Camp.

Q: What is the essence of Brazilian jiu-jitsu?

A: Brazilian jiu-jitsu has a good reputation as a combat method. We don't need to do crazy things to prove that anymore, because everybody knows it. All instructors should try to teach the art in the right way, emphasizing the basics and fundamentals that will allow the practitioner to evolve in their future years. They should also keep in mind that the way they behave outside the school will affect the public perception not only of jiu-jitsu, but also of our reputation as martial artists in general. We should all keep in mind that giving is a way of receiving. Once you have gained skill and a position of responsibility, it is your obligation to help others to grow. Blue belts should help white belts, purples should help blues, and brown and blacks should help everyone.

As president of the Brazilian Confederation of Jiu-jitsu, it is my responsibility to help younger competitors find their way, and to make things easier for them to succeed in the sport. This involves working for the good of others, not only for myself. In the big picture of jiu-jitsu, we all share that responsibility. We need to put our own selfish interests aside and do things for the benefit of others and for the benefit of the sport. That's what a good leader does - care for others and do things so others can benefit. We are all the leaders of our own lives, so we should all do this. This is the how the sport of jiu-jitsu, with all of us working together, can leave a mark in history. This is the true way of Brazilian jiu-jitsu.

CARLSON GRACIE

The Brazilian Legend

A LEGENDARY JIU-JITSU EXPERT FROM BRAZIL, CARLSON GRACIE WAS AN ACKNOWLEDGED MASTER OF AN ART THAT IS SYNONYMOUS WITH CHAMPIONSHIP GRAPPLING AND MMA FIGHTING. IN HIS YOUTH, CARLSON ASSUMED THE RESPONSIBILITY OF FIGHTING STYLISTS FROM OTHER MARTIAL ARTS TO PROVE THE EFFECTIVENESS OF GRACIE JIU-JITSU. HIS MOST FAMOUS FIGHT OCCURRED IN FRONT OF MORE THAN 20,000 SPECTATORS IN MARACANAZINHO STADIUM. AT THE TIME, HE WAS ONLY 20 YEARS OLD. HIS GOAL? DEFEAT WALDEMAR SANTANA, THE MAN WHO HAD PREVIOUSLY INSULTED GRANDMASTER HELIO GRACIE. AND A VICTORY MEANT THAT CARLOS COULD REGAIN THE FAMILY HONOR. AFTER THAT FIGHT, CARLSON GRACIE BECAME A NATIONAL HERO. FOR MORE THAN 30 YEARS, HE DEFENDED THE FAMILY NAME IN NUMEROUS VALE TUDO FIGHTS. IN HIS LATER YEARS, HE BECAME ONE OF THE MOST SUCCESSFUL TRAINERS IN THE HISTORY OF SPORT JIU-JITSU, AND HE COACHED AND TRAINED A LONG LIST OF WORLD CHAMPIONS.

Q: Professor Gracie, please introduce yourself.

A: I was born in Rio de Janeiro on August 13, 1938. I began training in jiu-jitsu at age three under my father, Carlos Gracie, the oldest of the four famous Gracie brothers and the originator of Brazilian jiu-jitsu. I am the founder and head of the Carlson Gracie Jiu-Jitsu Team, and I created Carlson Gracie Jiu-Jitsu. My style differs from other styles of Brazilian jiu-jitsu in the sense that I am always inventing and evolving new techniques and fighting strategies, refusing to let my jiu-jitsu become stagnant or outdated. If you're not going forward, you're going backward.

Q: What is your fighting record?

A: At 16, I was the Brazilian jiu-jitsu champion in the open weight class, which was the only class at that time. I fought 18 no-holds-barred matches, ending up with a record of 14-1-3. My 14 wins were by submission or knockout, and my three draws included two against Waldemar Santana. My one loss was a controversial decision that caused a riot when I was not awarded the victory. During the fight, my opponent tapped, so I released the finishing hold. Afterward, he denied he had submitted. My most well known victory was against Waldemar Santana. I was 17, and Santana was 24. Santana had beaten my uncle, Helio Gracie.

Q: How did your family get involved in the art of jiu-jitsu and what do you remember about your training days under your father, Carlos Gracie Sr.?

A: Esai Maeda, also known as Count Koma, was a jiu-jitsu champion who was head of a Japanese immigration colony to Brazil. Gastao Gracie – my grandfather, Brazilian politician and scholar – helped Maeda establish the colony. As a show of friendship, Maeda taught jiu-jitsu to my father, who then taught it to his younger brothers. Anytime I had a question about a position I would ask my father. He would always have an answer, but he would never directly come to me because he was so busy. Nevertheless, I wanted to learn so I would ask. He never gave me a formal class. I would just watch him and then practice. This not only helped me to think on my own, it also helped me come up with new techniques based on things that I had seen others do. It trained my mind as well as my body.

Q: Tell us about the fight against Waldemar Santana.

A: Santana was actually a good friend of mine, even though he was older than me. We liked each other very much. After his fight with Uncle Helio, however, I called him and told him that we now had a big problem! I was 20 at the time. Normally, the authorities would not have allowed me to compete. However, I lied about my age and was eventually given permission to try and restore the family honor. None of Helio's sons was old enough to fight. So even though I was young myself, I was the only family member available. I could have finished the fight earlier because I had many chances for submission. Normally, I would not have punished a man so much, but I wanted to make an example of him for the disrespect he had shown to Uncle Helio. I wanted his face to tell the story of the fight – not his words.

Q: Did you enjoy fighting from the bottom?

A: Not at all! For quite awhile I was the only one fighting for the Gracie family. There wasn't another Gracie fighting except for my brother Robson. Robson was a phenomenal fighter – outstanding really. But at 118 pounds, he was too light to face many of the big and strong men who challenged the art of jiu-jitsu. I was always fighting against people who were bigger than I was, so naturally I would end up on the bottom. Fortunately, I could dish out a lot of punishment from there.

Q: Rolls Gracie, your brother, died in a tragic hang gliding accident. He is regarded as one of the four greatest jiu-jitsu fighters ever. The others are Helio, Rickson and you. Did you have much to do with training Rolls?

A: Rolls originally trained with Helio, but he didn't do very well. In a challenge match that many people watched, Rolls fought Cicero, a fighter from Nitorei, which is an island off Rio. Cicero, who weighed one kilo less than Rolls, beat him badly. Because it was submission only, it was ruled a draw. Using modern scoring it would have been 20-0. I was cheering for Rolls, but I was very upset when he was beaten so badly. I told Rolls that Cicero was nothing, and that he should not have lost to him. I opened a school a few months after that in Copacabana. Six months later Rolls left Helio's academy and came to train with me. Later, he became my partner in the school. Rolls bugged me all the time about how to do things. He would bother me constantly, so he learned a lot. After 18 months of training, he became a phenomenon and beat everybody. He is by far the best jiu-jitsu man who ever lived. Before me he wasn't learning all the updated techniques. He was frozen in time. To be good in jiu-jitsu you have to be always moving forward.

> **"Rolls bugged me all the time about how to do things. He would bother me constantly, so he learned a lot. After 18 months of train ing, he became a phenomenon and beat everybody. He is by far the best jiu-jitsu man who ever lived."**

Q: How has your teaching changed since you became better known in America?

A: I have taught jiu-jitsu classes and seminars in the U.S., Canada and Brazil for more than 40 years. I have popularized jiu-jitsu in Brazil by spreading it beyond my immediate family and teaching the general public. My greatest joy has come from producing numerous world champions from all races and walks of life. I would never prepare a fighter to face a Gracie family member in a no-holds-barred match, but everybody knows I have prepared many to fight against other Gracies in jiu-jitsu tournaments. Don't forget Wallid Ismail, who beat Royce Gracie.

Q: How do you see Brazilian jiu-jitsu competitions these days?

A: Jiu-jitsu is so competitive now that it is hard to predict who will win. In my school, for example, I consider everyone above purple belt to be at the same skill level. In Brazil, the technical level is very good. It is no longer the privilege of only the Gracie family to know the best techniques. All the academies have great knowledge.

Q: Do you think no-holds-barred fighting requires different skills from jiu-jitsu?

A: No. 1, I require my fighters to be good at jiu-jitsu, because that is the basis of what I teach. After that, I adapt the style to whatever the rules are in the particular event. I personally have done a lot of boxing, so I show that to my fighters. You see, you always have to be moving forward and learning different things. If you fight a boxer, you better know how to slip a punch or you're going to get nailed. Being successful in jiu-jitsu is as much about being open-minded to learning new things as it is about learning a particular set of techniques.

> "Japanese jiu-jitsu at one time was the best jiu-jitsu, but they began hiding so many techniques that they forgot them. We were lucky that Count Koma, who came to Brazil, knew the original jiu-jitsu and taught it to my father [Carlos]."

Q: How close is Brazilian jiu-jitsu to Japanese jiu-jitsu?

A: Japanese jiu-jitsu at one time was the best jiu-jitsu, but they began hiding so many techniques that they forgot them. In Brazil, we were lucky that Count Koma, who came to Brazil from Japan, knew the original jiu-jitsu and taught it to my father [Carlos]. He then passed it down to everybody. So that is why I don't hide anything. I have to be intellectually honest and show everything I know. Otherwise, how can I live with myself?

Q: Is there any position or technique more important than another in Brazilian jiu-jitsu?

A: All positions are important. You should not concentrate on just one thing and neglect another. You might start out learning slowly, but you'll eventually be well rounded then when you catch on. And don't get too specific as far as learning techniques. Learn them all equally as you go, and don't get impatient. One day you will wake up, and you will be comfortable [performing the techniques]. Don't try to force your learning. It should be natural.

Q: What has made Brazilian jiu-jitsu so popular in the U.S.?

A: Of course, Royce Gracie's victories were good for everyone, and he is probably the single reason you see jiu-jitsu everywhere. Because of Royce, everyone knows about jiu-jitsu now. He did everyone a great service, and he deserves to be admired for what he did.

Q: Who is the greatest fighter in the world today?

A: People ask me this question all the time, but it is honestly hard for me to say. There are so many great fighters that it is not fair for me to mention one because I admire so many. I don't want to disrespect the ones that I don't mention. I could name 20 fighters I consider champions and that I like to watch, and they are not just Brazilians, either.

Q: Some of your previous students broke away from your "Arrebentacao" (Demolition) team and created the Brazilian Top Team. What happened?

A: All these guys studied and trained here with me. The members of this so-called Brazilian Top Team were all my students, and I taught them everything. They never paid any money to train at the academy, and I taught them everything. But what can I do?

Q: How do you see the American students?

A: They have excellent backgrounds. Many of them are already wrestling champions, and they have tremendous physical qualities. Best of all, they are very determined and focused. You only need to tell them what to do once, and they go off on their own, following your instructions to the letter!

Q: You had great moments in your life. Which ones were the worst and the best until this day?

A: By far, the worst moment of my life was the death of my father. It is the single most striking moment of my life. That loss was enormous. To this day I still feel it as if it occurred yesterday. The biggest joy and my most important moment was my win over Waldemar Santana. The Gracie name was low at the time, and I was able to bring it to the top again. I take great pride in the fact that I was the only one able to defend the family name for quite some time. There was my brother Robson, but as I told you he was very light. There were many women in the family but no fighters. There was a long gap there, and I carried the torch for all those years against one and all. Now I look to my new crop of future champions to defend my name in the years to come.

CLEBER LUCIANO

The Brazilian Volcano

CLEBER LUCIANO IS ONE OF THE MOST WELL-KNOWN AND RESPECTED JIU-JITSU FIGHTERS AND TEACHERS IN THE UNITED STATES. A CHAMPION IN BRAZIL, WHERE HE BEGIN TRAINING AT AGE 5, LUCIANO TRAINED AND COMPETED AGAINST THE BIGGEST NAMES IN THE SPORT. HIS EXPERTISE WAS REWARDED BY A BLACK BELT BEFORE HE REACHED AGE 20. WITH COUNTLESS MATCHES IN JIU-JITSU TOURNAMENTS WITH THE GI, AND GREAT EXPERIENCE IN NO-GI SUBMISSION GRAPPLING, LUCIANO IS VERY FAMILIAR WITH WHAT TECHNIQUES WORK WITH THE GI AND WITHOUT. BUT MORE THAN THAT, HE IS FAMILIAR WITH HOW LIFE WORKS WITH JIU-JITSU AND WITHOUT IT. A "HYPER" KID WHO LIKED TO FIGHT ON THE STREET AND WHO WAS HEADED DOWN THE WRONG PATH, JIU-JITSU GAVE LUCIANO AN OUTLET FOR HIS AGGRESSION AND A STRUCTURE THAT GAVE HIS LIFE NEW MEANING. WITH A COMMITMENT TO GROW JIU-JITSU AROUND THE WORLD. AND TO USE IT TO HELP KIDS BETTER THEMSELVES, CLEBER LUCIANO IS AT THE FOREFRONT OF THE MODERN JIU-JITSU AND GRAPPLING REVOLUTION.

Q: How did you get started in jiu-jitsu?

A: I started because I was very hyper as a kid in the Rio area. So my mom wanted to put me in sports to calm me down. So I had two friends who did jiu-jitsu and the mother of one of them took me to watch the class one day. So I went and checked it out and liked what I saw and so I started training. This was with one of Helio Gracie's students who was a very high black belt. I was just a kid, only six years old, but I knew that it was fun. I loved to train, I loved jiu-jitsu, and I loved grappling. So I just kept going. So I also took a lot of judo classes, because judo is also very popular in Brazil. So I eventually got my black belt in judo also.

Q: Did you start taking judo after you started jiu-jitsu?

A: I started both at about the same time. Because I figured that judo would help me in my jiu-jitsu. But I always liked jiu-jitsu the best between the two. It was just more fun for me. Now, even though I have a black belt in judo, I've forgotten most of my moves. I probably still do some of them without thinking, but I don't compete in that or teach it formally or anything. Part of it was just that I got a little bored with judo. When you do a match you just start to get going and they end the match after only a minute or two. I didn't like how fast it was. One takedown or throw and the fight was over – even when you were not hurt or in any real danger. So it was too far removed from a real situation for me. So I figured out that jiu-jitsu was more complete. You can do everything – takedowns, throws, pass the guard, get points, get submissions – everything.

Q: When did you become closely associated with the Gracie family?

A: When I was 15 I was a blue belt and I went to the Gracie Academy and started training with Carley Gracie and got to know Royler, Rolker, and all the rest. Everyone really accepted me and made me feel like I belonged and was part of the family. So I continued to train there with some of the top guys in the world like Royler Gracie, Saulo Ribeiro, Carlos Barreto, and all the top guys. I got my black belt together with Saulo and Carlos and several other guys. I guess that I was at the Gracie Academy for nearly 5 years before I got my black belt. I felt like I really got a great jiu-jitsu education and got my black belt just before I turned 20. I was very proud of that because it is very young in jiu-jitsu to get it then.

Q: When did you decide to move to the United States and teach?

A: I did some tournaments in Brazil – some really big ones – and in one of them I beat Leo Vieira, who is really good. We were both at the same level and the two top guys, so everyone really wanted to see us compete to see who would win. I won that – and don't know how – but I beat him. After that I started getting a lot of calls from people wanting me to go to different places to open a school. A few of the calls came from this area, and I knew that there was already a lot of Brazilians teaching in Southern California, and I decided to come here. I wanted to come to a place where my students would have a chance to compete against other schools. Los Angeles probably has the most jiu-jitsu schools in the United States of any city. So that was a big part of it for me.

Q: What it hard when you first came?

A: Yeah, it was. But I knew I wanted to be in Huntington Beach the moment I got off that plane and came here. It is a great area with the water very close and a lot of nice people and also a lot of people who want to train jiu-jitsu. So I just immediately loved it here. I want to be here forever. When I first came I started the school with two American guys and that didn't work all that well because I was working for them at a school called Brazilian Martial Arts. But I was the one who knew jiu-jitsu and knew how to teach. So after a year I left to open my own school – Cleber Luciano Jiu-Jitsu. With my own school I can teach the way I want to on my own schedule – so for me it is better. I have more freedom. So I've been here at my own school for five years now and I have over I'm very grateful to my loyal students and I'm committed to teaching them the best jiu-jitsu in the world to show them my appreciation.

Q: You're known as one of the world's top tournament fighters. What is your philosophy of competition?

A: My strategy is to be very relaxed. In all my fights I relax and make sure in the first two or three minutes that I don't make a mistake and get behind on points. So I'm very careful early in a match. I don't want to get taken down, let someone get to my back, let someone get cross-side on me – things like that. I just try to figure out my opponent's game and get a feel for what he likes to do and what he is trying on me. It is very important to be patient. Once I get an idea of what he is doing, I can play my strategy and decide which attacks to use. I don't want to get crazy early, try to hard, and then get points scored on me or, even worse, get submitted. Relaxation and breathing is my game.

Q: What do you do once you've figured out your opponent's game plan?

A: Then I start to attack. But I always attack with good balance and good grip. Those two factors are the most important things to establish when you start your attack. As soon as you have a good grip and good balance then you can go for the takedown. If you're grappling with a good wrestler, for example, you can really feel his balance and so you need to be rock solid in your base.

Q: In a tournament situation do you like to fight from the guard or do you like to operate from on top?

A: You need to go for a superior position from the top. I don't believe in falling back into the guard and pulling your opponent on top of you. I teach my students to try to establish a strong top position during the first two minutes. In your first minute, if you put somebody in the guard, they are very fresh and will be alert and able to defend any submissions you might try. So if you work for two or three minutes, then you can get your opponent a little tired and also confuse him a little so when you get the position you want, you have a much better chance of your attacks working.

Q: What is your favorite position to work your attacks from?

A: I like the cross-side position a lot. There are more opportunities for submission from this position. The good thing about the cross-side is that you can apply it with equal success whether you are fighting no-gi Abu Dhabi rules or fighting with jiu-jitsu rules with the gi. This is because you are able to use the weight of your chest to pressure your opponent, but yet your hips and legs are free to move with him when he tries to escape. I work a lot of neck cranks and a lot of arm-neck combination chokes so it doesn't matter to me if I compete with a gi or without one. Of course there are a lot more moves that you can do with the gi – I can make a thousand moves with it. My whole life I trained with the gi for tournaments in Brazil. Plus you have material to grab at the lapel and the elbow and the back of the neck, et cetera that you don't have without the gi. So you have a lot more options. Without the gi I can do my basic positions, but I can't do all the advanced moves that I can do with the gi. With the gi it is really more fun because there are a lot more options.

Q: Is it difficult to transfer submission sport techniques into no-holds-barred?

A: My techniques are very effective in vale tudo fighting. So I don't have a lot of problems transferring them over. But kicking and punching do add a lot more dimensions to the grappling game, so while the sport techniques do work when you get into position, you have to be much more careful coming in, so you don't get caught during the entry. Plus, when you get on the ground you can use strikes to set-up your submissions. If you're cross-side, for example, and going for a choke, and your opponent is tightly guarding his neck, then you can drop a few elbows on him to make him block, which will then expose his neck for the choke. The same thing can done in different situations with the knees. The old technique of circling and then shooting in on him just doesn't work as well as it used to. People practice against it. Three of four years ago it was much easier to take strikers down. Now with everyone practicing kickboxing and Thai boxing there is a lot more danger coming in. So timing is the more important aspect for grapplers now. Saulo Ribeiro got caught with a knee by Yuki Kondo in an MMA match when he was shooting in and lost by a cut. I remember Renzo Gracie had the same problem a couple of times. You have to come in behind a kick and you have to time your entry very carefully.

Q: Do you think the guard still works for no-holds-barred?

A: If you lock somebody in the closed guard, but then only defend from it, you are going to have problems. You can defend for two or three minutes but after that you will get tired and the punches will start to get though. So you can't stay in a defensive guard for a long time like a sitting duck. However, if you work from the open guard, where you move your hips, use the inside hooks, and use sweeps and half-guard moves to keep your opponent off-balance, then you can survive and potentially even submit your opponent. The key is to be active from the guard – you have to have mobile hips, legs, and feet.

Q: What is best way to mentally prepare for a tournament?

A: In any tournament I do now I am very relaxed beforehand because I have done so many. Ten years ago I was really tense before a competition but I did so much that I don't worry about it so much anymore. Mental relaxation is as important as physical relaxation. The more you compete, the more relaxed you will be. When I was younger I made a big mistake of going into a fight as if my opponent was my enemy – I took the competition personally. I was like a volcano waiting to erupt and when I did I just forgot everything and I would not do well. I don't want anyone to make this same mistake and I don't want to make this mistake again, either. Every time you go into a fight you should worry about yourself, and not worry about your opponent. Your goal is to fight the fight, not fight the opponent. If you do your job the outcome of the fight will take care of itself. What happens is that you get so intense that you forget all your techniques and your entire game plan and you just brawl mindlessly. It happened to me. Everything went out the window – all I could think was "Kill! Kill! Kill!" When I fought it was as if I had never taken a single jiu-jitsu lesson. But I learned from that mistake big time. Now when I fight I don't care if my opponent is screaming and cursing at me – it doesn't matter. Let's just do the fight in a professional manner and then forget about it when the fight is done.

Q: Do you see a big potential for jiu-jitsu in the U.S.?

A: The key to the future of jiu-jitsu is the kids. Jiu-jitsu is great for kids because it teaches them respect and discipline and gives them something positive to do. I have about 60 kids who train in jiu-jitsu now, and as those kids grow up they are going to compete in tournaments. They will tell their friends about it and they will want to compete. I see so many kids who are as young as 5 years old and they already know how to move on the mat really well! These kids are going to be very hard to beat as they get older and move into the higher divisions. But more than that, it will help kids to become better much better persons. When I was a kid, for example, I was really hyper and I loved to fight on the street. So jiu-jitsu took me off of the streets and gave me an outlet for my aggression. Jiu-jitsu calmed me down mentally and gave me a much more cooperative attitude towards my family and people in general. Jiu-jitsu teaches fighting techniques to kids but it also teaches kids not to fight. It will change your attitude for the better. Without jiu-jitsu I don't think I would be here today.

FABIO GURGEL

The Lion of Jiu-Jitsu

A VETERAN OF MANY TOURNAMENTS, FABIO GURGEL HAS LEFT HIS MARK JUST ABOUT EVERYWHERE HE HAS COMPETED. HE DECIDED TO PUT HIMSELF TO THE ULTIMATE TEST BY COMPETING IN THE ULTIMATE FIGHTING CHAMPIONSHIP AGAINST JERRY BOHLANDER FROM KEN SHAMROCK'S LION'S DEN. AFTER RUNNING OUT OF TIME INSIDE THE OCTAGON AND LOSING, GURGEL DECIDED TO TACKLE AN EVEN BIGGER FOE.

AGAINST THE ADVICE OF NEARLY EVERYONE GUGEL FACED MARK KERR, THE GIANT AMERICAN WRESTLER. THIS MATCH WOULD GO DOWN AS ONE OF THE GREATEST FIGHTS IN THE HISTORY OF NO-HOLDS-BARRED. GIVING AWAY OVER 50 POUNDS, GURGEL TOOK KERR TO A DECISION. ALTHOUGH GURGEL LOST THE MATCH, HIS INCREDIBLE TECHNIQUE EARNED HIM A MORAL VICTORY. WATCHING FABIO GURGEL PERFORM JIU-JITSU IS LIKE WATCHING A BALLET DANCER – HE IS GRACEFUL, EFFORTLESS, AND PRECISE.

GURGEL RETIRED FROM COMPETITION TO DEVOTE HIS TIME TO TURNING OUT FINE MARTIAL ARTISTS AND PROMOTING THE ART OF JIU-JITSU AROUND THE WORLD. FOR HIM, SPIRIT AND HEART ARE THE MOST IMPORTANT ATTRIBUTES IN MARTIAL ARTS TRAINING. "IN ORDER TO BE THE BEST," GURGEL SAYS FIRMLY, "YOU MUST HAVE THE WARRIOR'S SPIRIT AND THE WARRIOR'S HEART."

Q: When did you start training?

A: I was born in Rio de Janeiro, January 18, 1970. When I was 13 years old I started training in a small gym with Professor Toninho, who I trained with for 10 months. Coincidentally, this was the same master that Romero "Jacare" Cavalcanti started training with – Jacare later became my instructor. I was taken to Toninho's gym by a friend who used to train with Carlos Gracie Jr. He thought I should start in a smaller gym so I would get more personal attention. My original goal was simply to learn self-defense, nothing else. But I quickly fell in love with jiu-jitsu and just couldn't stop. I finally received my black belt from Jacare at the age of 19, after being a Brazilian champion several times in all the lower ranks.

Q: What titles do you have?

A: I have all the titles a jiu-jitsu fighter can have. To begin with, I am a four-time world champion. For my first title I defeated Murillo Bustamante. In 1996, for my second title, I defeated Daniel Gracie. Then in 2000 I won again against Ricardo Arona. Then in 2001 I got my fourth title defeating Fabio Leopoldo in the semi-finals and then Rodrigo "Comprido" Meideros in the finals, even though he was much younger than me and was considered the favorite. After that I decided that I had nothing left to prove because I had beaten everyone, and so I decided to stop competing.

Q: What was your first big vale tudo fight?

A: It was against Denilson Maia and was very important since it was my debut and I had the responsibility of defending the honor of Brazilian jiu-jitsu. At that time all the Brazilian jiu-jitsu teams were united with the goal of proving that jiu-jitsu was more effective than luta livre. We all trained together, proving that union makes a group stronger. The fight went 100 percent as planned – training for the fight was way harder than the fight itself. It was an unforgettable night for myself, Murilo Bustamante and Wallid Ismail as well as for all the people who watched it.

Q: How did you get involved in the UFC?

A: At that time the UFC was the biggest vale tudo event in the world. I was invited to participate and that alone was already an honor and a great responsibility too, since in those days jiu-jitsu had the reputation of being unbeatable, I trained very hard for that fight. I moved to Los Angeles and trained with Rickson Gracie for two months, plus I trained boxing with Claudinho. I was truly in top shape, but unfortunately I did not fight well and my opponent, Jerry Bohlander, held the fence the entire time and left me with nothing to do. Since that fight, all events in the world have made it illegal for a fighter to hold the fence. If you watch that fight you will understand why. I had to keep him in my guard in order to control his movements. At the final bell, I knew I given everything I had and had done my best.

Q: Some people said that you should fought with an open guard.

A: It's very easy to make comments from outside the Octagon. I saw the fight on video and saw some mistakes. Jiu-jitsu is a perfect art, but it doesn't mean that everybody can use the art perfectly. Since I made some little mistakes, I ended up losing the fight. After that fight I went to train with Rickson Gracie to correct the mistakes in the positions. I'm sure that if I knew about those aspects before, that the fight would have been completely different. I was very frustrated by what happened and a promoter later brought Jerry Bolander to Brazil when Ruas had his revenge against Oleg Taktarov. That night they brought us both into the ring and I challenged Bolander to a rematch. He agreed but later on backed down from the deal. I learned later that the UFC had offered him an easier opponent. To me, however, I was freed from my frustration because he backed down from the fight. I did what I had to do and he did what he thought was the best for him.

Q: Was the criticism hard to take?

A: Nobody likes harsh words. But the point is that everybody likes to talk. Some people think that because they do few leg press repetitions with 300 pounds they can control Mark Kerr with an open guard. Why they don't they try to keep pushing the leg press with 300 pounds for thirty minutes nonstop?

Q: You then won three vale tudo fights in a row in Brazil, right?

A: I had to fight three opponents on the same night. The first one was Pat Smith, the UFC II runner-up and a great stand-up fighter at the time. He had just KO'd Andy Hug, the late K-1 champion. He was very explosive and strong when the belt rang he came ready to fight. But then shortly into the fight he started holding the fence, and the rules were clear. so he was disqualified, My second match was against Michael Pachoulik, a wrestler who had just defeated luta livre's Denilson Maia in Japan. I fought a good fight and brought him into my guard and punished him as much as I could. After five minutes, he tapped out. This brought me to one of my greatest tests in life as I then had to face Mark Kerr.

Q: How do you remember that fight?

A: It was 30 minutes of fighting without rounds or breaks. I weighed 200 lbs and Kerr was 245. It was the first time I had faced a world-class wrestler who trained as a professional bodybuilder as well. He was heavier and stronger than any of my sparring partners. Even though I felt he was strong in the beginning, I was very comfortable and had total control of the situation. Since my strategy was to take the fight the distance, I waited for him to get tired, hoping I could capitalize on any mistakes. Everything was going as planned, and then 15 minutes into the fight Kerr bit my finger real hard – I still have the scar to prove it. So I turned to the referee, who was new at vale tudo, and showed him my bleeding finger. Kerr then headbutted me right above my eye. After that he spent the last half of the fight punishing that eye. During that fight I experienced every single feeling from tiredness to pain to the will to survive. It was a great feeling to hear 1,200 people cheering my name. It was a great fight and a great experience that taught me a lot about myself.

Q: Is it true that Mark Kerr visited you the day after the fight?

A: Yes, he did. He had a problem with his hand. Dr. John Keating asked me if I knew a specialist on infections. So I recommended a doctor that lived very close to my house. They visited him and Kerr got better. Mark then came to my place to express his gratitude. We talked about the fight and he told me that he knew I was not going to quit and that at a certain point he didn't know what to do. We respect each other very much.

Q: If you had to fight Mark Kerr again, what would you do differently?

A: I would not change positions as much as I did. I would adopt one and let him get tired. I would also try to stay on my feet longer. I have better coordination and could have done more damage on the feet. He needs the ground to win.

Q: Didn't you also train under Carlson Gracie?

A: Yes, I did. It was a great time because everybody was together, training and working for the good of all jiu-jitsu. Carlson was teaching all the time and I learned a lot of tactics on the ground. He knows a lot about jiu-jitsu and how to use it properly.

Q: What was your most important sport jiu-jitsu match?

A: There are many fights that were important and unforgettable in my career as a sport jiu jitsu practitioner, however one that I truly remember happened in 1990 in the Rio de Janeiro Championships against Amaury Bitetti. I was losing the match by two points and there were 30 seconds left in the match. I took him down and immediately won the match. He made his two points in the first minute of the match and I spent the rest of the fight trying to score. Fortunately, I was able to win. It was without a doubt a great moment in my career and I keep this fight in a very special place of my heart. It is a great memory.

Q: Do you think Brazilian jiu-jitsu is the best style?

A: Nowadays, vale tudo is about the best man. Styles help, of course, but today you see jiu-jitsu people beating wrestlers and wrestlers beating jiu-jitsu fighters. This is because it's about individuals. For me, jiu-jitsu is the best because it can help you in your life. Vale tudo events are a very small part of the whole picture. You can't educate kids with no-holds-barred events but you can help kids with jiu-jitsu.

Q: What is your opinion about the new techniques compared to the old basics?

A: The technical evolution of jiu-jitsu techniques is based on sport competition. Many people criticize sport jiu-jitsu but they never participated in a competition. New ideas and concepts are always hard to accept. It is natural not to accept them. The level of the game has increased and keeps evolving so that new ways of preventing attacks have to be developed. If you are not willing to change you are going to lose. Your approach is going to die out because what works is what people will use. This applies not only to jiu-jitsu but to everything in life including business. Anyone running a business for more than ten years knows that changes have to be made to adapt to changing market situations.

Problems can arise, however, when someone with not enough skill in the basics wants to invent and create new moves. This is stupid. The basics movements of jiu-jitsu are the ones everybody should use and apply. The new techniques are mostly the product of high-level champions. They are capable of executing these techniques but most can't do them. So if your are not a full-time competitor, stick to the basics and you'll be surprised how good you can perform.

> "Rickson is a scientist of jiu-jitsu. His knowledge and skill is far and away above everybody else – not only in America but in Brazil as well. There's another level in the art of jiu-jitsu and Rickson lives on that level."

Q: What is your opinion of Rickson Gracie?

A: Rickson is a different fighter from anyone. He is a scientist of jiu-jitsu. His knowledge and skill is far and away above everybody else – not only in America but in Brazil as well. There's another level in the art of jiu-jitsu and Rickson lives on that level. I would like to reach it some day. He sees things in a fight that nobody else can see. Training under Rickson is a very revealing experience even if you're a world champion. With him I began to understand the 'real' essence of jiu jitsu principles. Some people say that I talk a lot about Rickson but let me tell you something, if you haven't been with Rickson on the ground, you don't know what jiu-jitsu is all about.

Q: Is jiu-jitsu strong or weak in Brazil right now?

A: The jiu-jitsu situation in Brazil is not a good one, because the sport has split into two separate groups. It is an ego fight between those who want power at any cost. In this ego fight, the people involved do not realize how much damage they are doing to our sport. It is sad to see that happen right in front of our eyes. It seems that other martial arts styles went through the same thing and have gotten weaker. Even with plenty of examples, jiu-jitsu does not seem to have learned from it. If history teaches us something, it is that human beings never learn from their mistakes. We should work together and try to push the sport in a strong direction instead of weakening it by fighting and arguing among ourselves.

Q: What is the future of jiu-jitsu?

A: I believe that jiu-jitsu will never stop being part of the lives of the people who have dedicated time and effort to it. However, as a sport, I am not sure what the future holds because there are too many variables. I hope the work that has been done by the Confederation of Brazilian Jiu-Jitsu (CBJJ) keeps growing and those who are trying to destroy the sport for personal gain lose credibility and eventually realize that it is better for all of us to stay together. On the other hand, I am a believer in submission fighting as a sport. I truly think it has huge potential, even though is still in the beginning stages. It is practiced in many countries around the world, which brings a healthy balance to the sport. I believe it does not help nor hurt jiu-jitsu. It is simply another grappling sport for the jiu-jitsu practitioner to enter, just like a judo or sambo tournament.

Q: Do you like the new fighting rules?

A: I believe any attempt to improve the sport by making changes in the rules is good and positive, since they make it possible for the art to develop. We are no longer trying to prove who is a bigger man, what we are trying to accomplish is to professionalize the sport of jiu-jitsu and find new ways of making it more profitable for the competitors and sponsors. I agree with any new rules for the simple reason that anyone trying to improve the sport will eventually bring something new and good – it does not matter what kind of rules they are. If a participant does not agree with the rules they should find another tournament or create another event that they agree with and compete there.

Q: How has Brazilian jiu jitsu and vale tudo developed in the last decade?

A: The major change I see is that in the old days we used to fight for the simple pleasure of defending our art and to be recognized as a fighter – fighting for your style was the main reason for vale tudo fights. Today, the events have become professional and the fighters focus only on the money. Since the industry generates so much cash, it is logical for fighters to take advantage of that for their financial security. Another important point is that the jiu-jitsu that was only known by a very few 15 years ago has now become popular and everybody knows the art. Today, the art of Brazilian jiu-jitsu is practiced by all fighters. Without a knowledge of jiu-jitsu, no fighter has any business being in an MMA event. However, and this is a very interesting point, jiu-jitsu fighters also had to add strikes and kicks to their arsenal – which was unheard before. So now all fighters know a little of everything, and the best man wins, independent of their style of fighting. A true mixed-martial-arts style has been developed due to the UFC and other similar events.

Q: Is there still a big rivalry in Brazil between jiu-jitsu practitioners and other vale tudo fighters?

A: Definitely, it is not the way it used to be. Before, luta-livre fighters wanted to compete directly with jiu-jitsu practitioners in Rio de Janeiro and there was a big rivalry between them. Today there is room for everybody, and luta livre fighters are respected all around the world. No style needs to prove that their fighting method works. Everyone has matured and realized that times have changed and that there is no room for the childish rivalries we had in the past. Everyone is trying to improve what they do and all the problems are solved in the ring now, with no hard feelings after the fight.

Q: Can you talk about the Professional Jiu-Jitsu League that you have created?

A: In my opinion, the Professional jiu-jitsu League is the best vehicle to have jiu-jitsu seen as a professional sport. It pays the fighters to participate in the tournaments, and it keeps the big jiu-jitsu stars fighting with the gi for the sport of jiu-jitsu, instead of going to Abu Dhabi and no-holds-barred which eventually will distance them from the art they learned in the beginning. In the event that took place in 2000, we had the cream of the crop from the jiu-jitsu community. The best 50 athlete in the world participated, going through a very clear and fair formal selection process.

The formula to participate was very simple. The fighter must be among the top eogjt athletes that have the biggest number of gold medals in each weight division. The Brazilian media said it was the best jiu-jitsu tournament ever. And the other interesting thing was that it was on TV and they received money to be in it. You have to come up with a complete package that allows the competitors to make money and became professional. This is the only way to keep them in the sport and away from vale tudo. Don't get me wrong, I love MMA, but sport jiu-jitsu is a great art that everybody can practice for the rest of their lives.

Q: In your opinion, who are the best Brazilian jiu-jitsu and vale tudo fighters today?

A: This is a very hard question to answer because there are many good guys out there, especially after the push the sport experienced in the last 10 years or so. The sport is moving in new directions and this simple factor opens more opportunities for all the new practitioners. The same thing happens with MMA. The sport is evolving so fast that new great champions are coming out all the time. Sometimes it is impossible of keeping track of everything is happening.

Q: What is next for you?

A: I am involved in the production of professional events, will continue giving my seminars in Brazil and around the world, and managing the several gyms that I own. All these things keep me very busy and I'm the kind of guy that I think the busier you are the better you'll be. In short, keep your eyes open and your mind busy!

FABIO SANTOS

Synergy in Motion

FROM RIO DE JANEIRO TO SAN DIEGO, CALIFORNIA. FROM SURFING IN IPANEMA TO THE BEACHES OF LA JOLLA. FOR FABIO SANTOS, ALL THESE CHANGES HAVEN'T BEEN A CURSE. INSTEAD, THEY HAVE BEEN A BLESSING. A GIFT FROM HEAVEN, IN FACT. HE IS DEFINITELY ONE OF THE MOST CHARISMATIC BRAZILIAN JIU-JITSU INSTRUCTORS IN THE UNITED STATES OF AMERICA. ARTICULATE, WITH A GREAT SENSE OF HUMOR AND A LOOK VERY FAR FROM THE AVERAGE BRAZILIAN FIGHTER, FABIO SANTOS NOT ONLY KNOWS HOW TO USE HIS BELOVED ART OF JIU-JITSU IN A VERY SYSTEMATIC WAY, BUT HE CAN USE HIS MIND AS WELL. HIS VIEW OF JIU-JITSU TRAINING IS BASED ON A SYNERGISTIC APPROACH THAT RESULTS IN A BETTER TECHNICAL SYSTEM. ALTHOUGH ALWAYS LOOKING INTO THE FUTURE AND WILLING TO CHANGE WHATEVER MAY BE NECESSARY TO IMPROVE WHAT HE DOES, FABIO SANTOS CONSIDERS HIMSELF A TRADITIONAL INDIVIDUAL IN THE ETHICAL ASPECTS OF THE ART. "I ALWAYS TRIED TO UPHOLD THE MEANINGFUL AND ETHICAL VAL- UES THAT THE PREVIOUS MASTERS HAVE CULTIVATED AND DEVELOPED," HE SAYS. NEVER TO GLORIFY HIMSELF, BUT RATHER TO PRESERVE ALL THE KNOWLEDGE PASSED ONTO HIM BY HIS TEACHERS, FABIO SANTOS HAS BEEN VERY ACTIVE IN PROMOTING THE ART OF BRAZILIAN JIU-JITSU THROUGH CLASSES AND SEMINARS AROUND THE UNITED STATES OF AMERICA AND OTHER EUROPEAN COUNTRIES.

Q: How many years you have been training in Brazilian jiu-jitsu?

A: I started in 1969. More than three decades of dedicated training.

Q: Who was your teacher in Brazil?

A: My training began under the late Rolls Gracie, who was one of Carlos Gracie's sons. Unfortunately, Rolls, to whom many people looked upon as the best jiu-jitsu practitioner in the whole Gracie family, passed away after an accident at a delta.

Q: Did you stop your training after his death?

A: No, not really. Of course, I felt down after he passed away. It was a very emotional time. He was not only my teacher but also my friend... a friend who influenced my life in many ways way beyond the jiu-jitsu. But life had to go on. So, thanks to Rickson Gracie, I started to feel motivated again. I started to enjoy the training, and I finally regained the passion for what I was doing. Rickson already knew me from Rolls' school so he kindly accepted me as student.

Q: Did you get your black belt from Rickson Gracie?

A: Yes, I did. I was only a purple belt when Rolls passed away, and Rickson took me all the way up to black belt.

Q: Did you ever have ups and downs in your regular training?

A: Yes, of course. Everybody who has been practicing something for more than 40 years has gone through that. Not in a sense of stopping or quitting the training but being a little bit burned out from the pressure of doing it. I was training every single day, even weekends. When I got to high school, I kind of relaxed a little bit. I mean, I wasn't spending 10 hours everyday at the academy as I used to. Sometimes you have to adapt to the circumstances and roll with the punches. Adapting to your current life situation is something that a lot of people don't know how to do. Life changes and you have to schedule your training sessions accord- ingly — especially if you are not a professional jiu-jitsu teacher.

Q: Why did you decide to move to California?

A: It is a long story, but I'll try to make it short. I got my major in Physical Education from the University of Gama Filho in Rio de Janeiro. Then Rorion Gracie called me and invited me to come here to teach at his school in Torrance. At that time, there were names like Royce Gracie, Rickson Gracie and Royler Gracie at the school. As you can see, it was a great opportunity for me. I was there for more than two and a half years. Afterwards, I decided to move to San Diego and open my own school under the Rickson Gracie Association.

Q: What is the most important aspect in training in Brazilian jiu-jitsu?

A: To understand the main concept of the art.

Q: Which is?

A: The Brazilian jiu-jitsu practitioner must know how to wear his opponent down. When the opponent is worn out, he's unfocused and his concentration level is down. That is when we use our brain and intelligence because our opponent can't think clearly. Jiu-jitsu is about using the proper strategy and tactics at the right time. You don't look for the technique. On the contrary, you set an environment in which the opponent gets himself in trouble. The sub- mission technique is there waiting for you, but you need to know how set it up.

Q: And how you do that?

A: Good question. I'll try to answer the best that I can. The submission technique is the tip of the iceberg. You can only get the submission technique if you control the opponent at will, and the only way you can control the opponent at will is through perfect positioning. That is the secret... positioning. What do I mean by positioning? Well, every jiu-jitsu position has a certain amount of details that should be perfected. The closer to perfection you are on these technical points the less chance the opponent will have to escape. Then, he is under your control. Now, when he is under your control, finding the sub- mission technique is simpler.

Q: Do you think the time limits affect the outcome of the fights in events such as the Ultimate Fighting Championship?

A: Definitely and positively! The time limit changes the whole conception of the fight. It affects the fighter's mentality and state of mind, and I'm going to give you an example. Let's say that I drop you right in the middle of the desert. No food, no water, but I tell you that I'll be back in 24 hours to pick you up. All you have to do is hold on there. But, let's say that I leave you there with no food or water. And then, before I take off, I tell you that I'll never come back for you. Your state of mind is going to be very, very different. Do you understand me? In this second case, you've got do something. You've got to move because you're going die there if you don't. You've got to react. There's no "time limit" that you can hold on to. You've got to take your chances ... now! This is what happens in events like the UFC in which you've got time limits. The only thing a fighter with a less technical arsenal has to do is hold on to the opponent. He is not going take any chances, because someone will "pick him up from the desert." Then, he gets a draw against an opponent who is probably much better than him. But, if that fighter is in a match that does not have a time limit, then my friend, he has to move. He has to know what to do. He has to take his chances to win. Therefore, he will need strategy and tactics. As you can understand, the whole concept of the fight changes immediately.

Q: In some sport jiu-jitsu tournaments, you can see some practitioners using too much muscular strength when trying to apply the techniques. Is that right?

A: No, it is not. That's a big mistake. Win or lose, I demand that my students use technique — not strength. When my students test for a higher rank or belt, it's the same thing. I demand that they use jiu-jitsu techniques that display the "jiu-jitsu personality." There is no brutal force. That's not jiu-jitsu.

Q: So, you can tell the level of the practitioner according to this, right?

A: Pretty much. A good jiu-jitsu man knows how to "place" the technique on time. He is able to feel the right moment and the right energy to insert his movement in the flow of the action. This little detail tells a lot about the practitioner. Look at the way he moves when he is on the mat, how relaxed he is, how he breathes. There are a lot of small details that make all the difference in the world when it comes to applying a jiu-jitsu technique.

Q: How is your academy in San Diego?

A: It is a quiet place where I try to do my best to share the art to which I dedicated my life. It is important to me that the atmosphere at the academy is the right one so everybody enjoys training and being there.

Q: So, you still have relationship with Rickson?

A: Of course, I do. If you never have been on the mat with Rickson Gracie, you simply don't know what Brazilian jiu-jitsu is all about!

Q: You don't look like a "tough guy." The huge muscles, big neck and all that. How come?

A: Well, you're right. I don't look like that, but I don't need it either. I don't pump iron. I "pump" bananas and carrot juice! A man of jiu-jitsu does not need to pretend to be a tough guy. He doesn't display aggressive attitudes and all that. I'm a simple guy. All I need is to know my art and that is more than enough! I look for functional strength. Anything else is dead weight, and that won't help you in a fight. The right weight and endurance is the key. I'm not interested in adding muscle for muscle sake. I have a lot of confidence in jiu-jitsu so I know I can win no matter how big the opponent may be. Technique is what is important.

Q: Do you follow a particular diet?

A: Diet is very important. It doesn't matter how much you train — you need the right kind of food in your body to perform at a high level. I try to eat healthy, and I take supplements. Sometimes it's very hard to eat six or seven times a day. When I began fighting, there were no weight classes.

Now there are. As a result, I had to put some weight on, and that changes the whole game, believe me.

Q: In the last few years, American wrestlers have taken the Mixed Martial Arts events by storm. What's your opinion on this?

A: I've seen some great wrestlers fighting in MMA events, and I guess they are learning how to compensate for their lack of finishing techniques. A lot of them have changed the whole wrestling approach and strategy to fighting, and they are using many of the tactics used in Brazilian jiu-jitsu to fight in these types of competition. The smart ones have also added striking tools, particularly low kicks and Western boxing.

Q: Do you believe in cross training?

A: Yes. You need to incorporate different training to be a complete MMA fighter. I have enjoyed training and studying boxing. A lot of jiu-jitsu guys can't punch or kick efficiently. You have to strive to be a well-rounded fighter if you want to do well in MMA events. Your training has to be very balanced. It's very easy to train and get in shape, but you need a lot of heart to be a champion and keep it going. I really think that if you don't have any heart, it doesn't matter what kind of techniques you've been learning. They won't work.

> **"All the supplementary training in the world won't help you if your cardio- vascular system is not working at the right level."**

Q: What's the secret of the great Brazilian fighters?

A: There's no secret — it's just a good, effective, realistic system, and it takes a lot of hard training to polish the technical aspects of the art. You have to sweat for many years to be a good fighter. There are no shortcuts. You have to pay your dues, my friend. Nothing happens overnight.

Q: How do you keep motivated year after year?

A: I don't have a problem keeping my motivation up. I'm a very calm person, and it's easy for me to focus on things. I also like to work hard. So, when I want to do something, I just do it. My family and my friends support me in everything I do, as well, so that has been a great help over the years.

Q: Is there anything else you would like to add for our readers and practitioners?

A: Yes. I'd recommend finding someone who has the same goals in jiu-jitsu that you have. Find the right kind of partner. Don't hurt yourself training with reckless people who don't care for technical refinement and are only interested in an uncontrolled grappling situation. These training partners won't help you improve. Be focused and train hard.!

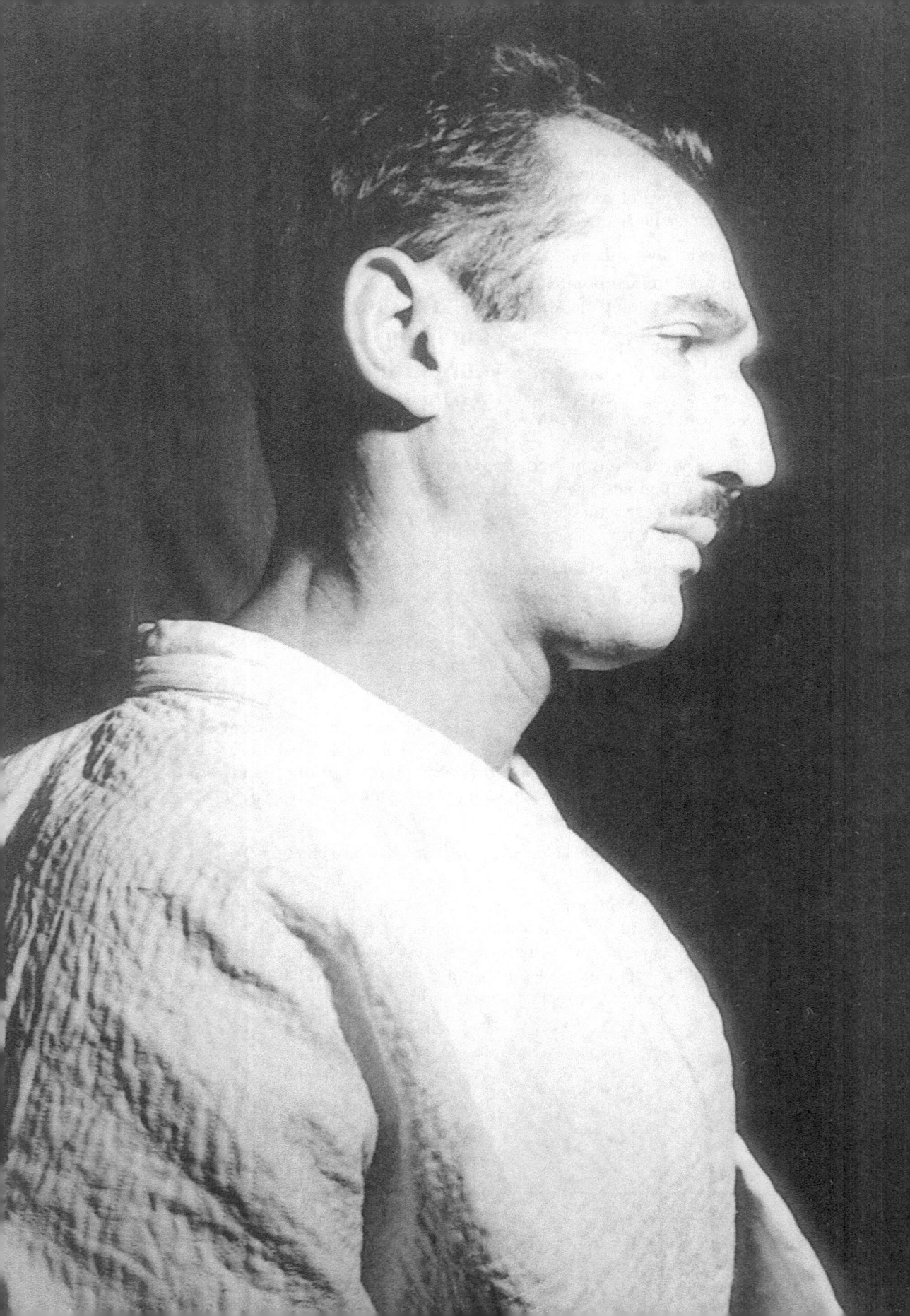

HELIO GRACIE

The Jiu-Jitsu's Greatest

FROM A SICKLY CHILD TO A FEARED JIU-JITSU CHAMPION TAKING ON ALL-COMERS, HELIO GRACIE'S BELIEF IN HIMSELF AND HIS SYSTEM OF FIGHTING ENABLED HIM TO TURN HIS LIFE AROUND AND NOT ONLY HELP HIMSELF, BUT ALSO HELP OTHERS.

HELIO GRACIE, THE FATHER OF THE GRACIE JIU-JITSU SYSTEM, WAS BORN THE YOUNGEST OF FIVE BROTHERS ON OCTOBER 1, 1913 IN THE BRAZILIAN CITY OF BELEM, IN THE STATE OF PARA. A SICKLY CHILD, HELIO SUFFERED FROM AN INEXPLICABLE WEAKNESS THAT RESULTED IN SEVERE FAINTING SPELLS. DUE TO THIS PROBLEM, HE WAS FORBIDDEN FROM ENGAGING ANY KIND OF PHYSICAL ACTIVITY. BY WATCHING HIS OLDER BROTHER, CARLOS, TEACH EVERY DAY, HELIO MEMORIZED EVERY SINGLE MOVE SHOWN AT THE CLASS. ONE DAY, WHEN CARLOS MISSED CLASS, HELIO HAD THE OPPORTUNITY TO TEACH ONE OF HIS STUDENTS. THE MAN WAS SO IMPRESSED WITH HELIO'S TEACHING SKILLS THAT HE ASKED CARLOS TO LET HIM KEEP TRAINING UNDER THE "YOUNG GUY." THE REST, AS THEY SAY, IS HISTORY.

HELIO GRACIE MODIFIED THE JAPANESE VERSION OF JIU-JITSU, CHALLENGED OTHER FIGHTERS AND NEVER HESITATED TO STEP ONTO THE MAT AND PUT HIS SYSTEM TO THE TEST. THIS WAS THE BEGINNING OF THE FAMOUS "GRACIE CHALLENGE," WHICH PUT THEIR GRAPPLING STYLE OF COMBAT TO THE TEST AGAINST ALL FIGHTERS FROM THE STRIKING ARTS. IT WASN'T UNTIL HIS SON, RORION, CREATED THE ULTIMATE FIGHTING CHAMPIONSHIP, THAT THE GRACIE METHOD OF JIU-JITSU BECAME KNOWN AROUND THE WORLD. SON ROYCE GRACIE, SHOCKED THE MARTIAL ARTS WORLD BY WINNING THE UFC THREE TIMES, AND ANOTHER SON, RICKSON GRACIE, A LEGEND IN HIS OWN RIGHT, WENT TO JAPAN TO REPEAT HISTORY AND DEFEATED JAPAN'S BEST MARTIAL ARTISTS USING THE TECHNIQUES HIS FATHER DEVELOPED. BY FIGHTING ALL-COMERS, AND STANDING UP FOR WHAT HE BELIEVED, HELIO EARNED A REPUTATION AS A MAN OF HONOR, SKILL, AND BRAVERY THAT ENDURES TO THIS DAY

Q: How did you start your jiu-jitsu training?

A: My older brother Carlos learned the art its Japanese version, from a Japanese immigrant named Esai Maeda, who taught him the art out of respect for my father, Gastao Gracie, who had helped him get established. Maeda was a fighter who had studied judo, sumo, and several forms of wrestling. A little bit later my brother Carlos began to formally teach. I watched the classes but I wasn't allowed to participate due to my physical condition. I used to sit there every single day, memorizing all the moves in my mind. One day, Carlos was late for a private class, so I just walked up and told the student I'd teach him that day.

Q: What happened afterwards?

A: Carlos came and said to the student, "OK, let's get started." But the man said that I had already taught him. He said that he was very happy with me and he would like to have me as instructor from that day on. That man turned out to be the President of the Bank of Brazil!

Q: Why weren't you allowed to teach at first?

A: As a child I was always sick and very small for my age. When I attended school I used to experience fainting spells. I guess that I was very allergic to the school! The school forbade me from engaging in any kind of physical activity because the family doctor said that I was a physically deprived child.

Q: Did they find the problem?

A: Yes, they found out that I had a problem in my nervous system. Pretty much everyone in my family suffers from this, but I had it the worst. This is why my brother Carlos developed the Gracie Diet.

Q: How were your days at the school?

A: I didn't attend very much and I wasn't a good student. I was smaller that the other kids and I had a real smart mouth, so I used to get in trouble very often.

Q: When did you start to modify the techniques?

A: Well, it was not that I intentionally wanted to change anything. I lacked the physical power to make some techniques really work, so I began to adapt what I had seen to my own physical limitations. It was something very instinctive.

Q: So you didn't change for the sake of change?

A: No, I had to make things work for me. Sometimes I'd find myself in a situation, using the technique the way it was taught to my brother, Carlos, by the Japanese teacher. But I couldn't get it to work because the classical techniques would require a lot of strength. So I had to find a way to make it work using leverage, not muscle strength.

Q: When you began to think about improving the whole system?

A: Pretty soon, I realized that what I was doing was something that anybody could do. The techniques that I was developing would work for anyone, not just for me. At that point I decided to devote my life to jiu-jitsu.

Q: Did your health improve?

A: Yes, very much. I guess the correct diet and the right exercise made me healthier. But also, and this is very important, I began to get rid off the mental complexes that I had as a weak child. I was not insecure anymore and I became more confident and outgoing as I began teaching and helping other people to improve.

Q: Do you think martial arts training can change people's lives?

A: Sure it can! I always say that when you can handle a physical situation you are more confident. When you are more confident and secure, you become much more tolerant of others because you don't need to prove yourself. It's like if you win the lottery-you don't have to worry about money anymore so you're happier. If you know how to defend yourself properly you don't have to worry about being victimized. It clears your mind to concentrate on other things.

> **"I guess the correct diet and the right exercise made me healthier. But also, I began to get rid off the mental complexes that I had as a weak child."**

Q: Isn't this a direct contradiction of the famous Gracie Challenge?

A: No, because the Gracie Challenge was a way of improving our system and letting the people see how good the techniques were. It was not a personal thing, or an ego trip. If you really look at it from the right perspective, the challenge was very much for ourselves because it put us in constant difficulty and we had to develop new techniques and strategies to deal with other systems. It never was a personal thing.

Q: You challenged the great boxers, Joe Louis and Primo Carnera, correct?

A: Yes. I wanted to prove the effectiveness of the system. I personally had nothing against them. They were just big men and big names and I was sure that I could take them.

Q: Didn't you once fight for three-and-a-half-hours straight?

A: Yes, they were going to enter it in the Guiness Book of World Records, but they finally decided against it because they felt it would push people into fighting to beat the record.

Q: How did you became so famous in Japan?

A: I don't know. Maybe because of my many fights in Brazil.

Q: How did you come to fight Kimura?

A: Kimura was considered "the toughest man who ever lived," at that time. He heard about me and decided that he wanted to fight me. I said, "Fine, let's go." In Japan, they have a tradition that the top guy doesn't fight challengers unless they defeat his best student. So I had to fight Kato, who was Kimura's top student and 40 pounds heavier than me.

Q: What happened?

A: I defeated Kato. I choked him into unconsciousness. All the Japanese were shocked because no foreigner had ever defeated a Japanese jiu-jitsu champion before. So that gave me the chance to fight Kimura.

Q: Was he good?

A: Yes, he was very good. In fact I never felt I could win because he was over 80 pounds heavier than me and greatly skilled.

Q: Why did you fight him then?

A: Because I always enjoyed fighting against the odds. Kimura was so sure about his victory that he said if I lasted for more than three minutes, I would be considered the victor. And I did. I lasted for 13 minutes and I was still fighting when my brother Carlos threw in the towel because he was afraid that the arm-lock Kimura had would shatter my arm.

Q: What did Kimura say afterwards?

A: He was so impressed that he invited me to Japan to teach at his academy. But I kindly refused. I was very honored but I couldn't leave my family and go.

Q: What is your teaching and martial arts philosophy?

A: I firmly believe in helping people. That's why I departed from tradition, because I wanted to find better and easier ways of doing the things. I've seen a lot of instructors throwing the students when in fact the students are paying for throwing the instructor. No one learns being thrown!

Q: Do you teach women?

A: Yes I do. Women are more concerned about self-defense and don't train to fight as men do. But even that is changing now.

Q: Are you happy with the great popularity the Gracie Jiu-Jitsu these days?

A: Yes I am. I'm so very proud of my sons. Rorion worked very hard in the United States to promote jiu-jitsu. Of course, Royce and Rickson also did a great job and they have great reputations as fighters and teachers.

Q: Is it true that you wear a blue belt?

A: Yes, this is out of protest for all the so-called Gracie Jiu-Jitsu and Brazilian jiu-jitsu masters. Everybody is a black belt or a master in jiu-jitsu these days. But there is a big difference in the way my system is taught in the Torrance Academy and the way others teach their own version of jiu-jitsu. That's why we registered Gracie Jiu-Jitsu name. The way, the art and the values I developed during my whole life as Gracie Jiu-Jitsu can be taught correctly. Other people might have the arm lock or the choke and that's fine. Anyone can train the way they like but I only endorse the teachings at the Torrance Academy and legitimate affiliated schools.

Q: Do you still teach?

A: Yes, a little. I know my sons are spreading the art around the world and I'm very happy that my work is appreciated by those who want to keep the knowledge alive for the future generations. If teach it the right way, Gracie Jiu-Jitsu can make you a better person and make you happier with yourself.

Q: Many modern fighters have as many MMA fights in one or two years as you did in your whole life. Do you feel no-holds-barred fighting has taken on a different meaning today?

A: I didn't have that many vale tudo fights but definitely the things are different today. When I fought I did it for a cause and for a reason. The reason was to prove the efficiency of the method of jiu-jitsu that I was developing. I never did for money. Today, fighters do it simply for money, that's their only objective and goal. It's understandable that when the reason why a person is doing something changes, the whole picture changes too. Fighters today are truly professionals, there is a whole industry that allows a lot of people make a lot of money fighting in NHB. As far as that is concerned we cannot compare my times with the current ones.

Q: When you fought, it was your strategy to remain on the bottom, tire your opponent, and then submit him?

A: Absolutely not. My strategy never was to remain on the bottom and tire my opponent. That's something that I had to do for obvious reasons. It was a consequence, not my way of fighting. I have always fought bigger and stronger opponents, some of them simply grabbed my gi and put me on the ground. Because of my light bodyweight I always ended up on the bottom, but that didn't happened because I wanted to fight from that position! No way. What I wanted was to mount the guy and submit him from there but the weight difference always made that difficult to me so the most of the time I was having the guy on my guard. When you are on the ground the bigger opponent always will use the bodyweight advantage to stay on the top. It's a natural thing but once again no, remain on the bottom was never my strategy, it was the result of circumstances and never my goal. I couldn't choose. Fortunately, when I found myself on the bottom the technical resources I had in jiu-jitsu allowed me to become victorious.

> **"When you are on the ground the bigger opponent always will use the bodyweight advantage to stay on the top."**

Q: Do you feel that modern fighters have figured out how to beat the guard?

A: Let me tell you something about the guard and how people are using it today. It is not that the new fighter totally figured out how to pass the guard-which it is partially true because they have began to learn jiu-jitsu to do that. The problem is not in the guard, the problem lies with the fighters whom don't know how to properly use the guard. If you are not fully capable of using the guard, then it doesn't take a great fighter to pass the guard, but this doesn't mean the guard is not good anymore or you shouldn't use it because people now know how to pass it. The guard is like Michael Shumaker's F-1 car; if you drive it I'm sure you won't win a Grand Prix, but if he does it, he will. The problem it is not the car is not good-you are the problem because you are not good enough driving the car. If you don't know how to properly use the guard, people are going to pass it, but that's not the guard's fault, it's your fault. And that's what is happening today.

> "Although it could be advantageous for our opponents, I believe that jiu-jitsu should be represented by a fighter wearing a gi."

Q: If you were in your fighting prime of 30 years old, how do you feel you would do against the top MMA fighters today and what would be your strategy against them?

A: I'm sure that I would find a lot of difficulties mainly because my body weight-but I had this problem when I was younger anyway. Fighters nowadays are extremely big-some of them due not to natural foods, that's obvious. Technique-wise, since everyone is learning jiu-jitsu it would make it more difficult but I am yet to see a fighter with a technical level that could defeat me. The only way you can win a top jiu-jitsu fighter is with jiu-jitsu. The way I developed the jiu-jitsu techniques make the art almost an inexpugnable fortress. The fighters nowadays use a lot of strength and force when they fight. I never used those because I have always fought bigger and stronger opponents. It could have been suicidal to do it. My strategy was always based on technique, not strength. That's why I could fight for 3 hours and 45 minutes. Nobody can fight that long if all what he uses is pure force.

Q: Do you feel that the gi is an advantage or disadvantage in a no-holds-barred fight?

A: Although it could be advantageous for our opponents, I believe that jiu-jitsu should represented by a fighter wearing a gi.

Q: Do you think the jiu-jitsu techniques that are taught and used today are more effective than the techniques taught and used 60 years ago?

A: The new "modified" techniques are not better than the old techniques. What is an "old" technique? This is ridiculous! The problem lies in that modern practitioners are stronger than in the past-they don't really need to polish their technique to make a basic technique work because they compensate with brute force. For instance, you can apply a choking technique and apply the technique wrong, but if you are 220 pounds and you have arms like a bodybuilder, you are going to choke the guy out, no matter what. But it doesn't mean you are doing the technique right. If I use the incorrect way of doing it-like the bodybuilder did-I won't be able of apply it effectively. Why? Because I don't have the force to apply a movement that is being performed technically wrong. I can't compensate my lack of technique with strength because I don't have it. I have to make sure I do the technique 100 percent perfect. Then, I don't need all this muscle. In modern jiu-jitsu competitions, fighters are using force and pure strength to compensate for the lack of polished technique. And that is not good. Maybe you'll be able of winning some tournaments with the modern and inconsistent rules but this approach is a shortcut that will take you nowhere.

Q: What is your opinion of all the modern competitors talking about "new" and "modified" techniques?

A: When a fighter is not competent using the basic and fundamental techniques, he always tries to compensate and create new things to cope with that. Then they criticize the basics describing them as "old." This is a non-sense affirmation. Modern boxers are using the same boxing techniques that Joe Louis did. The overall approach to boxing training has changed but they still doing the jab, cross, hook and uppercut. It's that simple. Once you have a good and strong technical arsenal and game plan, all what you need is to be able of apply all the basic at will. To be able of funtionalize what you have. That's what your dedication and training should be focused on, and not trying to create new things that are simply a reflection of your lack of skill in jiu-jitsu basics. All these new and modified techniques are no more than try to reinvent the wheel. They are simply a modification of principles and concepts already established in the basic techniques. Nothing new. The funny thing is that some these "new" techniques can only be applied against a less skilled opponent-no way you'll be able of apply them against a good fighter-and having to use and develop "modified" and "new" technique to beat a less-skilled opponent doesn't say much about you as a jiu-jitsu fighter and practitioner.

Q: What the major risk for a jiu-jitsu fighter in a MMA fight?

A: The difference here is that the jiu-jitsu fighter has the risk of being punched and get knocked out. That's why I have always covered myself to avoid being knocked out. If my opponent didn't knocked me out, then everything was going to be alright. A victory throughout a knockout is what I call an "accidental victory." Not a victory based on technique and strategy. Anyone can get knocked out with one accidental punch but it doesn't mean the opponent is better and more technical than you.

Q: You're generally acknowledged as the originator of the modern Gracie jiu-jitsu style. Excluding yourself, rank the top jiu-jitsu exponents, technique-wise, in the Gracie family?

A: Definitely my sons. They are the ones I have spent more time with and you can see that in their technique. I haven't dedicated myself that much to my nephews, cousins, et cetera, so I can say that my sons are the more technical exponents in the Gracie family. Even today my sons have their own lives and I don't spend much time with them.

Q: Rickson is regarded as the number-one fighter in the Gracie family. What are his qualities as a fighter?

A: At the time Rickson was representing the family in the fights in Brazil, it's true that he was without a doubt the best fighter in the family. Now there are other members that are coming close but at that time he was the absolute champion in the family. His qualities as a fighter are many and he was gifted with a great and strong body. This makes everything easier. Then he has always been very dedicated to jiu-jitsu, and last but not least he has the right mentality and temperament to be a fighter. You put everything together and that's Rickson Gracie.

Q: Outside of the Gracie family members, which modern fighters do you feel have good jiu-jitsu technique, and that you like to watch?

A: I don't really watch many fights. I'm sure there are many good fighters out there but I'm not interested in watching other people fight.

Q: Many people recommend doing yoga as a great complement to jiu-jitsu, what do you think?

A: Yoga is a good activity regardless if you do jiu-jitsu or not. I never did, I never need it. Sure it can be good for your body, but all what I needed were the specific drills and exercises I developed for jiu-jitsu.

Q: When you started teaching martial arts, did you ever think that Gracie jiu-jitsu, a style that you developed and made famous in Rio de Janeiro, would ever become as popular all over the world as it is now?

A: No. I never practiced jiu-jitsu with the popularity and money goals in mind. I never cared about it. My only objective was to make the art better and make myself better to better protect myself. Then pass it onto my sons and students. My goal in teaching was always to teach my students to be able of defeating me, because when they got better, they pushed me harder and I had to get better too. I never taught in the wrong way or hide things from my students. The popularity the art has today, it is due to my son Rorion. He is the person who really made the name of Gracie jiu-jitsu well-known around the world. Very few people knew my jiu-jitsu and my name before Rorion came to America and created the UFC. After that a whole business was developed for all Brazilians to come to the United States and other countries around the world, open schools, teach jiu-jitsu and for people to start organizing MMA events and make a lot of money. Now it is a new ball game but when I was teaching and fighting I never had money in mind. Never crossed my mind or thought about it.

Q: What is the difference between Gracie jiu-jitsu and Brazilian jiu-jitsu?

A: My brother Carlos introduced me to the jiu-jitsu he learned from Esai Maeda. As I modified and perfected those techniques a Brazilian style of jiu-jitsu was born. We never changed the name. It remained simply jiu-jitsu. When my son Rorion came to America in the '70s he decided to pay tribute to the teaching method I have developed and started calling it Gracie jiu-jitsu to differentiate from the Japanese method of jiu-jitsu that some people in the United States had heard about during the war. Through his dedication and great business sense, Rorion made Gracie jiu-jitsu the most popular martial art in the world today. So directly or indirectly, everyone that practices Brazilian jiu-jitsu is using the moves I have developed, some with better techniques than others. What surprises me, it is that some members of the Gracie family and individuals that really know that both styles are the same, prefer to call it "Brazilian jiu-jitsu." Credit should be given where credit is due. If what I have developed is internationally known as Gracie jiu-jitsu, that is what it should be called. There is no other way around it.

> **"Today the competitions are built on commercial bases. The goal of jiu-jitsu is to win, not to play silly games to win a match. That's not jiu-jitsu."**

Q: If you could change anything about modern Brazilian jiu-jitsu competitions today, what would it be?

A: The rules. Competition rules and time limits of today are ridiculous and change everything. Today the competitions are built on commercial bases. The goal of jiu-jitsu is to win, not to play silly games to win a match. That's not jiu-jitsu. Unfortunately, that is what it is right now. I have created a new set of rules and regulations to make jiu-jitsu competitions more real and less manipulative. You are there to win by submission, no by playing and trying to stall a fight without doing anything, letting the time pass and win without haven't done anything at all. A jiu-jitsu fighter must enter in a competition to win, not to compete. Today the people fight in competitions to not lose, and that's embarrassing for the art.

Q: When you fought you did it for a cause. Today fighters and even members of the Gracie family do it for money. How do you feel about it and how do you think it affects the mental state when you fight for honor or fight for money?

A: Of course! There are a lot of things that money can buy, but let me tell you that it won't buy courage and passion for something. You can fight hard for money but there always will be a limit-a line you won't trespass simply for money. When you fight for honor or because your life is at stake, you can do things that you'll never do for money-you can endure punishment that no money will make you to. There are a lot of crazy things a professional fighter can do for big sums of money but when you fight for other reasons bigger than money, then you can do and endure things you can't even imagine before. Today people simply fight for money, not because they are brave and want to prove something to the rest of the world. They simply do it for money, and there are things money can't buy and there are things no money in the world will make a person do. There are limitations for everything, even for what money can do in people's behavior. Money doesn't bring an interest for the individual in evolving and improve as a fighter either.

Q: What it would be you final message to all practitioners of jiu-jitsu around the world?

A: To be honest, grateful and true human beings. I would like to remind them to always give credit where the credit is due. We all have our own lives but it doesn't mean we have to negate our roots and recognized those who opened the doors for us. Today the art is well known all over the world and many Brazilian instructors are making their living thanks to what my son Rorion did here in the United States. He opened the doors for everybody. I would like to see people recognizing that and then go on with their lives and business as usual. The worse thing is life is not to be grateful. Technique-wise I would tell them to stick to the basics and train hard to make the basics work against any type of opponent and under any kind of situation. Don't waste time with new "technical fantasies" that will take you nowhere. Stick to the basics.

> "Today the art is well known all over the world and many Brazilian instructors are making their living thanks to what my son Rorion did here in the United States."

"Jiu Jitsu is a mousetrap. The trap does not chase the mouse. But when the mouse grabs the cheese, the trap plays its role."
~ Helio Gracie ~

HELIO "SONECA" MOREIRA

High Energy Jiu-Jitsu

WHEN YOU MEET "SONEQUINHA" YOU WILL FEEL NOTHING LESS THAN THE ENERGY OF SOMEONE SERIOUSLY DEVOTED TO THE STUDY OF BRAZILIAN JIU-JITSU. ALTHOUGH HELIO MOREIRA STARTED HIS TRAINING A VERY EARLY AGE, HE IS EXTREMELY UNDERSTANDING, APPROACHABLE AND RESPECTFUL – NOT ONLY AS A JIU-JITSU INSTRUCTOR BUT AS A HUMAN BEING AS WELL. HIS LONG YEARS OF EXPERIENCE HAVE ALLOWED HIM TO INTERNALIZE THE IMPORTANT MORAL ASPECTS OF JIU-JITSU AND USE THEM IN HIS DAILY LIFE. INTERNATIONALLY RECOGNIZED AS A MARTIAL ARTS AUTHORITY, HE CURRENTLY MAKES HIS HOME IN THE U.S. WHERE HE TEACHES AND SHARES THE KNOWLEDGE HE HAS SPENT A LIFETIME ACQUIRING. BORN IN RIO DE JANEIRO, HE FIRST BECAME INVOLVED IN THE ART WHILE LOOKING FOR A METHOD OF SELF-DEFENSE. INSTEAD HE FOUND A WAY OF LIFE AND BECAME OBSESSED WITH SHARING HIS DISCOVERIES WITH STUDENTS BOTH YOUNG AND OLD, REGARDLESS OF THEIR ABILITY. WHAT SETS HIM APART IS THAT HE IS READY AND WILLING TO NOT ONLY TRAIN HARDCORE MARTIAL ARTISTS, BUT ALSO INDIVIDUALS INTERESTED IN PERSONAL DEVELOPMENT AS WELL. HE IS A KNOWLEDGEABLE AND FASCINATING MAN, FULL OF INTERESTING STORIES, AND BRIMMING WITH A POSITIVE ATTITUDE TOWARDS TEACHING AND TO LIFE. IN THE MODERN WORLD OF DISILLUSIONMENT, HE IS TRULY A UNIQUE INDIVIDUAL

Q: When did you start training Brazilian jiu-jitsu?

A: When I was 9 years old. My main teachers were Cirilo Azevedo, Zé Beleza, the Machado brothers, Renzo Gracie and last but not least, the president of the Brazilian Federation, Carlos Gracie Jr. Although all of them practice the same martial art, they are very different in the way they teach and perceive jiu-jitsu. Even the same techniques have a different flavor depending of who is teaching it.

Q: Do you recommend training under different teachers?

A: Not in the beginning, because students can get easily confused and their progress will be slowed by all the information coming from different people. Later on, once the student has a brown or black belt, it is okay to learn different approaches to the same techniques and positions. It is very important to get the basics from one instructor and develop a deep understanding of them. Later, if you have the opportunity to expand your training under other instructors, they may give you some personal points to add to your previous knowledge. This can not only improve your techniques but also your level of understanding.

Q: What attracted you to Brazilian jiu-jitsu?

A: In Brazil, it is simply jiu-jitsu and it comes from the Gracie family. But I know it is important to use the term "Brazilian" in order for people to differentiate the system created and developed by the Gracie family from Japanese forms of jiu-jitsu. The reason I got involved in jiu-jitsu is very interesting and amusing. My mother has always been a very beautiful woman who attracted a lot of attention because of her looks. When I was in high school some of the guys started to joke about my mother, saying things that were offensive. One day I decided that I'd had enough and I confronted them. I fought all those guys at the same time and they were all older than me and much bigger. I got the worse part of that fight! I tried to face them again but they just got mad again and I got beaten again! It was then I decided that the only way out was to learn how to fight these guys with my bare hands, and jiu-jitsu was the answer. I spent three months training really hard with only the idea of getting revenge. After this time I went back to them and gave them what they deserved. They became my friends after they got their beating. We stayed friends all this time. I know this is not the reason an individual should learn a martial art but that is the way it happened to me. In a way, I'm very grateful things came out that way because jiu-jitsu became a way of life to me and opened a lot of doors.

> **"In Brazil, it is simply jiu-jitsu and it comes from the Gracie family. But I know it is important to use the term "Brazilian" in order for people to differentiate the system created and developed by the Gracie family."**

Q: Have you ever trained in other martial arts?

A: Only boxing. I really like it and I feel it is a very good complement to jiu-jitsu. It is a very efficient art for those who want to learn to use their hands for fighting.

Q: Was it hard for you to learn jiu-jitsu techniques?

A: I started when I was a kid. At the age of 9 your body absorbs and learns in a way that you can't believe. Give a kid a bicycle and leave him alone for a week – then you go back you'll find the kid doing things you have never seen. Kids learn at a very fast pace and this is what happened to me in jiu-jitsu. Because of the age I started, all the movements seemed to fit perfectly into my body. Since my physical structure is slim and limber, I had a lot of advantages when performing the techniques and positions. The way I learned was basically by playing. I loved to play, and when a kid plays without any pressure they learn really fast.

When I began to understand more about the art, I became more involved in the learning process. I believe that after all these years of training I have acquired the most important secret of the art – good basics and strong fundamentals. I have seen a lot of black belts with very weak and poor knowledge of the basics and this is very bad for the art. Some of them are what I call "three-position black belts." By this I mean those black belt who only know a few positions and everything they teach is based on what they do best. A teacher can't teach only the movements he likes. He needs to have a complete knowledge and understanding of the art and share all its possibilities with his students. Later on, the students themselves will decide which positions and techniques are better for them. It is the instructor's responsibility to give all his knowledge to the students. If a teacher saves a little here and there, eventually it will weaken the art.

Q: Why do you think some instructors do that?

A: I can only guess! Definitely there is insecurity about what they may know or not know. If you really know the art, you are not afraid of giving knowledge to students. But I don't agree with giving tons of information to a student too early, because the only result you'll get is to confuse them! A good teacher knows how much information should be given at any point in training, so the student can naturally absorb all the technical knowledge. If a teacher doesn't want the students to learn, all he has to do is give a lot of technical information in a random way. This will confuse the student but nobody will be able to blame the instructor for not giving information.

Q: How should a student's daily training be conducted?

A: Jiu-jitsu is an art that evolves constantly. It has to do with the way the art is practiced in Brazil and the great number of competitions every weekend. New movements and technical changes appear all the time. This is good because it makes the technical aspects of the art grow constantly.

On the other hand, we have to be careful because many people who are not interested in sport competition may end up trying to duplicate the latest techniques developed by the champions. Training for competition is a completely different thing than training for yourself and focusing on the true art of Brazilian jiu-jitsu. Competition goes away and disappears from your life when you reach a certain age, but the art stays with you forever if you are really interested in it. My advice for those who are not interested in competition is to focus on developing great basics. Don't try to learn 20 different ways of passing the guard. Learn three or four basic techniques that encompass all the fundamental principles of passing your opponent's guard and work hard until you have mastered them. Analyze the principles and then try to combine them according to the situation you find yourself in. You'll be surprised how strong your game will become, focusing on a limited amount of techniques instead of chasing thousands of movements without taking time to master any of them.

Since the art is based on a logical and progressive approach to techniques, it is very common to find new movements while training and sparring. Sometimes you get caught in a technical dilemma, and the natural way the body escapes from a position will allow you to develop a new movement. But it is important to keep in mind the essence of how jiu-jitsu acts and moves. See how you can escape or do a movement without using strength – use technique and not muscle. This is the main reason why basics are so important.

Q: What should a student look for in a school?

A: Students should be dedicated and loyal to their teacher and not jump from one instructor to another for no reason. They should be honest with themselves and keep training hard regardless of what their goal may be. Before starting to train under any given instructor, check his credentials and find a little about him. Check a class and see if what he is teaching is what you want to practice and train in. Many instructors put too much emphasis on one aspect and forget others – too much competition, too much fitness, or maybe too much self-defense. The teacher should have a balanced approach to jiu-jitsu and not teach only one aspect. There are also differences depending on the country. For instance, in Brazil almost every academy focuses on training to compete in tournaments because that's what jiu-jitsu is there. In the United States, 95 percent of the students are interested in self-defense and exercise. Your approach to teaching should be different then. Rice is rice but Brazilian and Chinese don't cook it the same! Jiu-jitsu is jiu-jitsu but it should accommodate the culture of the country where the instructor teaches.

Q: Do black belts only need to train with other black belts to improve their game?

A: Not really – not if the black belt wants to develop certain specific things. A technical jiu-jitsu practitioner, even if he is a high belt, can train with lower belts and get a great workout – but he will always be lacking something. For instance, an experienced and knowledgeable blue belt who has practiced for three years and is close to purple won't get much benefit from training with white belts all the time. He needs to train with higher belts because the way a purple or brown belt moves is more technical, polished and has more meaning and strategy behind each movement that he does. Jiu-jitsu is about technique and strategy, and the blue belt won't get much of that with white belts. He can train basics drills with the white belts but that will be it. The white belts will improve but not the blue belt.

> **"You simply start training because you want self-defense or to be in good shape, but after years of dedication you realize that you have gained many other more important benefits during this great journey."**

Now, picture the black belt. Of course, he can train with purple or blue belts but all he can really do are some basic drills and low-intensity sparring. If you want to seriously improve your game, you need to find the right sparring partners.

Q: What are the major changes in jiu-jitsu since you began training?

A: The rules established by the Brazilian Confederation under the guidance of Carlos Gracie Jr. is the major improvements in the sport. With these rules of engagement, practitioners have been able to face each other under safe regulations that allow the technical elements to keep evolving. Combat jiu-jitsu is a martial art that can't be trained unless you hurt your partner – but sport jiu-jitsu allows practitioners to test their skills safely. Of course, the Ultimate Fighting Championship brought everyone's eyes to Brazilian jiu-jitsu and spread it all over the world.

Q: Who would you like to train with that you haven't?

A: Rickson Gracie. I think any serious jiu-jitsu practitioner would love to train with him. He is a living legend to jiu-jitsu fighters and fans and the most technical practitioner of all time.

Q: What keeps you motivated after all these years?

A: My students are my best friends and I consider them like my brothers. Jiu-jitsu has helped a lot of us to find friends who become like a family. This is one of the many things the practice of a true martial art brings to your life. You simply start training because you want self-defense or to be in good shape, but after years of dedication you realize that you have gained many other more important benefits during this great journey. Jiu-jitsu and my family are the two most important things in my life.

Q: How do you mentally prepare for a fight?

A: To be honest I don't have a special mental and philosophical preparation for a competition. I know that whatever I may accomplish is coming from God, so I simply consider myself a vehicle. In both jiu-jitsu and life sometimes you win and sometimes you lose and you need to be prepared for both. Embracing everything we have in life, good or bad, is something that helps everyone have a better existence. We are only taught to win, and so we are only happy when things go our way and not when things come out differently than what we planned. If you accept the fact that things can go the other way and don't try to engineer your life too rigidly, you'll find out that you are happy with whatever comes your way.

Q: What has inspired you in your training?

A: Some time ago I had the opportunity to train with a student of Carlos Gracie Jr. This individual only has one arm. I also trained with a student of Jorge Pereira. It happens Pereira's student is paraplegic and has no movement in his legs. With the first student I sparred using only one of my arms – and with the second I tied my legs. I lost against both of them! This single experience allowed me to realize many things and opened my eyes. You have to learn how to use what you have and make jiu-jitsu work for you under your own circumstances, not somebody else's.

In 1995 I had a serious back injury. My doctor said I should start thinking about stopping jiu-jitsu completely. The back is a very important part of your body if you train jiu-jitsu. It is like having a shoulder injury in boxing; yes, you can use your hands but not the physical support system. That is what the back represents to a jiu-jitsu student. I had to re-evaluate my training, select the people I could train with, and what kind of techniques I'd do. My movements couldn't be as explosive as before. I needed to develop a new game plan so I could establish a more convenient position every time I sparred. I had to limit the weight of my sparring partners because heavier guys would seriously hurt my back. I also had to avoid training with people who used only brute force and pure strength. The funny thing was that I think that I improved my jiu-jitsu because of that and became a better teacher.

The moral of the story is to learn your limitations and then work around them. Jiu-jitsu has something to offer everybody, but we need to know how to find it. If you are a 40-year-old lawyer or an architect you can't train as crazy as a 20-year-old student. Also, you can't afford to get injured because you don't make a living with jiu-jitsu. Does it mean you can't get a black belt? No. Of course, you can! What is important is to find a teacher who understand this and will guide you to reach your goals according to your personal situation. Teachers can't teach the same to all their students – they have to vary their classes according to the type of students they have.

> "If you are a 40-year-old lawyer or an architect you can't train as crazy as a 20-year-old student. Also, you can't afford to get injured because you don't make a living with jiu-jitsu."

Q: How important is proper nutrition for competition?

A: One of the most important things a tournament competitor should have is a good diet. But this is true not only for a competitor but for every single student as well. A good diet is good for everybody! The right food is extremely important because if you don't put the right food into your body, it won't matter how many hours you train on the mat. Maybe when you are 20 years old your body will perform pretty much the same, but when you start getting older the proper diet will make a difference because your body will perform better. Once you take care of your body, then you need to put in many hours of training and do it intelligently, setting goals and improving at a steady pace. I used to love to eat junk food, but now I know I should have taken much better care of myself.

Q: Can weightlifting, running, swimming, et cetera replace time on the mat?

A: First of all, I don't think supplementary training will ever compensate for a lack of mat time. Train jiu-jitsu first, if it is jiu-jitsu you are interested in. Then when you get some extra time, use it for additional training that allows you to improve the physical aspects necessary to excel in the art. Keep in mind that this supplementary training should be very specific or you'll be wasting your time. Everything you do must have a purpose or an application to enhance your skills as a jiu-jitsu practitioner. Remember that there is no substitute for hard training and it is not the quantity of time spent training but rather the quality.

Q: How does fear affects a competitor's performance?

A: There are many psychological aspects that can really mess-up your performance in a competition. There was a time when I though I couldn't lose. I was winning every championship and I thought I was unbeatable. Well, it took a very short time for me to find out that I was wrong. I was putting too much pressure on myself because I thought I had an obligation to win. When you feel obligated to win you perform at a very low level. Jiu-jitsu is an art and a sport. In any sport sometimes you win and sometimes you lose, so be prepared for defeat, accept it and move on. This will take a lot of pressure off and you'll be able to perform at a much higher level.

Q: How important are proper breathing techniques?

A: Extremely important! Breathing is the key to relaxing, and relaxation is the key to performing jiu-jitsu techniques correctly. Many people don't realize that proper breathing and relaxation comes from a state of mind when you are confident with your jiu-jitsu skills. It is when you are not sure of what you know and what you can do, when you start to get nervous and your breathing becomes ragged and tense. The only way you can be confident of what you know is to have very strong technical fundamentals. Students need to reach a technical level where they can control the timing of their breathing in relationship to their physical movements.

Q: Where do you think Brazilian jiu-jitsu is going?

A: Jiu-jitsu is an art which doesn't need to prove anything. It is accepted that Brazilian jiu-jitsu is one of the most effective fighting methods known to man. The Gracie family, and especially Royce Gracie in the UFC, opened everybody's eyes to what the art has to offer. That happened in the early '90s. In the future, I would like to see the art become an Olympic sport, but I also understand that there is much work to do before this can happen. It is important that all practitioners, instructors, federations, and associations work together for the benefit of the art.

Q: Is it necessary to add other fighting skills to jiu-jitsu for mixed martial arts?

A: Definitely! In vale tudo, it is important to add some other combative elements – forget about doing only jiu-jitsu. You need to know how to kick, punch, and close the distance to get into grappling range. MMA is not jiu-jitsu and therefore some modifications should be made to cover all the necessary basics. Martial arts cross-training is necessary for any fighter who wants to be successful in mixed martial arts.

Q: What should jiu-jitsu practitioners mentally focus on?

A: Don't let anyone to steal your dreams and take attention away from your goals – because those dreams are pretty much all you've got. Work hard to reach those goals and remember that battles do not always go to the stronger man. It is important to believe in yourself, but do it realistically and with common sense. One should know his own limitations and work hard to at least reach those limits. If you give your best to anything in life, you will surprise yourself and find that you can exceed the limitations that you thought were impossible to pass. Professor Helio Gracie, for example, is more than 90 years old but yet still trains and challenges people to get on the mat with him. Many people say that he is an old man, but they are wrong. He is far younger than many others who are not nearly as old as him. He has proven that age is just a self-imposed limitation that can be exceeded. What a great example and what a courageous mind.

"**Be so strong that nothing can disturb the peace of your mind.**"
~ Carlos Gracie Sr. ~

JEAN JACQUES MACHADO
Choking the Fear

It would have been easy for Jean Jacques Machado to give into fear. Born without fingers on his left hand, Machado seemed forever fated to sit on the sidelines and watch his athletic brothers rise to sports stardom. But Machado had no quit in him and refused to listen to those who said that it was too dangerous for him to compete. Supported by parents who taught him that he had no limits, and encouraged by brothers who taught him to never back down from a challenge, Jean Jacques soon realized that he had athletic gifts that a mere handicap could never stop and a fighting spirit that fear could never conquer. Competing in jiu-jitsu, this "special" child was soon turning heads and winning trophies with his attacking, take-no-prisoners style of submission fighting..

Under the tutelage of the legendary Carlos Gracie Jr., his technical prowess became breathtaking. Absorbing every single detail of the art of jiu-jitsu, Jean Jacques learned how to decipher every subtle sign his opponents gave, and to use his mind to more than make up for any physical deficiency. His attitude of "no limits, no fear" spread to his personal life as well, and Jean Jacques gained a reputation as a true gentleman and a worldwide ambassador for the sport. His technical mastery was in full force when, in the 1999 Abu Dhabi Submission Wrestling World Championships in the United Arab Emirates, Machado faced four of the toughest fighters on planet earth and submitted them all including Sakurai and Uno-the only time that feat has ever been accomplished.

A fierce competitor on the mat, but a compassionate and supportive teacher off, Machado has used his life lessons to transform himself into a complete individual in an incomplete body. An inspiration and a role model as a fighter, teacher, and devoted family man, Jean Jacques Machado is truly an international emissary for all the grappling arts.

Q: How did you get started in jiu-jitsu?

A: Carlos Gracie Jr. was our teacher from the beginning. When you say jiu-jitsu you have to link it to the Gracie family. That's the family that started our jiu-jitsu style and we're just one part of that clan. I think that everyone today that knows Brazilian jiu-jitsu learned it, directly or indirectly, from a member of the Gracie family. Everyone should be grateful to them for that. I also learned a lot from my older brothers. Since they have been training for so long, even when I was just starting, they always taught me new techniques and corrected my positions-I learned a lot from being the youngest. Even today I'm still learning; every time I train with my brothers I feel I learn something new. When I have questions it's always good to have more than one head think about the movement. You get more answers than you can come up with yourself.

Q: Did you ever think that you weren't going to be as good as your brothers?

A: No, I never had that thought. My coach, my cousins in the Gracie family, and my brothers, never said anything like that-I never had any time to think like that. I was always very athletic and I really liked to do sports. Sometimes, though, a normal sport for someone else would be a dangerous sport for me. For example, I used to play hockey where you have to use your hands all the time. You can hurt your hands or your fingers very easily. I remember my parents being very worried, but they didn't want to tell me that I couldn't do it. They didn't want me to get it in my head that there was something other kids could do, that I couldn't. But still you wonder and sometimes feel a little bad. I remember one time that I felt very bad and my brother John said to my parents, "I want to be like Jean Jacques and cut off my fingers, too, so I can be good like him." So when you hear something like that it makes you feel good about life, not just about jiu-jitsu.

> "In Brazilian jiu-jitsu we have four belts: blue, purple, brown and black. I have to say that there's not a huge difference between the blue and purple; nor is there a huge difference between brown and black."

Q: Explain the ranking system in jiu-jitsu.

A: In Brazilian jiu-jitsu we have four belts: blue, purple, brown and black. I have to say that there's not a huge difference between the blue and purple; nor is there a huge difference between brown and black. The purple belt knows a little bit more than the blue as far as the amount of techniques, but the real difference is based on his experience and the ability to apply these techniques. The purple belt can apply all the moves while wrestling. The blue belt is someone who has already developed some sort of "game" idea, but the purple belt is someone who has a better application of the game. From purple belt to brown belt is a big step. The brown belt has to know a lot more physical techniques and have a higher level of understanding about the art. He needs what we call "body intelligence." A brown belt has some positions that are perfect; if he gets these positions, there's no escape for the opponent. He has to be able to do whatever he wants.

Q: What is your philosophy on submission fighting?

A: In jiu-jitsu, submission is the only thing I ever go for. It is the reward for the art. If you see a lot of the jiu-jitsu fighters, each one has their own style. Some guys like to fight from the bottom, some guys more from the top. But my style is that I just want to finish. No matter where I am I'm looking for the finishing move. I learned this way and I feel that it is a very creative style. In order to get a good finish, of course, you should have some type of control of the other person. It doesn't have to be a physical control. Control can also mean forcing the person into a position where you know how they're going to react.

If I try to get 20 submission attempts but I fail, I don't go and play the points game. Not being able to get the submission only makes me feel that I have to work more on my game. I give all the credit to that person who survives all my finishing attempts-the bottom line is that I didn't finish him so I deserve to lose. But I won't try to just get points. To me the only true proof of how good you are is to finish by submission. It is the true measure of the art.

Q: You did very good in no-gi tournaments like Abu Dhabi. Why?

A: I think Abu Dhabi was and is a great opportunity for any fighter to show how good they are. I've never seen a tournament that has so much money involved and so many great athletes from all kinds of styles: no-holds-barred, wrestling, judo, jiu-jitsu, shooto and even sumo I think. If you see the names of the people that fought over there it's really the best of the best. I saw it as a great opportunity to try my jiu-jitsu against other jiu-jitsu guys, or some wrestlers, or just any style. I was looking for that challenge and I think I had success. I proved my point that the Machado style of jiu-jitsu is very good.

Q: Did you do any kind of mental training before a fight?

A: Well, competing was extremely important for me, so I didn't feel like talking much. I was always just focused on the particular fight that I have ahead of me. I was there to fight and to compete. After the competition was over and everything had settled down a little, then I could have a nice time and relax a little. But I was always really focused on the event.

Q: Do you fight on instinct and reaction or do you have a set plan?

A: I think that you have your game by the time you get to fight. After training so much, your body and mind develop their own reactions. When you train grappling, which I have been doing all my life, you pretty much feel all the reactions that are possible in a given situation. Because when you are training with students there will be some beginners, some intermediate, and some advanced ones that will all react differently to a move you apply. Then your body pretty much absorbs and learns what to do when somebody reacts this way. So when you train a lot, after a while you don't have to think anymore - your body just reacts. It's the same as if you touch your finger to something hot. You're not going to think, you're just going to pull your arm back. That's the way I look for perfection in a technique. The more automatic I am, that's what I'm looking for. If I have to think, then I don't know the move.

Q: Your attacking style was always very popular...

A: My fighting style was and is well-known by everybody in jiu-jitsu-I'm always looking for a finish. Even if I don't win the match, they will know that they almost lost to me by submission. The lucky guys who escape from that don't want to face me again because they know how close to the cliff they were. Because I was away from competition since my brothers and I came to America, and it was hard to return to Brazil for the big tournaments because of the distance, I think maybe some people forgot how hard I try to finish a match by submission. A lot of them came up to me afterwards and said, "Man, I haven't seen that in a long time. It was great. Just like the old days."

Q: So you didn't get that much satisfaction just winning by points?

A: Not really (laughs). As I said before each fighter is different. Some are more aggressive and some more defensive. Each one has his own way of thinking. If you have a jiu-jitsu class with each of my brothers, teaching the same position, they'll show you a different angle that ends in the same submission. But each has a different way to apply the action or the movement. So I think I'm very aggressive in submission and I think that my brothers are like that too and are very submission oriented.

Q: You train with everyone straight-up, but yet you have no fingers on your left hand.

A: The way my parents raised me was to tell me that I could do anything I wanted. That's the way I still think. And for a lot of people they're not used to thinking like that. For myself, for example, I don't have four fingers on my left hand, but I was born like that. And I had to learn how to deal with it. Martial arts, and especially jiu-jitsu, is like water: it fits in every shape and in every body. It doesn't matter how big or small you are, or what kind of physical problems that you have. You're just going to have to adjust the jiu-jitsu to you, not adjust yourself to the jiu-jitsu. And that's what happened with me-I do movements that a person with a normal left hand doesn't do, because that's the way that jiu-jitsu fits me. I have developed jiu-jitsu to fit my touch. And I don't see any other person who trains jiu-jitsu that does it with the same type of problem that I have. I see it as a challenge and it empowers me and stimulates me to do better.

Q: How about when you were growing up?

A: I think I surprised a lot of people. Here I have pretty much no left hand, and most people in jiu-jitsu use both their hands to grab and to hold, but I did very well. I was always rated number one, or close to number one, in my weight class. So I tell my own students, "Look, if I can do it, you can do it." Success is in your spirit-it's a very spiritual thing. You really have to believe in yourself. And I think that if you really believe in yourself, you can do anything you want. No doubt about it.

Q: What is jiu-jitsu like in Brazil in comparison to Abu Dhabi?

A: The rules in Abu Dhabi are very different than Brazilian jiu-jitsu rules. In Brazil, every month the rules change a little bit, because the promoters are trying to make the matches more exciting. Sometimes the changes work well, sometimes they don't. I went back to train a while ago and saw that they were really trying to win by using the rules to only score points. And that really surprised me. I was only playing for submission like I had always done, but the other guys were just looking to get control of a position and then hold it to just score some points. I would say they weren't doing bad. They were playing by the rules and that is why there are rules. But like I said, each fighter has their own style. There are a lot of great champions in Brazil, but each one of them chooses a little different direction to apply their game. So it is different from here, but there isn't all that much more submission attempts there, either. The art of the submission is being a little lost everywhere, I think.

Then we have the vale tudo format. There are many jiu-jitsu fighters that try vale tudo as an extension of what they are already doing. They find there is no more room for them to grow inside jiu-jitsu and they take the game to a different level. Some fighters are great in jiu-jitsu but are not good in vale tudo - others are great in vale tudo but not good in sport jiu-jitsu.

Q: Do you think that all the different branches of the Gracie family are as close as they were before coming to the U.S.?

A: I believe so. I believe everyone has the common direction to show the world the Brazilian jiu-jitsu style. That's what the family is doing now. Each member is going their own way by doing challenges, by competing in sport, or by going no-holds-barred. By having a lot of students and giving a lot of seminars everyone is spreading the art of jiu-jitsu. I think that each member of the family has a mission to pass along the style. It doesn't matter if the direction of each family member is different. I think it's good, actually, because there are a lot of different types of people that wouldn't be drawn to just one thing. You know, different people/different choices!

> "Success is in your spirit - it's a very spiritual thing. You really have to believe in yourself."

Q: The Machado name has really grown worldwide. What do you think is the main reason for that?

A: People know the link of our family with the Gracie family and that means quality in the art. Our jiu-jitsu came from the Gracie family, and we are happy to admit that æ we're proud of it. I learned from Carlos Gracie Jr. and he was not just my coach but also my cousin. We have the same blood. So with that knowledge we gained, we used it to make friends. We have lots of students that we treat like family, also. I think it counts a lot with them. I believe that's how martial arts should be used-to make friends, and bring people together, and grow inside. Our goal in the Machado schools is not just to see the students become better fighters, but for them to become better persons as well to accept the challenge of life, to grow in life, to be a better father, to be a better friend, and to be better in their work. And we use the jiu-jitsu as a support for that. And I believe that most of our students feel that way and they like it. So we just keep making more and more friends as we teach more. I consider all my students in America to be part of my family. I'm very close to all my students. And that is the most important part of the martial arts to me.

> **"Our jiu-jitsu came from the Gracie family, and we are happy to admit that we're proud of it. I learned from Carlos Gracie Jr. and he was not just my coach but also my cousin."**

Q: How do you train outside of jiu-jitsu?

A: I lift weights three times a week. I also do cardio every day. When I'm at the gym I use the machines. I go for an hour-and-a-half without stopping æ a half hour on each machine. I do the bike first, then I do the rowing, and then I end up with the stairclimber, sometimes I do the climber. I even do step aerobics. It is very important to understand that today being good in jiu-jitsu is not enough anymore. Years ago if a bigger and stronger guy didn't know jiu-jitsu it was easy to defeat him. Today the big and strong guys know jiu-jitsu so if you are not in top physical conditioning you are going to be in hot water! You need a complete package that involves cardiovascular training, weight training, jiu-jitsu training and proper nutrition. If you lack of one of these elements, it is going to be very hard for you to become a world-class jiu-jitsu athlete.

Q: Do you have plans to build-up sport jiu-jitsu in the United States?

A: Absolutely. If you go to any school of Brazilian jiu-jitsu you will find only a small percentage of people who actually fight vale tudo. Most of them do jiu-jitsu for health or exercise or self-defense or sportive reasons. So most people don't have an outlet to try what they know unless they enter a sport contest. In sport, also, there is not the same intensity and anger that you can get in vale tudo. You're not trying to hurt your opponent, as is the case in vale tudo, but you're trying to submit him or out point him. So this gives students a less intense outlet for what they practice. I think the potential for jiu-jitsu is much greater overall, in terms of actual competitors, than for vale tudo. We have just scratched the surface and my brothers and I are really concentrating on having a lot of tournaments that people can go to, and compete in, and have fun. We've very excited about it.

LEO VIEIRA

The Young Gun Of Brazilian Jiu-Jitsu

LEO VIEIRA'S SPECTACULAR VICTORY AT ABU DABHI 2003, WHERE HE GAVE A CLINIC ON JIU-JITSU TECHNIQUES TO THE BEST GRAPPLERS IN THE WORLD, MADE THE NAME "LEOZINHO VIEIRA" STAND ALONE. AS INTENSE AS HE IS ON THE MAT, HIS FRIENDLY MANNER AND GREAT SENSE OF HUMOR HAVE MADE HIM JUST AS WELL-LIKED OFF OF IT. STRONGLY ROOTED IN TRADITIONAL VALUES, THIS YOUNG GUN OF BRAZILIAN JIU-JITSU IS A LIVING ENCYCLOPEDIA OF THE MOST ORIGINAL AND UNEXPECTED TECHNIQUES OF THE "GENTLE ART." THROUGH MANY YEARS OF DEDICATION AND TRAINING, LEO VIEIRA HAS DEVELOPED A DYNAMIC WAY OF ADAPTING AND INTEGRATING THE FUNDAMENTALS OF BRAZILIAN JIU-JITSU WITH UNIQUE, ACROBATIC MOVEMENTS THAT FIT HIM PERFECTLY. EXTRAORDINARILY TALENTED, HE HAS REACHED A LEVEL WHERE "AVERAGE" OR "MEDIOCRE" IS NO LONGER ACCEPTABLE, AND "EXTRAORDINARY" IS HIS MINIMUM ACCEPTABLE STANDARD.

Q: How long have you been practicing jiu-jitsu?

A: I began training in jiu-jitsu when I was 7. My instructor is Romero "Jacare" Cavalcanti. He is one of the best jiu-jitsu teachers in the world with a very special skill to bring out the best in a student. There are teachers who only teach, but Jacare can look at you and see all the aspects you need to improve on to reach your potential. He is very analytical and a very giving person. I have learned from him how to deal with situations where the pressure is extremely high, when a fighter usually gets very nervous and can't his emotions. His knowledge of the art is amazing and his ability to show how to make different technical concepts work together is really amazing.

Q: Have you ever trained in other martial arts styles such as karate or kickboxing?

A: Not really. In Brazil, if you start training jiu-jitsu is very uncommon to go into another martial art. Only those who want to fight vale tudo train in other styles like Thai boxing or boxing to complement jiu-jitsu. I have always felt attracted to jiu-jitsu and so never felt the need to go to another martial art. I don't recommend that anyone jump from style to style to find the perfect style. I believe this is not a good way to bring out your best, especially when you don't have a strong foundation in any. Only when you have a high level in one art can you add other things effectively.

Q: What was your early training like?

A: I remember a long time ago that I was watching white belts train. They were doing something weird so I asked them to show me what they were doing. They started laughing and showed me. There was common sense in the position, so I took that movement, added some logical elements of jiu-jitsu, and started practicing it. As it turns out, that particular technique is now one of my favorites. Some of the details had to be changed, but the funny part is that two white belts, using common sense, created a new position! I know there are people in Brazilian jiu-jitsu who don't like to change, evolve, and create new things. I am the opposite. I like to analyze and study different ways of improving whatever technique I'm doing. You must keep an open mind to be able to see and adapt new movements.

Q: But don't people sometimes train too many techniques instead of sticking to the basics?

A: Unfortunately this is something that I see all over the world. Blue and purple belts see techniques used by world champions in tournaments and they try to learn and sue them immediately. This is not bad, but beginners need to work the basics to the level of a black belt. Only then can you start to add variations from other people. For instance, I have seen people that started to use the open guard, simply because they didn't take the time to master the closed guard! If you train hard and develop a strong closed-guard then you won't necessarily need to open your legs all the time and work from the open position.

Of course, there are times when you face a bigger and heavier opponent when your leg can't wrap the opponent's waist. Then you need to use the open or spider guard. My advice is to stick to the basics and work very hard until you can make these basics work any time and under any circumstances. This way you'll have very strong basics and will be capable of surprising your opponent with strong techniques. Train the basics first because they are the foundation for everything else.

Q: Has your personal jiu-jitsu developed over the years?

A: I have never stopped learning! The fundamental techniques are the same for everyone, but after many years of training you develop a personal way of doing jiu-jitsu. I always compare this to cooking – rice is rice, chicken is chicken, and carrots are carrots, wherever you live. What makes a difference is the way a good cook combines and prepares these elements. Jiu-jitsu is the same. We all know the same techniques but we spice them up with a personal approach that gives each game an individual flavor. Then when you start competing, your jiu-jitsu becomes more streamlined and direct. You start using only those things that really work. It doesn't mean that you don't train all the moves, but when you compete you have to become really good at a few things in order to win.

> **"My advice is to stick to the basics and work very hard until you can make these basics work any time and under any circumstances."**

Q: Has jiu-jitsu changed over the years now that so many people are cross-training?

A: Jiu-jitsu has evolved a lot in the last few years with new techniques and positions that have been developed by young champions. There is nothing wrong with that because that's the nature of competition. When you test yourself in different environments like Abu Dhabi where we fight without a gi, you need to incorporate technical elements like takedowns and reversals used in wrestling. Later on, when you go back to a jiu-jitsu tournament, you may end up using these techniques even though they were not originally from jiu-jitsu. Personally, I don't see a problem with this. It is a logical evolution based on achieving your competition goals. I don't spend time arguing philosophically about whether it is pure or impure. I leave that for the philosophers. I just know that you have to do it to win.

Q: What is opinion of MMA events?

A: Vale tudo fighting is not Brazilian jiu-jitsu. Jiu-jitsu practitioners do very well in these types of events because of the effectiveness of the art, but it doesn't mean that vale tudo exemplifies the essence of Brazilian jiu-jitsu. This type of fighting has been very important in giving credit to the art of jiu-jitsu. Royce Gracie made a tremendous world impact fighting in the UFC and defeating all his opponents with jiu-jitsu. In short, I believe these events are positive for jiu-jitsu but we can't mistake one thing with the other because they are very different.

Q: Do you think that the ADCC competition system is the future of the sport?

A: It is very difficult to say where the sport will be ten years from now but the truth is that mixed martial arts is not a sport that everybody can play. It takes a certain kind of individual, with the right attitude and the time to train properly. Many jiu-jitsu champions don't feel like entering MMA – they simply don't like it. It is here when grappling competitions like Abu Dhabi come into play. You can be a wrestler, a jiu-jitsu guy, a judoka, or a sambo practitioner and compete with a good chance of winning. Different grappling methods can compete against each other under basic rules that are fair to all styles. Regardless of your original method, you have to understand and even learn technical aspects of the other grappling systems you'll face. In MMA, a simple wild punch can finish the fight, but in a grappling competition like Abu Dhabi you have to be very technical or you will lose your first match.

> **"Martial arts get recognition through these events, but people then assume that jiu-jitsu and other martial arts are simply an MMA style for cage fighting."**

Q: Is MMA good for martial arts?

A: It's a double-edged sword. Martial arts get recognition through these events, but people then assume that jiu-jitsu and other martial arts are simply an MMA style for cage fighting. The true art of jiu-jitsu embodies much more than vale tudo, MMA, and cage fighting.

Q: Do you think that jiu-jitsu level in the U.S. has caught up with Brazil?

A: The skill level found in American jiu-jitsu practitioners has improved substantially. There are more competitions in the United States and more Brazilian champions are invited to compete, which also increase the level. The main difference lies in the fact that in Brazil we have competitions every weekend. Practitioners are competing all the time in regional, state, or national tournaments. The level is very high and practitioners are used to the pressure of elite competitions. This makes a difference. It is difficult to say when the U.S. will catch Brazil. If you ask me when Brazil will catch the U.S. in baseball, it is impossible to say. In Brazil, jiu-jitsu is like baseball in the U.S.

Q: Do you consider jiu-jitsu to be only a sport?

A: Jiu-jitsu is more than a simple sport. It has a certain philosophy to its practice. It can be used as a sport but the right jiu-jitsu training develops more than the practitioner's body. I don't want to sound religious, but the deeper aspects of any martial art bring a certain spiritual meaning and benefit to the student's life outside the academy. A sport is simply a sport. Once you can't play it anymore you are done. Jiu-jitsu is something that you can practice all your life and always enjoy.

Q: Do you feel that you have further to go in your training?

A: Of course! I keep training because I see that I still have to improve many aspects of my jiu-jitsu. I'm far from being a master. It doesn't matter if you win ten world championships and everybody tell you that you are the best. That means nothing to me. I try to keep my center even and my focus consistent – not only in my jiu-jitsu but also in other aspects like family, friends and business. I would like to have the opportunity to spending more time with my teacher, because every minute I spend with him gives me information that stays with me forever. Since I can't train with Jacare all the time, I value every single minute that I spend with him on the mat or simply talking about jiu-jitsu. I also enjoy spending time with my brother, who is a great reference for me in the art of jiu-jitsu. He complements me greatly and we are good friends, too.

Q: What would you say to someone who wants to learn jiu-jitsu?

A: I would tell them to find out about the teacher the are planning to train under. Find out what his reputation is, not only in competition but also in life. You are going to spend a lot of time with him in the Academy, so check out some of the classes and observe his teaching. How does he speaks to his students? What kind of attitude does he have about life? That person is going to be someone that you look to for jiu-jitsu advice, but who will also influence you in many ways that you won't even notice. Make sure he is a good human being, not only a good jiu-jitsu instructor.

Q: What keeps you motivated to train?

A: Motivation is something that you always need to work on – not only in jiu-jitsu but in everything in life. I'm Christian and I believe in Jesus Christ. I don't want to sound too religious but I truly think that man needs a philosophical or religious belief to guide him through life. I have found that anchor in a particular belief – someone else can find it in Buddhism, Zen, Taoism, et cetera. Motivation usually is based on a reason to do something. If you have a strong reason to do a task, then the motivation is there. In jiu-jitsu, my motivation is in the joy of training and competing, challenging myself every time I step into a mat. In life, it's another story. It is important to have a reason to do things in life – to have a destiny and a destination. Unfortunately, I see people living and passing through life with no sense of leaving a legacy. I think this is sad.

Q: Do you think street fighting is necessary to develop good self-defense skills?

A: I don't look for fights. I don't need to brawl in the streets to prove that I can fight. I don't need it and I don't think it brings a good reputation to the art of jiu-jitsu either.

Q: Do you have any particular mental or psychological preparation that you use before a fight?

A: I think about what I'm going to do, but I don't stress or put unnecessary pressure on myself. I like to surround myself with people who say positive things and who have the right attitude towards life and training. I try to keep people who bring negative energy, far from me. As I said before, I'm a religious person so I read the Bible and try to keep focus and relaxed all the time.

Q: Do you feel that breathing exercises are important for jiu-jitsu?

A: Jiu-jitsu is an art based on using leverage, not brute force. In order to use leverage you need to position yourself in the right place so you can exert leverage. In a grappling situation, you can't position yourself in the right angle without subtlety. In order to place your body in the right position to use proper leverage, you have to pace yourself. You can't force it. Breathing allows you to stay calm, to control your body properly, and to save energy for later use. You need to understand when to inhale and when to exhale while performing the technique, because this is a very important factor in producing momentum and creating additional space for the technique. It is difficult to explain without physically showing a technique. That's the reason it takes a knowledgeable instructor. There is more to the art of jiu-jitsu than simple physical techniques.

Q: How important is finding the right training partner?

A: In Brazilian jiu-jitsu you practice with a partner all the time, from the very first day. The effectiveness of the techniques lies in making it work against an uncooperative opponent. No motions are performed in the air. It is true that we have several solo drills that help to develop the necessary body mechanics for grappling, but this is neither the essence nor the basic training method of jiu-jitsu.

Training with a partner involves relating to a moving body all the time. You learn to "feel" another person and to adjust to your opponent in order to make a technique work. While in punching and kicking methods timing is the secret, in jiu-jitsu "feeling" is the key. You have to develop specific physical attributes to make the techniques work. Wrestling is similar. With no partner, there is no way of making the techniques really work.

The importance of having the right training partner is extremely relevant to improving. During all my years of jiu-jitsu I have seen many practitioners who didn't know how to help and cooperate with their training partner. They try to fight instead of cooperating, and never create the right circumstances for their partner to improve and master techniques. Unfortunately, many practitioners fight too much; they approach training like a competition or a fight, and make of a training session a nightmare where many students get hurt. I have seen people cracking elbows in training and breaking bones. I have seen people getting choked-out because they don't tap. All these attitudes are nonsense and stupid. Find a training partner who helps you to train and improve your technique, not a brainless tough guy who is going to hurt you.

With the right kind of training partner you can train hard and safe. It is the instructor's responsibility to control these situations so the tough guys don't hurt the rest of the students who are there to learn. In Brazil, a purple belt helps a blue belt, a blue helps a white belt, and a brown and black belt helps all the students. Unfortunately, I have seen blue belts badly beat white belts and purple belts punish blue belts instead of helping them to progress. If you want to play "tough guy" then enter a vale tudo competition or do it against a black belt.

> **"The key to making jiu-jitsu techniques work is leverage, but strength is also necessary. Don't think that technique will work by itself because it will not."**

In Brazil, the training is harder because the 90 percent of the practitioners compete. In the United States maybe only 20 percent the students compete; the rest simply train for pleasure and fitness and to enjoy learning the art. In order to attract people to jiu-jitsu schools instructors need to make everyday people feel comfortable and safe whatever their reasons for coming are.

Q: You are known for having very creative and unorthodox techniques. How did you develop these amazing moves?

A: I have to tell you that all these creative movements are very natural to me. I am not doing anything that doesn't fit my body and my physical attributes. If doing these techniques were something unnatural, then I wouldn't be doing them. You have to find what it works for you – the things that you can naturally do. These movements will be your basics, the foundation you'll build your jiu-jitsu on. In training I advise students to work and experiment with all types of techniques, but in competition to stick to the things that are natural for you.

Q: How much strength is necessary in order to make jiu-jitsu techniques work?

A: The key to making jiu-jitsu techniques work is leverage, but strength is also necessary. Don't think that technique will work by itself because it will not. A certain amount of physical strength is necessary to make leverage possible. What jiu-jitsu students must understand is that before applying force to the technique in order to make it work, they have to work on pure technique and leverage until they master the movement and can apply it with only technical skill, without using more than the required strength to make the body move. Then when they master this phase of the technique, they can start to add strength accordingly, but never trying to substitute a lack of skill for brute force.

Q: Can you imagine life without jiu-jitsu?

A: Training jiu-jitsu for me is both a mental and physical therapy. It is an important part of my life. Honestly, I can't picture myself without jiu-jitsu being part of my life. But don't get me wrong, life is bigger and more important than jiu-jitsu.

Q: What advice would you give to students about weight training, running, stretching, et cetera?

A: I study physical therapy, and definitely all these supplementary aspects of physical training can help any practitioner of Brazilian jiu-jitsu. What is important is that the student knows how to apply these other elements to jiu-jitsu. Hardcore weight training, running and stretching are not beneficial for a jiu-jitsu practitioner. The weight training, the running and the stretching exercises have to be adapted and fit into the jiu-jitsu format of moving the human body. If you simply run, stretch, and lift weights you won't necessarily be improving your jiu-jitsu. More exercising does not necessarily mean better results. You have to be specific in what you do and how you do it, otherwise you risk wasting your time.

> "Hardcore weight training, running and stretching are not beneficial for a jiu-jitsu practitioner."

Q: Has fear and nervousness been difficult for you to overcome?

A: Fear is not something anyone should be affected by. If you know how to transform that fear into a useful tool to boost your training and skills then you're on the right track. Unfortunately, many practitioners let fear take them over, and then they cannot react quickly to an opponent's moves. They freeze and all the hours of training are useless. Fear makes you be cautious, and this can ruin your performance. Use fear for your own benefit.

Q: What did your ADCC 2003 win mean for you?

A: That victory was a very important moment and a turning point in my career. From the outside it might have seemed that I won easily, but all my opponent were very tough. I only had two weeks to prepare for that event because my university studies take a lot of my time. Then I have my regular day job, so I didn't have that much training time. I had a good group of people who helped me in every aspect of the preparation. I was confident of my ability but also very respectful of my opponents. My team, my friends, my wife and my family were really important in keeping me relaxed and focused for that tournament. They all had a great deal of patience with me and supported me in each and every way they could. Of course, the advice and attention given to me by my teacher, Jacare, every step of the way, was priceless.

Q: What advice would you give to new students?

A: I can only say the things that work for me. Find a teacher that is a example to follow not only in jiu-jitsu, but also as a human being. Have faith in everything you do, leave room to learn from others, and always be humble.

Q: What does the future hold for you?

A: I really don't know what the future holds for me but I'm sure of what I want. Regardless of how far I go in jiu-jitsu as a competitor, and eventually as a teacher for future champions, there is one thing most important to me – to spend time with my family and close friends. When you are on top everybody loves you, but once you start losing then nobody but your family will stick around. I take popularity for what it is and nothing more. Family and true friends are what really counts in life

LUIS HEREDIA

SEARCHING FOR MEANING

A MASTERFUL TECHNICIAN, AND ONE OF BRAZILIAN JIU-JITSU'S MOST RESPECTED TEACHERS, HEREDIA HAS BEEN ON THE CUTTING EDGE OF THE BRAZILIAN JIU-JITSU REVOLUTION SINCE ITS EARLIEST YEARS. TO GET A FEEL FOR THE PASSION THAT LUIS HEREDIA HAS FOR JIU-JITSU AND LIFE, ALL IT TAKES IS FIVE MINUTES WITH THIS HAWAII RESIDENT. HIS WORDS CONVEY HIS THOUGHTS BUT HIS EYES TELL THE REAL STORY ... A LOVE STORY WITH AN ART HE'S BEEN DOING FOR 30 YEARS.

AFTER WINNING THE 2007 PAN-AMERICAN JIU-JITSU CHAMPIONSHIPS, HEREDIA SAID MATTER-OF-FACTLY, "I HAVE WON MY DIVISION FIVE CONSECUTIVE TIMES, AND I AM PRETTY HAPPY." HE SAID THIS WITHOUT A SMILE, BUT HIS EYES REVEALED THE PASSION, THE ENJOYMENT, THE PRIDE AND THE SATISFACTION HE RECEIVED FROM ACCOMPLISHING THIS FEAT. WHEN YOU'RE READING THIS, PAUSE AND CLOSE YOUR EYES. IMAGINE, JUST FOR A SECOND, THAT YOU'RE SITTING ACROSS FROM LUIS HEREDIA, AND YOU, WITHOUT A DOUBT, WILL SEE THE PASSION IN HIS EYES.

BRAZILIAN JIU JITSU MASTERS

Q: How long have you been practicing Brazilian jiu-jitsu?

A: I have been doing jiu-jitsu for 26 years, uninterrupted. Each and every competition has meant something special to me. For the last eight or nine years, the Pan-American Jiu-Jitsu Championship has been my main priority. Why? I really believe that the Pan-American games set the standard for jiu-jitsu competition worldwide. I have memorable lessons from those tournaments since the beginning. I have learned a lot from competing. They were all tough matches, and I gained as much from my losses as my wins.

Jiu-jitsu has been my main focus; however, I have spent some time training in judo and boxing. When I first started training in jiu-jitsu, there weren't many schools around. The ones that were there, however, were full of students. I grew up in Copacabana, Rio, where most of the schools were located. Because of my location and transportation, it was easy to train close to home. At that time, the number of different schools to choose from spoiled me. One of my friends took me to Master Oswaldo Alves. Then I went to Carlson Gracie's school. From there, I was taken too Rickson's and Royler's training facility. I found my home right away. It was a lot of training and fun. I grew up training with guys like Pedro Sauer, the Barreto brothers, Tita, Paulo Barroso, and many other champions. There were so many. It is hard to mention them all. I miss those days.

> **"My real learning process started when I came to the United States with Rickson Gracie. Jiu-jitsu went from being fun training and competing with some great friends to a whole new challenge."**

My real learning process started when I came to the United States with Rickson Gracie. Jiu-jitsu went from being fun training and competing with some great friends to a whole new challenge. That has become my lifestyle and focus. I am proud to be one of the pioneers of the Brazilian jiu-jitsu revolution in this country. I have to give most of the credit to the person who believed in my potential, even more than myself at times—Rickson Gracie.

Q: Tell us some interesting stories of your early days in training.

A: As I mentioned before, there have been so many good times, but the first days in America with Rickson … they were the best. I did not have to teach much; I just had to learn how to teach and train. I ate jiu-jitsu for breakfast, lunch and dinner. I miss being a student sometimes. That's when I miss Rickson's teaching the most. He is the best ever.

I've got cauliflower ears as a blue belt. You know what that means? Lack of technique! I guess I always had more heart than technique. Then I met Rickson and things got more technical. I noticed that my ears were getting less attention. I wasn't a "natural" fighter, so I had to make up for it with lots of hard work and patience. It wasn't until I started teaching that

I found what I was "naturally" good at. I owe this to Rickson. He gave me lots of time to teach. I think about jiu-jitsu 24 hours a day. There is a lot of room for improvement in my career as a teacher and I just love to see how many people are benefiting from jiu-jitsu.

Q: Why did you come to the United States?

A: I was only a blue belt when we came here. Rickson and I always got along really well, and I think it was important for him to have someone come along who he could trust. So when he asked me if I wanted to come, of course I said yes. It was a little scary but it was also a great adventure.

Q: You were first at the Gracie Academy in Torrance, but then left to follow Rickson, correct?

A: Yes. When we left the Gracie Academy to strike out on our own, it was like starting over again. We didn't have a school of our own so we rented space all over the place. We were always on the road. We didn't even have mats, so one of the students who came with us scraped some money together and bought some, and we took those around with us.

Q: How was that experience for you?

A: Running the West Los Angeles school for Rickson was the first time that I really had to make the calls on what to teach and how to run the class. Rickson has guidelines, of course, but he was very flexible and left the decisions of what techniques to teach up to the instructors. About that time, a lot of people started to hear about Rickson Gracie, and he couldn't be there all the time, of course, so there were judo champions, wrestling champions, you name it, real top guys, coming into the school all the time to check out the style of Gracie Jiu-Jitsu. So I got to train a lot with world-class guys and just naturally kept improving. I mean, I had Rickson Gracie, the best grappler in the world, to teach me, and really tough guys to train with. How could I not get better?

Q: You were there the day Rickson was challenged by the Japanese champion, correct?

A: The school was in a building between a cell phone store, a clothing business, and an auto body shop. It just didn't look like a place where you'd find the best grappling school in the world, but the top guys came in. After Rickson's first win in Japan in 1994, a Japanese wrestler named Yoji Anjoh came in to fight Rickson, and brought a group of news people and TV cameras. He called Rickson a coward in front of his students and his family. Rickson trashed the guy because he was so disrespectful. I have never before seen Rickson so mad. He was scary that day because he is usually is so much in control, but I had to drag him off of the guy, and the Japanese fighter had to be taken to the hospital. I think that one fight is the reason that Rickson doesn't do any kind of challenge now. So I am sure if that same thing happened today, Rickson would just walk away.

Q: You also were in Japan when Rickson won the Vale Tudo in 1995 and gave a seminar where the best judo, jiu-jitsu and shoot wrestling fighters showed up to 'test' Gracie Jiu-Jitsu.

A: Yes, that one was a very good experience. After Rickson won the tournament for the second straight year, he gave a seminar the following weekend. Predictably, with all the attention in the Japanese media surrounding his win, the seminar was packed and attracted top fighters from the arts of judo, jiu-jitsu, shoot fighting, shoot wrestling, aikido, and even karate. There had to be 200 guys there, and everyone wanted to test themselves against Rickson Gracie, of course.

But there were too many people for him to train with in. So Rickson took all the big guys, maybe a hundred, then Royler took some, and then I took some, too—maybe thirty or forty. And everyone wanted to beat you. So I just put my mind on autopilot, let my body respond to the attacks, and just started grappling. Some were my size but a lot of them were twenty or thirty pounds heavier, too. I didn't know it at the time, but there were members of the Japanese National Judo Team there, some shootfighting champions, and also quite a few traditional jiu-jitsu guys. These were all very skilled and in-shape fighters. But I made them all tap. That day I was very proud of both myself and of jiu-jitsu. For me, it was a personal thing.

Mainly, what you get out of those types of events is admiration from people around you. But what really matters in the end is the satisfaction that you get inside of yourself, knowing that you have reached a certain level of achievement and knowledge in whatever you have chosen to pursue in life. So for me, that seminar was my own personal world championship. It was when I could look at myself in the mirror afterwards and know that I was where I wanted to be in jiu-jitsu.

Q: How has your personal jiu-jitsu system developed over the years?

A: Brazilian jiu-jitsu in America is not like it used to be, but maybe that's not such a bad thing. In one way, there has been a lot of change. It is a natural evolution; things tend to improve over the years: better athletes, more techniques, marketing ... the revolution of professional fighting. The basics stay the same, though. "The interpretation of leverage" will never change.

I believe that it takes a long time to really learn how to teach and develop your own style of teaching. As I mentioned before, I had a great mentor in Rickson. He taught me how to treat people and he taught me patience in my training. Teaching for Rickson was a very positive experience for me. I was able to learn from him and at the same time develop my own skills as a teacher. My teaching style has evolved over the years. I enjoy creating new ways to explain leverage and establish new training methods. I am better now than I was 10 years ago, and I plan to keep on this path for the next 10, 20, 30 years.

I got very interested in health after the Pan American Jiu-Jitsu Championships in 1996, because I suffered a very bad back injury and was laid up for a long time. I started thinking about how related exercise and health were, and how much more valuable I would be as a teacher if I understood nutrition and its effect on the human body better. Through my study and practice of nutrition, I also hoped to speed up the healing time. This is a life commitment. Water always is fresh and pure at the source.

Q: Do you have any general advice to pass on to the martial artists and BJJ practitioners?

A: All I have to say comes from my own life and experience in training. This is what I tell my students. First, listen and observe the more experienced ones, and be patient, very patient. In jiu-jitsu, you need discipline. It is like life itself; there are good and bad days. Always believe that something positive will come together. Be humble, but have heart.

Q: With whom would you like to have trained that you have not?

A: Really, nobody. Only, if I had never trained with Rickson, then I would have to say him. But I also have to say that I have trained with really good fighters, and I am still looking forward to more learning and training.

Q: What keeps you motivated after all these years?

A: I was born and raised in Rio, Brazil. I was brought to the United States by Rickson to start a school in L.A. Now I live in Maui and run my own school. I have a great situation now, with great students all over the world. I don't know what God has planned for me next, but guaranteed it will be awesome. I consider myself a very blessed man. Motivation is a positive attitude. I just want to enjoy where I am now—super healthy, competitor, business owner, teacher, surfer, father, and husband. My priority has always been on jiu-jitsu. I would encourage those students who are thinking about making jiu-jitsu part of their life [to pursue it] and ask them what are they waiting for? It is one of the best paths you will take in your life.

> "In jiu-jitsu, you need discipline. It is like life itself; there are good and bad days."

Q: Do you think it is necessary to engage in free fighting to achieve good fighting skills in self-defense?

A: I do believe that you can't rely on theories all the time. Training inside a professional school with proper guidance would be a safer way to practice techniques and theories, because fighting on the streets always has unpredictable results.

Q: What is the philosophical basis for your jiu-jitsu training?

A: It is a very simple one. It's either in your hands or God's. This is my formula. Jiu-jitsu equals life and life equals jiu-jitsu. Sorry, if some people do not understand that yet. Life is all about balance. When you have an important fight or commitment, you should balance that with more dedication and discipline.

Q: Do you have memorable experiences that have remained with you as an inspiration for your training?

A: All of them. All of my experiences have become my strongest lessons. In those early days in the West Los Angeles school, there still were a lot of people who didn't think that Brazilian jiu-jitsu worked. I think there definitely was a martial art bias against grappling and wrestling in general. It was hard for us to understand because in Brazil, the jiu-jitsu is king. Karate, boxing, kung-fu, and all the other martial arts are good, but whenever there was a Vale Tudo match, jiu-jitsu would dominate—everybody there knows that. But when we came here, all we ever heard was that grappling would fail against a good puncher or kicker. So when people would come in to train, they would want to go really hard to test the style. But Rickson is so good, that for him to wrestle someone his own weight is a mismatch, really. Plus, he is strongly built. A lot of the guys his own size who wrestled him would say, "You're a lot stronger than me; of course you beat me." So Rickson would say, "Then roll with Luis. He is a lot smaller than you." So I would get to train with a lot of guys that were a lot bigger than me.

> **"Jiu-jitsu is a great way to balance trust, confidence and humility. Jiu-jitsu means...soft art with a huge heart."**

In those days, I used to like to think of myself as Rickson's hit man. But I was probably more like a punching bag because I was the one getting hit. You see, in jiu-jitsu training, the beginners whom you spar with use a lot of muscle because they don't know anything else. So even if you eventually tap them in an armbar or a choke, you're the one that is bruised from getting throw wildly around. But in those circumstances, you do improve really fast. You have to, in order to survive.

Q: After all these years of training and experience, could you explain the meaning and philosophy of the practice of jiu-jitsu?

A: This is a very complex question. Like, life jiu-jitsu, has many different meanings. It has given me the opportunity to learn from and teach thousands of people. Right now, jiu-jitsu means being able to help as many people as I can by sharing my own philosophy. Jiu-jitsu is a great way to balance trust, confidence and humility. Jiu-jitsu means...soft art with a huge heart. I want to share it and to help people, using jiu-jitsu principles of exercise, coupled with diet, in order to help to maximize health and well-being. Jiu-jitsu isn't good just for fighting; there are many benefits that can be gained, including mental ones. If there is one thing that I have learned from jiu-jitsu, it is that if you focus yourself and your mind to a task, you can accomplish anything. It doesn't matter what others think you can or can't do. If you think you can do it, then you will.

Q: What do you consider to be the most important qualities of a successful BJJ competitor?

A: Lots of heart and a humble attitude.

What advice would you give to students about supplementary training (running, weights, cardio, et cetera)?

Well, it's all good; they all can help to a certain degree. But if you aren't beating the crap out of your kimonos, tearing and ripping them apart, then you aren't training enough. I tell the beginners, "Buy at least two kimonos."

Q: Have there been times when you felt fear in your training, and how does fear affect a competitor's performance?

A: I've never felt fear when competing. I have felt lack of physical performance, but never fear. Jiu-jitsu always has been the most positive part of my existence. I really learned more when I lost. Competitors should not have fear. Instead, they should transform that into concern and attention to the situation.

Q: What are your thoughts on the future of the jiu-jitsu, and what you think should be done to improve the sport?

A: Well, they are two different paths, but I think that it is growing and getting more exposure internationally. If the heads of jiu-jitsu focus and improve the organization, I could see jiu-jitsu becoming an Olympic sport. This is one goal that I would like to contribute to. This is for myself and for my son, who I hope to see represent jiu-jitsu in the future Olympics.

Q: Is there anything you would like to add for the practitioners?

A: To all of them, keep believing in jiu-jitsu. Be kind to each other. Believe in God and friendship. Party hard, but train harder. Special thanks to my mentor and inspiration Rickson Gracie; to my wife, Thati; my son, Kaile; and my parents. And now to all the people I have had the opportunity to share some learning experiences.

MARCIO FEITOSA

Not Another Face in the Crowd

HE IS ONE OF THE GRACIE BARRA´S "OLD GUARD." BASED ON TRADITION, BUT OPEN TO NEW FORMS AND TRAINING IDEAS, THIS ICON OF BRAZILIAN JIU JITSU HAS EVOLVED TO THE HIGHEST LEVELS OF SKILL AND UNDERSTANDING. THE WAY HE EXPLAINS THE PHILOSOPHY AND TECHNICAL FOUNDATION OF HIS ART, USING COMMON SENSE AND KEEN LOGIC, IS REFRESHING AND SOOTHING IN THESE DAYS WHEN MARTIAL ARTS IN GENERAL ARE LEADING US TO MORE COMBATIVE AND VIOLENT APPROACHES. HE IS A LIVING EXAMPLE OF HOW THE PAST AND THE FUTURE CAN WORK TOGETHER. WITH COUNTLESS MATCHES IN JIU JITSU TOURNAMENTS, AND GREAT EXPERIENCE IN NO-GI SUBMISSION GRAPPLING, MARCIO FEITOSA IS VERY FAMILIAR WITH WHAT TECHNIQUES WORK WITH THE GI AND WITHOUT. MORE THAN THAT, HE IS FAMILIAR WITH HOW LIFE WORKS WITH JIU JITSU AND WITHOUT IT. A TRUE JIU JITSU CELEBRITY WHEREVER HE GOES, FEITOSA CONTINUES TO TEACH AROUND THE WORLD, SHARING HIS KNOWLEDGE AND EXPERTISE AS ONE OF THE BEST BJJ FIGHTERS IN HISTORY. WITH A COMMITMENT TO GROW THE ART IN THE U.S., MARCIO FEITOSA IS AT THE FOREFRONT OF THE JIU JITSU REVOLUTION.

Q: In how many styles have you trained?

A: I only trained in Brazilian jiu-jitsu. Carlos Gracie is the only teacher I have ever had. I have trained with a lot of people who have taught me a lot, but the technique that I use is only from him. When I was growing up, I was lucky to get teaching from Renzo [Gracie], Helio Moreira, and a lot of instruction from Leio Teixeira. He provided everything that I needed. Sometimes people think I have trained in a lot of judo because I go for takedowns in competition, but that is [actually] because I train in BJJ proper. Everyone should have takedowns in his routine. Jiu-jitsu has takedowns, but people only focus on ground techniques. When I am competing without the gi, I go for takedowns, but I have never gone to a wrestling class. At first, I got into BJJ because I believed that it was the only martial art. When it became divided, people got BJJ to build other styles. Judo is a piece of jiu-jitsu. If the owner of a jiu-jitsu school has an open mind, he should present or teach other styles that work well with jiu-jitsu. I have an understanding of a jab and a straight, even though I have not been to a boxing class. I touched on various arts in class when I was a kid because they knew that I would eventually need it. As another example, I can do a low kick, but I never took a muay Thai class. I learned this in jiu-jitsu class.

Q: Why did you get started in jiu-jitsu?

A: It was entirely by coincidence. The Gracie Barra Academy was right in front of my house. A friend of mine joined the academy, and he told me how fun it was. One day he took me there to have a look. As a result, I started to train and that was it. When I was younger, I wanted to be a soccer player. In fact, I used to play soccer every day. Since the first day I started in jiu-jitsu, I forgot [all] about the ball and my sneakers. When I was 12, I started to train. When I turned 14, my parents divorced, so my brother and I had to take care of my mother. Because of this, I did not have enough money to pay the academy. I went to Carlos and informed him that I had to stop training because I did not have any money. He told me that anyone who needs his teaching will not go without it, and he insisted that we will make it work out. I was always the first one to arrive and the last one to leave. One day, he asked me what I wanted to do when I grew up. I said I wanted to be a jiu-jitsu instructor. Well, he found a way, so I stayed there and trained. He said he will make me a machine if I followed me. I will never forget that day.

Q: Has your personal jiu-jitsu changed or developed throughout the years?

A: I was a really skinny boy and not very healthy. I always had asthma and bronchitis, so I had breathing problems. I had to work really hard to improve that. To be really good in Brazilian jiu-jitsu, you have to have more dedication. The gift [natural talent] is not as important as dedication. It is always changing. Each year, I learn so much, not only technically but also mentally. In fact, I believe that the biggest changes are not in techniques but in the way I face winning and losing, the way I deal with students and my instructor, and the way I see life. I never received too many compliments when I was a champion, but I never had any insults when I lost. What I am saying is that I knew how to lose with dignity. Before a tournament, Carlos would always talk about my dedication to training. After a competition, he always said something about how hard I have tried. When you think about it, winning a gold medal sometimes is not as good a memory as finishing second in another tournament in which the competition is much better. I win when I overcome myself and I lose when I stop and see my limits.

Q: Do you have any general advice that you would care to pass on to Brazilian Jiu Jitsu practitioners and martial artists?

A: Tell him that if the only thing he sees in jiu-jitsu are the techniques, and the only goal is the medal in the last match, he will not have the determination, discipline, and strength to train in jiu-jitsu all of his life. He needs to understand that jiu-jitsu goes much further. It is a metaphor of life. Inside the dojo, he has all the teaching/guidance he will need for his life. Jiu-jitsu does not work like other sports do. People not see the academies just as a club. Many people see it as a family, so they usually start in one academy and stick with a group forever. In the past, some people were too radical about it, so in Brazil people from one faction take it too personally with people from another faction, so they do not hang out or talk to each other. Now people are much more open-minded and each faction is trying to support each other. It is much better for the sport and for everybody.

> "Jiu Jitsu is a metaphor of life. I can say that at least half of my character and personality have come from the dojo."

Jiu Jitsu is a metaphor of life. I can say that at least half of my character and personality have come from the dojo. After that, I can say the choices that I have made, for the most part, have been the right ones. So, what I have gotten from the dojo has made my life better. I feel like I am just beginning and that is because my dream in jiu-jitsu is to become a master. I want to be able to do like Carlos does. I want to lead a big group of people, and I want to make their life better. I know that today I am reaching a few people and making their lives better. Ten years from now, I will know how to do it much better, and I will be reaching more people.

Q: What one person would you like to train with that you haven't had the opportunity?

A: Carlos Gracie Sr. Carlos Gracie Jr. (Carlinhos) always tells me stories about him, and it's awesome what people say about him. It's my understanding that you could improve simply by having a conversation with him. Let me also tell you an interesting story about Carlos Gracie Sr. Carlos told me that he used to go to the large statue of Christ every day before sunrise and meditate. This was high atop the mountain. Afterward, he would come back and carefully prepare his meal. Then he would go into the attic and spend almost half of his day studying. Most of the time he studied foods, nutrition, and how various herbs could cure diseases. He was very disciplined.

Q: What would you tell someone who is just starting to learn jiu-jitsu and/or mixed martial arts?

A: I would tell them to not only look at the credentials of the instructor on the technical level, but also to find a place in which you feel that the people there have something to do with you. What I mean is that you have to feel like their ideas are similar to yours, or that you can identify with their ideas and principles. When you go to a dojo, you want the atmosphere to be good for you. You want to feel that the philosophy inside the school is good for you. Techniques are only one part of the school. Jiu-jitsu gives you power, but you can't use it to harass other people. The ones who get the most exposure are not the ones who use it to harass others but the ones who use it [the art] to make life better. These are the real martial artists. Before you do anything, you have to wear your gi and get on the mat, regardless if you train hard or train light. It must become a habit. Once you build that habit, the gi, the dojo, your instructor, and your teammates will be a continuation of your body and your mind. On a physical level, I would recommend achieving a high level of versatility, the ability to think fast or a quick mind, and the ability to adapt. There are some really good fighters who have good strategy and good plans. Then there are some great fighters who, when a plan fails or when everyone thinks the door is closed, come up with something new. A lot of times that something is a plan or a solution that even he did not expect.

In the course of learning the martial arts, and even more so in competition, you have to learn how to deal with your fears. Otherwise, they always will be with you. Once you learn how to deal with them, they can be helpful. The fear tells you that you are in a tough situation, so you need to be alert. When the adrenaline comes into your body [as a result of that fear], instead of making you freeze, you can use it to make yourself stronger, help you escape, and enable you to think faster.

Q: After all of these years, what keeps you motivated?

A: Let me answer that with another question. Have you noticed that sometimes a person who is winning everything and is great in tournaments often has a drop-off in performance when he changes to a different school? Why is that? It's certainly not that the techniques are worse or better at one school or the other. It's because he lost something that was driving him and pushing him to keep going. Maybe it was his instructor or his teammates; it could be a lot of things. For me, what keeps me keep going is not to show people that I am good. That's never been my goal, and I am not that vain. I try to build or create situations in my training so they are as close as possible to the competition. Thus, the training not only reflects the time [of day] and speed [required for competition] but also the mentality needed for competition. I get completely into it; it's very realistic. I am fighting to make the Gracie Barra name grow. I want to show that in our school we build champions, and that we have people who face the open air with fair play and honesty.

Q: Is it necessary to engage in free fighting to learn self-defense skills?

A: No, because you can't build a situation that's really close to a real situation without taking the risk of being injured. If you don't train smart, you can train really hard for one day. If you train smart, you can train really hard for 100 years. Which way are you going to get better?

Q: Should a BJJ competitor study other combat systems, like boxing or muay Thai?

A: If they intend to focus on Brazilian jiu-jitsu competitions, it won't help. The stand-up martial art that can help them—if they don't get the proper training from their school—is judo. Boxing, muay Thai, and wrestling will help if they are going to compete in no-gi events or mixed martial arts. It's allgood, but you have to realize a balance is always the best. Moderation is the key. If you are well rested, you can do them. If you are tired, you need to rest. Think of it in terms of elastic or a rubber band. If you are really tired, the elastic is going to rip. Once you get the rest and the proper nutrition, the elastic reverts back to its original strength. What I am saying is that if you know when to do it and how to do it, supplementary training is OK. Keep that balance and you will be fine.

Q: What are your thoughts on the future of jiu-jitsu and mixed martial arts?

A: I think we should try to organize the tournaments better. In addition, people should know that Brazilian jiu-jitsu is not the same as mixed martial arts. People should realize, however, that BJJ is a martial arts style that can be used in MMA, and it does really well [in that forum]. But the training in BJJ is not as violent or as hard on the body as MMA competition. I guess that is the biggest reason that BJJ is not twice as big as it is today. Most are scared to train because they think they will get hurt. People need to realize that Brazilian Jiu Jitsu is the art of gentleness.

NELSON MONTEIRO

A Man of Vision

NELSON MONTEIRO HAS BEEN ONE OF THE LEADING FORCES OF THE ART OF BRAZILIAN JIU JITSU AROUND THE WORLD. AS AN INSTRUCTOR, HE UNDERSTANDS THAT EVERYTHING GOES BACK TO HOW WELL YOU CAN APPLY THE THEORY YOU HAVE LEARNED. THE SIMPLICITY OF WHAT HE SHARES IS PERCEPTIBLE IN THE WAY HE CONDUCTS HIMSELF.

HIS MARTIAL ARTS JOURNEY TOOK HIM TO THE UNITED ARAB EMIRATES, WHERE HE SPENT SEVERAL YEARS TEACHING PRINCE TAHNOON AND HELPED TO CREATE THE ADCC (ABU DHABI COMBAT CLUB). FOR NELSON MONTEIRO, TEACHING IS A LEARNING PROCESS IN WHICH HE CONSIDERS HIS STUDENTS TO BE PARTNERS IN A JOURNEY OF KNOWLEDGE, RATHER THAN HIS DISCIPLES FOR PERSONAL GLORIFICATION.

Q: How long have you been practicing jiu jitsu and who were your teachers?

A: I have been training since I was 12 years old. My first teacher was Carlos Gracie Sr. I have always been athletic, so I would have to say that the movements came somewhat easily because I started training at a relatively young age. Although some techniques came naturally, there was no substitute for repetition in practice. Keep in mind that we had highly skilled competition as well, which certainly elevated my game.

Q: Would you tell us some interesting stories of your early days?

A: I remember when I was a blue belt and feeling like a real "Casca Grossa." I went to Ipanema Beach with my friend Rigan Machado. I saw a big guy who was staring in our direction on the boardwalk. He was a big muscular guy and he was wearing sunglasses and looked menacing. Rigan had his back to the guy and the guy kept staring in our direction. He eventually started walking toward us and I thought, "Oh man, we are going to get in a fight with this monster! The guy tapped Rigan on the shoulder and said, "Hey Rigan." It turned out to be Rickson Gracie. Needless to say, I am glad that my pride of being a blue belt didn't convince me to make the wrong choice that day.

Q: Do you think that the Brazilian culture creates the right environment for the art of jiu jitsu?

A: I think so. The Gracie family always placed their "wares" on the mat or on the street with bigger opponents. The laws in Brazil, at the time, were also relaxed in regard to fighting in the street without getting into trouble. The weather promotes a healthy lifestyle as well.

Q: How has your personal approach to jiu jitsu changed and developed over the years?

A: The foundation is still the same. The way I teach is the way I was taught as a student. The learning is endless, so the experience of practicing with my students has indeed improved my game as I get older. However, it is akin to building a house in that it all starts with building the foundation first. Some moves I teach in class may never be used; however, learning and repeating the basic foundation techniques is always stressed. I have studied and still do all the movements, trying to adapt and find new ways of escaping and moving from one position to another. I try to be creative and the only way I can do that is by keeping an open mind. I love to look at other competitors and study what they do. The final idea when you develop your own game is to find what really works for you based on your physical characteristics. Find how your body moves, what are the strong and weak points of your physical configuration, and then develop what is specifically for you.

Q: Do you think it is necessary to engage in free fighting to achieve good fighting skills for self-defense?

A: I think a martial art practitioner should never use the knowledge to prove himself in street fights. Use it for your own well-being above all. The satisfaction of overcoming our own weakness and expanding our physical ability leads to the confidence needed in the ring. But I definitely don't agree with the idea of going out to the street and looking for fights. I try to teach students self-defense skills that can be applied in a real-world setting. The last thing that you want to do as an instructor is to foster a false sense of security within your students. Conversely, I know a lot of MMA trainers who have never fought in sanctioned MMA bouts, and they are phenomenal instructors. Many fighters I know also study video as supplemental training, so I believe the combination of training on the mat and visualizing off the mat are ideal for achieving solid self-defense skills.

Q: Tell us about your adventures in the United Arab Emirates. How and why did this come into fruition?

A: I had a student who joined my school in Del Mar in 1994. The student started taking a lot of private lessons and was set to graduate from USIU (US International University) that year. He used to drive in a lot of fancy cars and told me that he was in the construction business. Upon graduation, he told me that he was the Prince of the UAE and offered me an opportunity to become his personal jiu jitsu trainer and to open the Abu Dhabi Combat Club. Upon my arrival, I wasn't exactly embraced by Tahnoon's former trainers. One night, I was having a late dinner with my wife. I was summoned at 10:30 by a former instructor who said he wanted to fight me, and that he was "going to break my neck." I told the guys that I had just finished a peaceful dinner with my wife and was digesting my food, so it would have to be scheduled for the following day. Man, I didn't sleep a wink that night! (laughs). I didn't know anything about this guy and it was really stressful not knowing what the opponent looked like or what his skills might be. When I came down to the club (Abu Dhabi Combat Club), my challenger said he was going to kick me in the head and knock me out. He started doing spinning back kicks prior to our fight and his kicks looked really pretty. Prior to beginning the fight, we went over the rules and decided the term "street fight" would suffice. He came at me with a few kicks and I was able to take him down and eventually mount him while forcing his arms across his face. Rather than rain down a series of punches to his head, I slapped him repeatedly. He did not deserve my punches, but he did ruin my dinner the night before so I was a little put off by his challenge. After a few slaps, I took his back and applied the rear naked choke and put him

> **"I think a martial art practitioner should never use the knowledge to prove himself in street fights. Use it for your own well-being above all."**

to sleep, since he disturbed my sleep the prior night. After all, he did say those unpleasant words and disturbed my digestion, too!

Q: As a competitor, did you have any mental or psychological preparation method that you used before a fight?

A: I always tried to step in the mat with a clear strategy. Going to the fight and having a game plan makes it much easier to feel prepared. I also try to visualize the fight and try not to become predictable. I always try to be at least three steps ahead of my opponent. Long hours of hard training brought me confidence and security and I used those to move on in my career. Nothing can beat fear but confidence in what you do.

Q: What is your philosophical basis for your martial arts training?

A: My father was an inspiration, but not in the way you may think. Unfortunately, he did not train and was a heavy smoker. However, my Dad always encouraged me to train and live a healthy lifestyle. I always try to improve my weaknesses and I recommend getting on the mat to train a minimum of four times a week. Overall, I think that it is the sum of many things; however, discipline and humility in learning are fundamental. If a jiu jitsu practitioner thinks that all he has to do is train, he is definitely wrong. He needs to keep an open mind and be aware that he doesn't know everything; therefore, he needs to keep learning.

Q: What advice would you give to your students on the question of supplemental training?

A: I recommend programs like Cross-Fit. However, nothing will replace training in jiu jitsu. To really improve your stamina, you have to get on the mat and train consistently. I see many people improve their jiu jitsu though training with weights and other machines. The real fact is that supplementary training should 'supplement' your main activity. Training with weights like a bodybuilder does won't help your jiu jitsu at all.

Q: Then what is the right approach?

A: You have to understand how your body moves and works when performing a jiu jitsu technique. Then, analyze the physiology of the specific movement and go to other training methods to directly improve these areas or muscles, but always try to 'duplicate' the jiu jitsu move. This is the best way. Only by doing it this way can your jiu jitsu technique improve. You can run ten miles a day and lift weights for two hours everyday, but your skills in jiu jitsu won't improve at all. You'll get better at running and put some muscle in your body, but your jiu jitsu won't be better because of that.

Q: How does fear affect a fighter's performance?

A: When you train hard and consistently, there is a sense of knowing that you are ready. The only time fighters feel fear is when they know that they have not trained properly or enough to face their opponent.

Q: What are your thoughts on the future of jiu jitsu and MMA events?

A: I notice that many of your questions are geared toward MMA. I would not consider myself an expert on MMA and my school is not geared toward training fighters for MMA, per se. My role is to be an ambassador for Gracie Barra Brazilian Jiu Jitsu and I believe that the art of jiu jitsu as a viable approach towards self-defense is growing exponentially. The main thrust of jiu jitsu is to teach self-defense. The training should always have practicality.

Q: What is your biggest source of motivation nowadays after training all these years?

A: I am always looking to improve myself, whether it is physically, mentally, or spiritually. I am also inspired by my students. My motivation comes from the fact that I need to keep learning because I think that no one knows it all.

Q: Do you have any general advice for martial artists and BJJ practitioners?

A: You have to have courage and discipline. The most important thing is to put the time into training. There is no substitute for experience and training. Always do your research before joining a school, try to find out as much information about your instructor's lineage and the personality of the school. I highly recommend taking introductory classes and asking the students questions about the school prior to investing in a school. Given the amount of information available online, it is easy to separate the "wheat from the chaff" in regard to qualified instruction. My main advice for practitioners of the new generation is to follow the instructions of their teachers. They are experienced martial artist with more knowledge than us, and the wisest thing for us to do it is to listen to them and learn from their experiences. By listening to what they have to say, we'll save time and avoid making the mistakes we previously did in their lives.

> **"The only time fighters feel fear is when they know that they have not trained properly or enough to face their opponent."**

Q: What are your plans for the future?

A: Thankfully, my school is growing rapidly and I am blessed to have good health, family, and students. I will continue to compete and train.

Q: Why do most Brazilian jiu jitsu practitioners enjoy surfing?

A: There is something special about riding a wave. Nobody knows what is going on in the brain of a surfer when he is riding a big one. Surfing in many ways has more high-risk variables than other athletic activities because of the physical elements involved. Regardless of your spiritual background, there is something special about being in the ocean and feeling the connection with something greater than you. That feeling is something spiritual. If you think of how life is, you'll realize that is a flux of things. Well, that is sort of the way a wave is. It is a spiraling transmission of wind power moving through the water but it looks like a solid entity. You create a partnership with nature.

Q: Do you consider surfing something like a moving meditation?

A: I'm not sure how to describe it but there is a strange feeling about paddling out into a monstrous wall of water, popping out into one's feet and then gliding. You get the feeling that the wave controls you, but after few seconds you are one with it. I think surfing teaches us about commitment, fear, and harmony. Also, it teaches about falling and getting up again and again. You are in connection with something alive and greater than you. You are one with that big wave. You always feel better once you've gotten in the water…and gone surfing. No doubt about it.

"The Jiu Jitsu I created was designed to give the weak ones a chance to face the heavy and strong."
~ Helio Gracie ~

PAULO GILLOBEL

One of the Elite

Originally from Rio de Janeiro, Paulo Gillobel is recognized as one of the most knowledgeable Brazilian jiu-jitsu instructors in the United States. He recently won the 2003 Pan-American Championships, setting an example of how a dedicated instructor can also successfully compete in big tournaments. A persistent dedication to success, despite major obstacles, has always been Gillobel's driving force. Displaying the qualities of an original thinker, he has a very analytical approach to both learning and teaching: "Regardless of what style of martial arts you are practicing, you should always allow room for additional knowledge to improve what you have.

Don't think that you know everything – or that what you know is all there is to know – because you'll be digging your own hole." By combining the positive elements of athletic competition with the deeper aspects of true martial arts instruction, Paulo Gillobel has truly transformed himself into "one of the elite."

Q: How long have you been practicing Brazilian jiu-jitsu?

A: Since 1988. My first teacher was Jorge Pereira – a Carlos Gracie Jr. black belt – and I have been training with the Machado brothers for the last four years. During this time, I have successfully competed in many tournament and events. I won national and state competitions in Brazil, and since my arrival in the United States I have been competing in tournaments all around the country. In 2003, I won the Pan Ams. That was a great feeling because only the best compete in it. When I was in Brazil, I trained jiu-jitsu, judo and boxing, but I also started training in wrestling once I got to the United States. Wrestling is a different form of grappling that can create some problems for a BJJ practitioner due to its ways of attacking, defending, and controlling an opponent on the ground. It lacks submissions and other tactical aspects of jiu-jitsu, but it is very helpful in many aspects of ground control. I truly think that wrestling complements Brazilian jiu-jitsu very well. You need to know how to make both arts blend in a smooth way. Wrestlers have great training methods and drills that any jiu-jitsu practitioner can benefit from.

Q: Was jiu-jitsu easy for you to learn?

A: When I first started jiu-jitsu, it was very easy to learn the techniques. I felt like it was my martial art. I was always one of the best in my weight at every belt, but to get really good you have to train and stretch a lot in order to avoid injures and to get your game flowing. Physical talent doesn't mean anything if you don't put in time on the mat. You may be better than another guy in the first stages of the training, but if he trains more than you he will make you tap regardless of your natural talent. Hard work and consistent training are more important than natural talent. Talent without passion and dedication means nothing. But if you have natural talent and also work hard you can become a legend in any sport.

Every day at the academy I learn something new. When I got my black belt, I felt like I was starting all over again. Plus, the Machado brothers have plenty of things to show and I feel very lucky to have a chance to learn from them. A lot of my previous perceptions of jiu-jitsu have changed with the years. Today, we have great instructors all over the world and you have to be more dedicated if you really want to be good at it. I have been extremely lucky since I always had great teachers and excellent training partners. With a great teacher next to you, it is easier to improve your technique and performance. You have to learn to be patient and understand that the good things take time. In any sport or activity excellence won't happen overnight – and jiu-jitsu is no exception. Jiu-jitsu is not an easy art, which is why it is one of the best martial arts.

Q: What changes have seen in jiu-jitsu since you started?

A: Compared to 20 years ago, there are BJJ schools all over the world now. There are a lot of people in different cultures who see the same concept in different ways – this gives BJJ different options to expand. But the bad news is that jiu-jitsu used to be more relaxed and technical in the past. Now we have a bigger tactical arsenal but a lot of people lack the basic foundation that helps you to reach the higher levels of the art. Evolution is good as long as we don't forget who we are and where we came from.

Q: What should a person do if they want to train jiu-jitsu?

A: The first thing is that you have to look for a good school, because not all academies offer a good training and teaching method. Then when you start, commit yourself to the training and go for it – that is way to have fun. The better you get the more fun it will be. Also remember to train smart and don't go crazy. Injuries will come very easy if you don't train wisely and these injuries will slow your progress.

In Mixed Martial Arts, you need a good trainer and coach to guide you. Unfortunately, too many people jump into a cage without proper training. Some teachers send their students to fight too soon because they want to become championship trainers, but they don't realize that you can't do that unless you truly prepare your students. What is really unfortunate is that the students don't know any better and follow their teacher's orders – even if these are crazy! A good teacher prepares a student the right way before sending him to fight Mixed Martial Arts or Vale Tudo.

> "In Mixed Martial Arts, you need a good trainer and coach to guide you. Unfortunately, too many people jump into a cage without proper training."

Q: What drives you to keep training and teaching?

A: I love what I do and I think this is the thing that pushes me day after day. The fact that I keep learning every day – there is always something new on the mat – keeps me on my toes. I love to compete and BJJ helps me to keep in shape, too.

Q: Who would you have liked to have trained with?

A: There are two people I would love to have trained with – Rickson and Royler Gracie. I am a huge fan of those two. I have been watching them fight my whole life, and they have been the motivation for my personal training and for my desire to compete. They are the number one examples of what all jiu-jitsu practitioners want to be.

Q: How do you prepare yourself before a tournament?

A: I meditate a lot. I always try to connect with my inner self. I also stretch a lot and try to relax, focusing on my breath and my heartbeat. I also do the "Ginástica Natural," which helps me a lot on my moves and my speed when I'm using jiu-jitsu techniques. The bottom line is that jiu-jitsu has to be natural. If there is any technique that is not natural then you have a problem. That's why BJJ is so different from other arts – you have to adapt the techniques to your own body to make them work. Not everybody can perform the same jiu-jitsu technique the same way. A jiu-jitsu technique is not a ballet movement that all the dancers have to follow exactly. You have to understand the principles of why and how the technique works and then adapt it to your own body structure. Only then can you truly express real Brazilian jiu-jitsu.

Q: What fighter has inspired you?

A: I have always admired Jean Jacques Machado. Every time I look at him or train with him I realize here is a guy who was born with a limitation – only half a hand in a sport where grip is everything – but yet became the best pound-for-pound fighter in the world. If he could overcome something like that, then all my petty complaints mean nothing. He is my biggest spiritual inspiration.

Q: Why do you practice jiu-jitsu?

A: That is a hard question because the answer involves many personal factors that are different for each individual. Everyone has a different point of view about this subject; some do to get more self-confidence, some to learn to fight, others because it is a good workout and simply makes them feel good. I think BJJ is a way of life, a challenge, a physical chess game. It is far more than simply fighting or grappling with another person. In Japan, the symbol of jiu-jitsu is water – that's because water is adaptable to any space, is unbreakable, and flows – but yet it is always water. It changes its shape but not its form. That is how I see jiu-jitsu and that's how the art should be used in competition. I also think it is how we should act in our personal lives.

Q: What are the most important qualities of a successful BJJ competitor?

A: There are several. The first is determination – you have to focus on what you are doing and train hard to be the best. The next is humility – you need to be humble to respect who is at a higher level than you because you are going to have to learn from them. You have to respect everyone but fear no one. Finally, you need courage and lots of creativity.

On the physical level I would say cardio and flexibility are the most important aspects, but you also have to work also your strength – because sooner or later you are going to need it. You should never only lift weights, because you might get stiff and lose your endurance – which in jiu-jitsu is extremely important. Weeks before the competition, you got to work on sprints to get quicker; that will help you to gun your engine when you need it.

Q: Is it beneficial for BJJ competitors to study other martial arts?

A: That depends on your final goal. If you want to be a BJJ competitor, you have to spend all your time on the mat, training. Judo and wrestling will help in this. However, kickboxing, kung fu or karate won't do much for you. Therefore there is no need for a jiu-jitsu practitioner to spend time training in other arts. But if you want to be a MMA fighter, you have to study a martial art that teaches you how to strike and to defend against punches and kicks. This kind of training will give you more options when you are facing an opponent in the cage.

Q: How does fear affect a competitor's performance?

A: I have felt fear many times during my competitions. Fear of losing, of getting hurt, of not doing your best are all reasons why someone may feel fear. But you can use fear to your own advantage because you need fear to develop courage. A good fighter overcomes his fear, but if you let fear take control of you then it is going to be hard to succeed in a fight or in life. If something scares you then you should face it. If you do that, then you have beaten fear. Courage is nothing more than having done something before.

Q: What are your thoughts on the future of jiu-jitsu?

A: I think we need more organization. We have the best product but we don't know how to sell it. We have to go after the big sponsors and get them to invest money in what we are doing – but in return we need to show a cohesive structure they can rely on. I like the way NHB is been managed, it is helping jiu-jitsu grow. Sport jiu-jitsu and submission fighting need events with credibility and professional referees, judges, and accredited organizations. We're starting slow but we will get there.

Q: What's the key for beginning students to stay in the art?

A: Keep training and believe that you are learning the best martial art ever. BJJ is growing fast and one day, for sure, it will be a very big sport. But in order to make this happen we all need to work together with the same goal in mind! New students should learn how to be patient and remember to always show respect for your partners. Try to focus on what you are doing with determination. Have the courage to train with everyone and to balance all the aspects of your life. All practitioners should develop these qualities from the early stages of their jiu-jitsu training. And like Jean Jacques Machado likes to say, "Leave your ego at the door."

RALEK GRACIE

Being in the Present

HE SURPRISED ALL AND TOOK THE WORLD BY STORM. WHEN THE WORLD OF MMA AND BJJ FANS FROM ALL OVER THE WORLD WERE WAITING TO SEE EITHER ONE OF HIS OLDER BROTHERS ENTER IN AN MMA MATCH FOR THE FIRST TIME, RALEK GRACIE CUT THE LINE AND WENT TO JAPAN TO BE THE FIRST OF RORION GRACIE'S SONS TO ENTER AN MMA EVENT.

HE DID IT WITH STYLE AND USED PURE GRACIE JIU JITSU TO DEFEAT HIS OPPONENT VIA A PERFECT BY-THE-BOOK ARMLOCK. FOR THOSE WHO KNOW HIM, HIS FATHERHOOD MADE HIM MATURE QUICKLY. HIS WORDS ARE THE WORDS OR A YOUNG MAN WITH A LOT OF KNOWLEDGE AND EXPERIENCE BEHIND THEM, ALTHOUGH HE RECOGNIZES THE VALUE OF HIS PREDECESSORS. "IN THIS LIFE, YOU CAN LEARN EITHER FROM YOUR MISTAKES OR FROM THE MISTAKES OF OTHERS AND SAVE A LOT OF PAIN ALONG THE WAY. MY GRANDFATHER AND MY FATHER GATHERED A GREAT AMOUNT OF LIFE EXPERIENCE THAT PREVENTING ME FOR MAKING STUPID MISTAKES," HE SAYS WITH A SMILE ON HIS FACE. "IT SAVED ME A LOT OF TIME IN LIFE."

Q: How did that fight happen?

A: I think that everybody was waiting for either of my two older brothers (Ryron and Rener) to accept one of the many offers we receive all the time. The truth is someone came to me from K-1 Heroes (MMA version of K-1 Events in Japan), made an offer and I decided to accept it. I know that even my father and brothers were shocked by I knew what I wanted to do.

I always felt the fighting was inside of me and I knew I was going to be the first one. So when the call came, I took it. The birth of my son had a lot to do with my decision. He gave me the fire to do it. It was an honor for me to go back to Japan representing the Gracie name. Of course Rickson, Royce, and other member of the Gracie family did that already, but for me it was a very special thing that the fight took place in Japan.

Q: How did you prepare for that fight?

A: One thing I was sure of; I didn't want to go out there and change what I have been doing all my life. If I spent all of my life training in Gracie Jiu Jitsu, I was not going to try to kickbox the guy. I have seen many great Jiu Jitsu fighters who spend too much time training other methods, and when they get into the ring, they rely on these techniques that they have been training for a few months instead of using those that made them champions and they have practiced all their lives. I was not going to do that. My purpose is to win with Gracie Jiu Jitsu.

Q: Didn't you train in other styles, like most MMA fighters do?

A: I did train other technical elements like boxing and kickboxing but I did it in order to be fully prepared against these types of attacks and not necessarily to use them to finish my opponent off. I study them because for an MMA fight you need to know, understand, and be aware of what other fighters use, and kickboxing is a big part of it.

Q: Speaking of being aware, were you aware of the pressure of being the first son of Rorion Gracie stepping into an MMA match?

A: Of course, I was aware. Nevertheless, that awareness of my position and what my fight represented for our side of the Gracie family didn't prevent me from doing what I had to do. Pressure is not a bad thing. It puts you in a position in which you have to bring out the best of you and that is when you achieve great things. It doesn't matter if it is Jiu Jitsu, business or anything … pressure is good … makes us sharp. I don't see pressure as a negative thing.

Q: Did you have pressure growing up a Gracie?

A: All Gracies have pressure … are you kidding me? The thing is when we are kids, we really play and then there is no pressure. The pressure comes and knocks on your door in many different ways. But that pressure is good because your destiny already has been chosen and what you have to focus on is to do what you, as Gracie, are supposed to do.

Q: You have a child now; for a man of your age, how that has affected you training?

A: Becoming a father changes everything. It gives you a wider perspective of things but at the same time is a wake-up call. Anything you do after you have a baby is for you. All your actions are directed to that child. That is pressure. But it is a great learning experience and there is nothing but growing in that journey.

Q: You seem comfortable with your role of being a Gracie?

A: Why shouldn't I be? As I said, we need to be aware why we are here and what is our duty in this world. This is not a bad thing. It is a blessing. Once you know why you are here, and you are aware of what you are expected to deliver, there are no misunderstandings. All you have to do is ... just do it.

Q: How is it to grow up being beaten by two older brothers who are considered among the best in the world?

A: It is good because you have as training partners two of the most technical and best Brazilian Jiu Jitsu guys in the world. Taking that as starting point, anything else is good. It is true that during many years it becomes frustrating in a healthy way, because they are taller, stronger, with more experience, and it is very hard to catch them. Then, I started to grow up and my technical level improved. My body became stronger and it was harder for them to get me. That was when I truly felt my real technical level because if some of the best guys in the world can't choke me ... that means I am getting better.

> **"Reaching a high level in the art of Jiu Jitsu requires more than the overall physical and technical skill that can be gained from years of prac- tice and training."**

They spend more time teaching and sharing the art of Gracie Jiu Jitsu with the students while I focus more on training for fighting. As long as they keep choking me ... I have room for improvement and still can get better [laughs]. Gaining experience in combat is an essential element in Jiu Jitsu training. There is no better way to gauge your progress once you reach a certain level that actually sparring against an uncooperative opponent.

Q: What do you think of your father, Rorion Gracie?

A: I'd better be careful what I say here [laughs]. Seriously, I really admire my father for many reasons; he is responsible for the explosion of Gracie Jiu Jitsu in the world. He is the creator of the UFC, which brought MMA as we know it today in the world. As a father and head of the family, he knew how to manage every single one of us into a complete unity. The Gracie Academy is an example of dedication, Jiu Jitsu teaching, and a world-class facility. He had a vision and worked on it. He is a very special person.

Q: What do Royce and Rickson represent to you?

A: They are examples for me. Royce was the first to fight in the UFC. Rickson went to Japan. They were and are heroes for me. Just think for a second how the world of Martial Arts changed after these two men went out and fought.

Q: What does Gracie Jiu Jitsu provide to those who practice the art?

A: The Gracie Family has a purpose. We have a long tradition of philosophy, diet, and art. These aspects are something that the members of our Academy enjoy bringing to their lives. They don't have to adopt the "Gracie way" of doing things but if a part of our philosophy helps them in their lives, we are happy; if some ideas found in our diet help them to improve their health, we are happy, and if any technique found in Gracie Jiu Jitsu helps them to survive a physical attack in the street, the mission is accomplished. A good instructor should help students to achieve their goals in life. Eventually, those students will be able to draw on their own knowledge and experience to help the next generation. Gracie Jiu Jitsu and Martial Arts in general are not merely a bunch of fighting techniques but a reflection of the society it represents. No matter what you do in life, you need to have a sense of purpose; otherwise you are just floating in an empty space.

Q: What advice would you give to those practicing Brazilian/Gracie Jiu Jitsu?

A: Reaching a high level in the art of Jiu Jitsu requires more than the overall physical and technical skill that can be gained from years of practice and training. The student must acquire an inner understanding and personal maturity that goes beyond the mere performance of the Gracie Jiu Jitsu techniques.

Q: Your grandfather Grandmaster Helio Gracie passed away early this year; what can you tell us about him?

A: He was a man of conviction. He knew what his purpose in life was since he got involved in the art of Jiu Jitsu. He always did what had to be done … either in fighting or cooking. He analyzed the situation, made a decision and acted with 100 percent of focus and motivation. He always did his best and based his life on common sense. His life was governed by common sense.

Q: What are your plans for the future?

A: To do my best in whatever is that I end up doing – fighting or teaching. Being in the present is the secret … always in a state of awareness … like right now … here … with you.

“Look at things by the enlightened point of view and update your optimism on reality.”
~ Carlos Gracie Sr. ~

RELSON GRACIE

Passion and Art

AS A MEMBER OF THE WORLD FAMOUS GRACIE FAMILY, RELSON GRACIE LOVES SURFING, SOCCER AND, OF COURSE, JIU-JITSU. BUT BEHIND HIS RELAXED ATTITUDE AND HAPPY-GO-LUCKY SMILE IS A GREAT TECHNICAL KNOWLEDGE OF JIU-JITSU THAT GIVES HIM THE ABILITY TO CONTROL HIS OPPONENTS AND MAKE THEM TAP ON ALMOST A WHIM. BUT HE IS MORE THAN "JUST" A GREAT FIGHTER. HE IS A MASTER INSTRUCTOR WHO CAN TEACH A JIU-JITSU TECHNIQUE FOR ANY FIGHTING SITUATION IMAGINABLE. ORIGINALLY FROM RIO, HE MOVED TO HONOLULU AND OPENED A SCHOOL TO SHARE THE UNIQUE BRAZILIAN ART

DEVELOPED BY HIS FATHER, HELIO GRACIE. RELSON GRACIE RECEIVES VISITS FROM STUDENTS WHO COME FROM ALL CORNERS OF THE WORLD. AFTER HE HAS TAUGHT THEM A NEW "JIU-JITSU TRICK," HE KINDLY SETS AN APPOINTMENT FOR HIS SUNDAY SOCCER GAME. AND IF YOU THINK RELSON IS INTENSE ON THE MAT, YOU'VE NEVER SEEN HIM ON A SOCCER FIELD! KEEP YOUR ELBOWS IN, YOUR CHIN DOWN AND PREPARE TO MEET RELSON GRACIE.

Q: How difficult has it been to popularize the system developed by your father?

A: It wasn't an easy task. The Gracie challenge was created to put our system to the test and this is something very hard to keep up. During more than 70 years the different members of the Gracie family have been trying to prove that the Jiu-Jitsu method developed by the Gracie's is a great and effective self-defense system. I understand that this is a little bit dangerous but we are talking here about martial arts, not dancing. The only way of proving an art effective is putting it to the test. Fortunately, during the last decade, martial artists from all styles and systems understood the importance of knowing how to deal with an opponent on the ground. They greatly accepted the grappling methods and the Gracie Jiu-Jitsu system. Some of them not only have incorporated some techniques into their repertoire but became full time Jiu-Jitsu practitioners as well. This situation brings a great rewarding feeling to the Gracie Family-we had something important to share and we did. Fortunately, people accepted. The legacy is there to enjoy.

Q: What's your opinion of the UFC (Ultimate Fighting Championship) and other reality-based fighting events that revolutionized the world of martial arts?

A: I think today its format now it is very different than used to be. The original concept and idea is lost. I believe that the UFC has been a very revealing experience for a lot of fighters and it has opened the eyes to a lot of martial artist about the efficiency of some self-defense method when confronting an uncooperative aggressor. For some reasons completely political, the original idea of the UFC turned into a "sport event." I understand that PPV and politicians tried to regulate the shows so more people can see them and more money can be made from it but when we started the whole things was not about PPV or bringing sport sponsor into the show, it was about proving a point, about making people realize some important thing about fighting and fighting has nothing to do with sport. Basketball modified its format to fit TV, football also did and finally UFC did as well but not while the Gracie had a word on how to run the show.

> **"I believe that the UFC has been a very revealing experience and has opened the eyes to a lot of martial artist about the efficiency of some self-defense methods."**

Q: How would you define the essence of Jiu-Jitsu?

A: It's very difficult to describe the essence of a system on paper. Punches and kicks are okay but the most of the fights end up on the ground. Down there it's impossible to use these punches and kicks with the same efficiency that being on a stand-up position; the leverage and body mechanics are very different. On the ground the bigger guy is not always the one having the advantage. This was clearly proved by my brother Royce Gracie when he defeated bigger opponents at the Ultimate Fighting

Championship. Understand the grappling aspect of a real fight is something very important for all martial artists.

Q: Unfortunately, grappling is not very attractive for a television show when compared with boxing or kickboxing. Why is that?

A: The problem here is that in a grappling situation you won't understand what's happening unless you have been educated about the grappling techniques. In boxing, you see what's happening. In Jiu-Jitsu a small movement of the hip may mean a lot but unfortunately the spectator won't realize the whole game until the physical action is over. This is one of the reasons why the people controlling the "sport" are trying to change the format, in order to make it more appealing to the masses. And I understand their point of view but that is not what we are talking about. Grappling is much more subtle, requires an educated spectator to fully understand what the fighters are doing or trying to do. It's not something you can just sit down on the couch with a six pack (beer) and a pizza and you can appreciate. You can enjoy but definitely not understand what is going on there. You have to be educated to understand the subtleness of an expert grappler or Jiu-Jitsu practitioner-how he moves, what he does and why he is doing it.

Q: It has been said that strength is not necessary for using Jiu-Jitsu and many people disagree, what's your opinion about this?

A: I guess this concept has been misunderstood. The Brazilian Jiu-Jitsu practitioner uses leverage and body positioning above everything else. This is the only way of making the art work against bigger opponents. Therefore, the students are instructed to think about technique, not using brutal force to make the technique work. Of course, a certain amount of strength is necessary but the efficiency of the techniques developed by my father don't require a great deal of muscle to make them work. As I said there is a certain amount of force but never trade technique for strength. My father proved this theory for 65 years. If you use brutal strength to get your techniques, that's not Jiu-Jitsu. Using intelligence, leverage and body positioning-that is the key of the art.

Then you have another scenario; two fighters with equal skill and physical attributes. Then strength becomes an important factor. The technique may not require brutal force but because your opponent is as skilled as you are, then all the physical qualities will make the difference, and strength is not an exception.

Q: How do you feel now that everybody knows about Brazilian Jiu-Jitsu?

A: I am happy because the world has recognized my father work. I don't mind teaching people the Jiu-Jitsu techniques and secrets. Why should I? I'm very happy sharing a great self-defense system with everybody who wants to learn it.

Q: What style can beat Jiu-Jitsu?

A: Only Jiu-Jitsu. The art shocked the world and some great wrestlers, to win over sport Jiu-Jitsu champions, had to study Jiu-Jitsu so...Jiu-Jitsu wins again. In order to win Jiu-Jitsu you have to study Jiu-Jitsu. It is that clear...in order to beat Jiu-Jitsu you have to analyze and study Jiu-Jitsu so in the very end, the victorious needs to know Jiu-Jitsu. We came up in a moment in time when everybody thought a punch or a kick was all what they needed to defeat any kind of opponent. Don't get me wrong, it is not that you don't need to know how to punch and how to kick but everybody was lacking of a complete understanding of a ground work and even more, they thought they could use all these punches and kicks on the ground or that nobody could never ever take them down. Well, we proved the things to be very different and bring some kind of light into the martial arts world.

Q: Do you consider yourself a modernist?

A: To be totally honest I don't know how the term modernist or traditionalist applies to the martial arts. For instance...people like Gichin Funakoshi (karate), Jigoro Kano (judo) or Morihei Ueshiba (aikido) are considered traditionalists but if you read and look into their lives you'll find out they trained under different instructors and they did change a lot of the things they learnt under their teachers. They modified, re-structure and taught differently all the material they gather throughout their lives. They were "eclectic" and pioneers (modernist)...even more than many people nowadays. The difference is they kept the traditional values such as respect, ethics and morals. If you ask me if I am a traditionalist my answer would be "yes" because I kept all these important elements but if you consider to be a "traditionalist" to not evolve technically or modified things to make them better, then I'm a modernist. One thing doesn't exclude the other. It's a natural process and a necessary one if we want to improve what we are doing. It's that simple but unfortunately people love to fuss over it.

Q: After all these years of people wishing to learn the Brazilian Jiu-Jitsu "secrets," what's your perception of the art and its influence in the martial arts world?

A: As I said before I think a lot of people have been educated that in order to be a well-rounded martial artist you need to know and understand grappling. Now, our students like to practice Jiu-Jitsu just for Jiu-Jitsu sake. People understand how important Jiu-Jitsu is and is a great feeling to see how many thousand of practitioner around the world have kindly embraced the art developed by my father. It makes me proud. As martial artist we should look for quality and if someone is better in a certain fighting aspect there is nothing wrong with going to learn from that person. It's important to be humble and acknowledge that there are areas where you can improve. But to be a real martial artist is more than just training and fighting, many other mental components are involved. You have to be a martial artist 24 hours a day, live like one, think like one, be ready like one. This is the old Samurai attitude and it can be used in our times. For instance, I love to visualize attacks and reactions to those attacks. I like to train in a relaxed atmosphere so my motions become reflex, natural reactions, instinctive responses. This is the only way you can become one with your art, making your training melt with your human essence and inner self.

Q: Why did you decide to move to Hawaii?

A: I lived in Monterey, California during three years but my brother Rorion Gracie was already there so I thought that Hawaii, having its roots in Japan, could be a good place to live. The weather is very similar to Brazil and there's a lot of surfing, which I love! I don't think I could live anywhere else. I have everything I need and I enjoy all what I have.

Q: What is your diet and personal training routine?

A: I follow the Gracie diet developed by my family. Once in a while I enjoy having "something extra" but... only here and there. I eat a lot of vegetable, fruits and try to keep my vitamins and minerals in the proper proportions. As far as my personal training I like to think of myself as a technician with effective results so my main focus in training is the technique, the skill of Jiu-Jitsu. Of course you need other physical attributes to complement you basic skill as flexibility, strength, endurance, et cetera. Running, weight training, yoga, et cetera are good complementary methods that may enhance your Jiu-Jitsu. Just don't lose sight of your main goal.

Q: What are you plans for the future?

A: I'm teaching here in Hawaii where I feel very happy. People come from all over the world for Jiu-Jitsu training. Even from Europe! I have a good life here with my friends and my students. I related to all the Hawaiian environment and life style so I feel like a fish in the sea! I hope to keep learning, improving and teaching my dedicated students all the knowledge that I gather through my personal experiences in the arts. The instructor grows by his student's success. The better your students are, the better instructor and martial artist you will be.

Q: What do you do for relaxation?

A: What a Brazilian man can do for relaxing? Only one thing...play soccer!

RENATO MAGNO

Living the Good Life

ORIGINALLY FROM SAO PAULO, BRAZIL, RENATO MAGNO BEGAN HIS MARTIAL ARTS TRAINING IN JUDO, BUT BRAZILIAN JIU-JITSU WAS WHAT TURNED HIS LIFE AROUND. LUCKY ENOUGH TO SPEND TIME AND TRAIN EXTENSIVELY WITH SEVERAL MEMBERS OF THE GRACIE FAMILY IN RIO DE JANEIRO, HE BECAME AN ACTIVE COMPETITOR WITH AN IMPRESSIVE LIST OF ACCOMPLISHMENTS. IN KEEPING WITH HIS REPUTATION OF A TOP JIU-JITSU MAN, HE DISPLAYS ALL THE TRAITS OF A TRUE MARTIAL ARTIST. OUT OF DEDICATION, HE SPENDS LONG HOURS ON THE MAT TRYING TO PASS ON THE KNOWLEDGE OF HIS BELOVED ART TO HIS NUMEROUS STUDENTS AT VARIOUS MACHADO JIU-JITSU SCHOOLS IN SOUTHERN CALIFORNIA.

"NO QUESTION IS TOO INSIGNIFICANT TO ASK," SAYS MAGNO. "IF SOMEONE WANTS ME TO EXPLAIN A POSITION IT IS BECAUSE THEY DON'T UNDERSTAND IT. I'M GLAD TO HAVE THE KNOWLEDGE THAT ENABLES ME TO HELP SOMEONE. BEING AN INSTRUCTOR IS AS MUCH ABOUT HOW YOU RELATE, AS IT IS ABOUT HOW MUCH YOU KNOW. YOU CAN HAVE THE BEST TECHNIQUES IN THE WORLD, BUT IF YOU DON'T KNOW HOW TO GET YOUR POINT ACROSS THEN YOUR KNOWLEDGE IS WORTHLESS."

NO MATTER HOW REFINED HIS JIU-JITSU TECHNIQUES ARE, HOWEVER, MAGNO RECOGNIZES THE NEED FOR VERSATILITY. "NO MODERN MARTIAL ART IS A COMPLETE SYSTEM IN ITSELF. IT'S VERY IMPORTANT FOR GRAPPLERS TO UNDERSTAND THE STRIKING ASPECTS OF COMBAT," HE SAYS. "IF YOU DON'T KNOW HOW TO DEFEND AGAINST STRIKES, SOMEONE IS GOING TO HIT YOU AND KNOCK YOU OUT. BUT IF YOU KNOW HOW TO DEFEND AGAINST THEM, THEN YOU CAN TAKE A PERSON DOWN AND GRAPPLE." THIS REALISTIC APPROACH HAS CAUSED RENATO MAGNO TO BE WIDELY REGARDED AS ONE OF THE TOP BRAZILIAN JIU-JITSU INSTRUCTORS IN THE UNITED STATES

Q: How did you begin your martial arts training?

A: In Sao Paulo, my father loved judo and he used to train several times a week. I wanted to do the same so I began going with him. My judo was with the Pinero club, one of the best in the city. Many competitors from there were selected to go to the Olympics, so the level was very high. I used to workout with Joan Gonzalvez and Fuscao, two great Brazilian judo instructors who taught me many techniques. After I began studying jiu-jitsu, the combination of the two arts was very interesting. I used judo for the stand-up aspects of throws and takedowns, but on the ground my technique was pure Brazilian jiu-jitsu. I think they complemented each other very well-at least it worked for me. Judo is very effective in dealing with how to throw your opponent, and also how to control his balance and position while on the feet. Brazilian jiu-jitsu is, of course, is the best art in the world for submissions.

Q: Why did you compete in judo and not jiu-jitsu?

A: Mainly because there weren't many jiu-jitsu competitions. So to improve my ground skills judo competition was the perfect place to start. I had many opportunities to compete and that increased my technical level. Of course, once my opponent was on the ground, I used jiu-jitsu all the way. Later on, jiu-jitsu competition began to grow and it was easier for me to compete there.

Q: When you moved to Rio de Janeiro, did you keep training jiu-jitsu?

A: I did, but there weren't many classes for kids. The jiu-jitsu training was more for adults than for kids. The training at that time under the Gracie family was very technical and very specific and detail oriented. For instance, when you learned a technique like the triangle, you were supposed to train that single technique for the whole month-changing the angle, the position, applying leverage in different ways, and paying attention to the little details that make the technique work. You spent weeks or even months working on that. By the end of the year you might know only 12 or 15 basic techniques but your knowledge and skill was so good that you could pull them off anytime almost at will. The transitions from one technique to the other were very smooth, and the control over the opponent's body in order to apply the movement was very important part. The training was not competition oriented. It was very, very technical and we were not in any kind of rush to learn thousand of new movements to win a tournament. The basic were strongly emphasized and the technical level was very high.

Personally, I had to work hard in order to get better at jiu-jitsu. I know some people are very natural and able to duplicate techniques very fast, but I had to work at it. I believe that it was good for me because it made me learn the value of hard work. Since those days, I always try to work positions that I don't feel comfortable using. I always try to improve on my weak points.

Q: Was the training more for self-defense or competition?

A: There weren't many jiu-jitsu competitions so the focus was more on self-defense. The training was very quality-oriented and the sportive aspect was not fully developed. I don't even think too many of us were thinking about sport competition at all. A lot of the family members were training there together: the Machado Brothers, coached by Carlos Gracie Jr., Royler Gracie, Renzo Gracie, Ralph Gracie, Rillion Gracie and many other family members.

Q: There are competitions everywhere now. How has sport jiu-jitsu affected the art?

A: Now the whole thing is very different. The students who want to compete don't have time to spend an entire month polishing only one technique. There are new techniques all the time a as result of the tournaments. In some ways this is very good for the sport, but in other ways life in the fast lane is not all that. Competitors need to spend time catching-up with the new competition movements and can't spend hours and hours on the basics. It's very hard to find a good balance if the student's interest is in competition. The sophistication of the techniques is 100 percent superior to those in the past. There are new ways to hold the belt, better approaches to body controls, better entries and takedowns, et cetera. Unfortunately, some things have been lost along the way. That's the reason why it is more difficult to be a good teacher and a good competitor these days-you have to work twice as hard as in the past to get on top and stay on top.

Q: Are all jiu-jitsu instructors willing to change and adapt to the new techniques?

A: Regardless if your jiu-jitsu is more based on the old traditional techniques, or its focus is on modern competition, there is hardly ever an instructor who will not alter his methods to some extent. If he is convinced that an addition or change is more effective for a particular technique then he will replace it. In the end, the art of teaching is the sum total learned from theory and practice. But if you are not interested in sport competition then you have to train differently, maybe with a more traditional approach.

Q: Weren't you one of the first jiu-jitsu fighters to start training in boxing?

A: Yes, I was! I was living in Sao Paulo and I got interested in boxing, so I began to take classes. As time passed I became very good at it-or at least so I thought. I began to feel that boxing was the best art! Every time I went to Rio de Janeiro, I went to the Barra Gracie school. Carlos Garcie Jr. Renzo, Rigan and everybody else was there. I told them about boxing and they began to tease me over the whole thing. All of a sudden, everybody knew I was into boxing. So they put me on the training mat to show my boxing skills, and I ended up on the ground and being choked-out every single time by several students. I was embarrassed in front of everybody!

From that on every time I went to visit Barra Gracie everybody would yell, "Watch out for Renato's boxing!" They all had a ball teasing me about it!

Q: Did you keep training in boxing?

A: I quit! At that time I was so frustrated with the whole experience that I decided to stop my boxing training-although, now I know as a fighter you need to know how to use your hands effectively. So I guess I was just ahead of my time and didn't realize it.

Q: Living in Sao Paulo, how did you train with the Gracie family in Rio?

A: It's a long distance from Sao Paulo to Rio de Janeiro-around seven or eight hours driving. My father used to drive to Rio and that's when I went to Barra Gracie. Fortunately, Renzo Gracie had a girlfriend in Sao Paulo so he was there all the time. That was perfect for me because he would come to my house and we would spend a lot of time together-not only training jiu-jitsu but also having fun.

Q: Haven't you been closely involved with the Machado Brothers for many years?

A: Yes, I have. I still learn a great deal from them. It is interesting to note that each one has a different fighting style-Jean Jacques, Carlos, Rigan, John, and Roger have different strong points in their jiu-jitsu and I've had the great opportunity to learn specific information from each of them. I have also incorporated some other aspects like takedowns and controls from wrestling into my game. These days, everything happens very fast and you need to be explosive and powerful on the ground-much more than in the past, simply because good mat technique is not enough in competition. You need to be a very well-balanced competitor to make it into the top three. In the last few years, the technical level has risen enormously. The practitioners are more aware of others elements that make your jiu-jitsu better. The cardiovascular training, the nutrition, the stretching and flexibility aspects are really important these days and make a huge difference.

In the past we used to train straight jiu-jitsu-period. No weights and no concerns about cardiovascular training and endurance. We were not aware of the needs for specific training programs to gain strength and cardio, and of the importance of nutrition and rest in order to recover from training. Don't forget that if you don't sleep, your body doesn't rest-and if you don't rest you can't train hard. It's that simple; but unfortunately we didn't think about it in the past.

Modern training methods is one of the reasons why students are improving so fast these days-they know about all these elements. Even if they combine them at a very basic level, the overall result is far better than what we had 20 years ago. In some ways, you can't really compare what we have now with what we had in the early days. It's like basketball; you can't compare the NBA of today with the NBA of 15 or 20 years ago. It's still basketball, but all the training around it is 100 percent better. Today, jiu-jitsu is all about having a complete package.

Q: When is the appropriate time to incorporate other training elements into a student's routine?

A: Not as a beginner, that's for sure. Only when you have been training jiu-jitsu for a while-maybe around one year when you have the basic techniques down. But it should only be done if you have extra time. You should start incorporating weight training, cardio, plyometrics, and flexibility training but always as a compliment to your jiu-jitsu and not as a substitution. Running five miles a days, lifting weights for one hour, and swimming for another hour won't improve your guard or mount position. Don't get caught in the idea that because your body looks good after all the weight training and running that you are good at jiu-jitsu. Jiu-jitsu is about technique, not about the way you look.

Outside training also depends on the student's age and goals. For instance, if you are not interest in competing and just want is to be in shape and enjoy the training, then you have to focus more on techniques, positions, and pure jiu-jitsu. If you do a jiu-jitsu workout three or four times a week, you'll be more than OK. That's because a jiu-jitsu workout gives you all the basic fitness elements with the calisthenics, strength, and stretching exercises you do in class. But if you are interested in competing and winning tournaments, then your supplementary training has to complement your jiu-jitsu. You'll need that extra edge that comes from running, swimming, stretching, and specific weight training routines. You need to know the latest technical improvements so you won't get caught by surprise in the half-guard game or by the new leg-locks.

In sport jiu-jitsu, the techniques change and evolve all the time-a competitor needs to be updated constantly. A regular student who trains jiu-jitsu for self-defense and for fun doesn't need to worry about all that. The principles and concept s of Brazilian jiu-jitsu cannot be changed. They are the same for everybody and standard throughout the world and every student learns them. The techniques, however, can be changed. Brazilian jiu-jitsu is not a very old art and there are millions of practitioners around the world already. It is one of the fastest growing sports.

Q: Is sport or self-defense training more popular?

A: In the United States, people are interested in competition but not as much as in Brazil. In Brazil, there are competitions every weekend, and this raises the technical level very fast. In America only a small amount of students want to compete. Therefore the way we teach the classes has to fit into that. The importance is about how to master the basics and not in learning a lot of competition techniques. It's in separate classes for those who want to compete, where you can focus on technical aspects more suitable for sport. Also, you have to understand that most students have day jobs and can't afford to get hurt in class because they won't be able to work the next day. Jiu-jitsu may be their passion but not the way they make their living. Therefore, as an instructor, you need to control and regulate the classes so the students know how much pressure to apply without hurting each other. It's stupid to try to fight against an arm bar when your classmate has the lock 70 percent complete. That's the reason I don't like to let beginners to train with beginners all the time. I like to mix the students so the higher belts can control the techniques and don't get involved in an ego contest. You need to know when you can't get out of a technique and when to let your partner finish the movement. If you develop a feeling for it, very soon you'll be able to feel the position and escape the lock just as your opponent begins to apply it. If you always try to use strength to resist a lock, then not only will not learn anything but you'll get injured as well.

Q: Why does it take so many years to get a black belt in Brazilian jiu-jitsu?

A: The black belt is the essence of Brazilian jiu-jitsu. It is not like some other arts where being a black belt has been watered down and doesn't mean anything anymore. Although we have degrees within the black belt rank, the 'faixa preta' is the sign of the highest skill level in our art. Therefore, when a student reaches that rank he is pretty much on his own. There is not a lot of interest in getting the second or third degree black belt. It is simply not important to people. The first two belts in jiu-jitsu are the foundation for the rest and you have to spend time there. The blue and purple belts create a base for the student to grow. To a certain extent, a good purple belt knows almost every technique a black belt knows-he just lacks the time, fighting experience, and years of training and practice.

When you compare the jiu-jitsu belt ranking system to other martial arts, you'll notice that jiu-jitsu has only four belts (blue, purple, brown and black) while karate, for example, has six. So a Brazilian jiu-jitsu black belt is probably more equivalent to a second or third degree black in karate in terms of the time it takes to earn. So a BJJ black belt is better trained than black belts from other arts because it takes much longer to get.

On the other hand, there are undoubtedly BJJ who prevent or delay their students from getting their black because they're afraid of losing part of the business. Keeping a student in a belt rank too long is as unfair as giving out a belt too fast. In the very end, it boils down to the instructor's honesty. Nowadays, students train very hard and the time to achieve the black belt is shorter-not because of a lack of requirements but because people train harder and smarter than 20 years ago. There are exceptional people who achieve black belt rank in four or five years but these are very rare. They must train many hours a day, be physically gifted, and have a natural talent for jiu-jitsu. Their dedication to the art must be absolute.

Q: Is a black belt automatically a good teacher?

A: A black belt can teach anyone they want, of course, but it doesn't necessarily mean they know how to do it properly. I have seen black belts who have won major championships who cannot properly explain the most basic techniques to a student. They are great as fighters and competitors but their ability to communicate is not adequate enough for them to teach properly. On the other hand, I know purple belts who are not interested in competition, but yet who are extremely knowledgeable and can help a beginning student understand and apply almost any technique. They have the ability to transmit the essence of the art. In the future they will be the ones training the champions because they can pass the knowledge to future generations. Being a good fighter or competitor does not necessarily mean you'll be a good teacher. A good teacher will always know how to help the students recognize and deal with the important points of any technique. Effective teaching is the final responsibility of each instructor.

Q: What is the most important element in applying a jiu-jitsu technique in combat?

A: Relaxation is a big part of the game. Being relaxed is very important, especially when your opponent is in control. You want to be relaxed because that is the only way you'll eventually come up on top. When you are relaxed, good things just happen. Do not tense up or think too much because that is a waste of energy. When you are on the mat, you want to be relaxed physically and mentally. Your strong points should be your intelligence, your conditioning, and your ability to read your opponent. The essence of jiu-jitsu is to let the technique explode from within. You must use the art with feeling. It is vital to draw from all your physical and mental resources. To a true jiu-jitsu practitioner the words "try" and "impossible" do not exist-you simply execute a technique when the situation warrants it.

Q: What is the most important advice you can give a student?

A: Every time you train, do it with sincerity and heart. In all martial arts, sincerity is essential to building a credible technique, although many people can't see the relationship between sincerity and the actual physical movements of jiu-jitsu. You need to be serious and perseverant in your training, otherwise your training will have no value. You can't have the mindset that training is merely something to do to kill time. Don't go to the academy and merely go through the motions. Have a goal in mind every time you train-and train regularly.

Q: What have the martial arts meant to you?

A: The art of jiu-jitsu has given me everything I have in life. Jiu-jitsu keeps my body healthy and clean, relieves my mind of stress, and fills my life with goodness. If I live another thousand years, I'll spend them all studying the art of jiu-jitsu and living the good life in the company of family and friends. Life is good and I intend to live it to its fullest.

RICKSON GRACIE

The Brazilian Icon

RICKSON GRACIE HAS BEEN SAID TO HAVE THE MOST PERFECT TECHNIQUE OF ANY MEMBER OF THE LEGENDARY GRACIE FAMILY, CREATORS OF BRAZILIAN JIU-JITSU. RICKSON HAS DEDICATED HIS LIFE TO MARTIAL ARTS AND IS CONSIDERED BY MANY TO BE THE BEST FIGHTER ON THE PLANET.

A GENUINE LEGEND, RICKSON HAS GAINED WORLDWIDE ACCLAIM FOR HIS LEADERSHIP IN SPREADING THE ART AND PHILOSOPHY OF JIU-JITSU. HE IS MAN OF HONOR, TRADITION, HONESTY, AND KINDNESS. HE IS PROUD TO BE BOTH A FAMILY MAN AND A MODERN-DAY WARRIOR. RICKSON HAS WON SEVERAL OPEN VALE TUDO CHAMPIONSHIPS HELD IN JAPAN IN WHICH EXPERT FIGHTERS FROM ALL OVER THE WORLD, TRAINED IN A VARIETY OF MARTIAL ARTS STYLES, COMPETED. RETIRED FROM MMA EVENTS, RICKSON GRACIES FOCUSES TODAY ON SPREADING THE TRUE SELF-DEFENSE SYSTEM DEVELOPED BY HIS FATHER, THE LEGENDARY HELIO GRACIE.

Q: How old were you when you began to train?

A: We all started when we were babies; not so much for the techniques or the discipline, but to start getting the feeling of the grip using the legs. My dad played with me even on the bed. When we started to actually get the movements, we already had the reflex and the conditioning to feel comfortable. I started competing at six years old, and since then I've been involved in the sport aspect of Jiu-Jitsu, just training and competing.

Q: Is it a tradition in your family that everyone learns Jiu-Jitsu?

A: Yes. Since we were born, we've been involved (in Jiu-Jitsu). Jiu-Jitsu offers a very special way for you to understand yourself. You can understand your limitations; you can improve your patience, sensitivity, coordination, and sportsmanship; you learn how to lose and how to win; and you learn how to be respectful. It's a very gentle way to learn. By doing this, you become a better person just by learning how to fight.

Q: How far did you go with your studies?

A: I did the college entry exam for Physical Education and I decided to stop because it wasn't what I wanted. It was there that I chose Jiu-Jitsu.

Q: When you promote Jiu-Jitsu are you insinuating that no other style or system has any value?

A: No, that would be foolish. Many people don't know that my specialty is free fighting. I punch, I kick and I fight very well on my feet and on the ground. The goal is to be a well-rounded martial artist, especially when you are talking about real self-defense. I only say, "Look at what we have to offer before you make any decisions about our system." An understanding of ground fighting will make you a better fighter and martial artist, that's all.

Q: What are the origins of the Gracie family?

A: The Gracie family came from Scotland and arrived in Brazil around 1900. The first generation that became involved in Jiu-Jitsu was my father, along with his brother Carlos Gracie. A Japanese named Maeda Koma, who had come to work in Brazil as a Japanese immigration representative, became very close to my grandfather, Gastao Gracie. As a gesture of friendship, he offered to teach Jiu-Jitsu to his children. Consequently, my Uncle Carlos began to learn Jiu-Jitsu around 1912, 1915. Since then he began to participate in the development of Jiu-Jitsu, adapting a lot more leverage and other techniques than those that had been already taught. He became the highest expression of Jiu-Jitsu in Brazil for a long time and was very well known worldwide. The next five generations represented Jiu-Jitsu and the

> "The goal is to be a well-rounded martial artist, especially when you are talking about real self-defense."

tradition of the family. This is what keeps us connected to the sport and to this life that we live.

Q: There are some differences in the family. What is the reason for this? Is it different techniques or just different applications?

A: The family is enormous. My father had nine children. My uncle had twenty-one children; the oldest is already over fifty. I have even lost count of the number of grandchildren and great-grandchildren in our family. It's evident that in a family so large, among the great many different types of people, some differences are going to appear, which is normal in any family. But on the other hand, a common union exists which refers to the sport. Everyone is interested in seeing Jiu-Jitsu grow because all of us are linked to it in one way or another.

Q: About your father, Helio Gracie, he trained until his last days, correct?

A: Yes, he did. He was always an example for all of us. He was a person who left me without words to define him.

Q: In Japan, Ju-Jutsu (preferred Japanese spelling) was the main martial art until the 40's. Afterwards they developed Judo and Karate, right?

A: In the olden days, Jiu-Jitsu was the only art used by the Japanese people. When the Japanese had swords, they fought to kill with the sword. Whenever they lost the sword, they fought to kill with their hands, using different techniques, but always with the objective of ending the fight. This is the purpose of Jiu-Jitsu, whose literal translation is: "soft art." This art was altered a bit. As time went by, with the war and invasion of the occidental world into the Japanese culture, the Japanese hid this superior art and began to export a sportier side to the occidental world. This is where judo and karate come in: arts that are purely sport. The objective of these arts is not to kill your opponent, but to gain points. Even Japan itself, in order to maintain itself competitively in sports in the international arena, forgot the old Jiu-Jitsu and began to enter into a type of training that was a lot stronger than that developed for the world. They completely forgot the traditional Jiu-Jitsu, that has as its predominate objective the victory over its adversary. And today I am certain that long ago Japan had already forgotten the Jiu-Jitsu that was made and developed by my family.

Q: Why is such a dangerous art called a "soft art?"

A: It is soft because it is based on the movements of leverage. It does not have brutality stamped on the movements that are used; the movements are "gentle." Good Jiu-Jitsu doesn't use strength, it doesn't have to be brutal. Jiu-Jitsu is supposed to be a beautiful art. It's a matter of skill. You are supposed to feel it, and appreciate and enjoy it, and want to move your body and mind in oneness. That's what's you want to do. Unfortunately, that is not what people want to see today. That's the Jiu-Jitsu's old school of thinking, isn't it?

Q: What is so different about Brazilian Jiu-Jitsu as opposed to conventional Jiu-Jitsu?

A: There is only one Jiu-Jitsu in Brazil. It was all created by my family. Some have a bit more technique, others have less, but basically it's the same thing. Here in the United States there are perhaps fifty different types of Jiu-Jitsu, but they are totally based upon wrist locks and hip throws. It is as if they were aikido; they do not have much efficiency in the sense of a real personal defense or fighting. People from other styles of fight are really impressed with the efficiency our Jiu-Jitsu has shown.

Q: In Rio, you are a famous man; everyone knows who you are. How did you feel when arrived to LA., a city of many famous people?

A: In Brazil I felt like a sequence of tradition that was implanted by my predecessors. I feel very proud of being part of this tradition, this clan; but I never stopped being part of the sequence of work that has been developed for over 70 years. When we moved to the United States, few people knew what Gracie Jiu-Jitsu was; few people knew our potential. This has changed slowly, until we got to the point of giving classes to police academies and to the Marines. The events which were being promoted at that time by Pay-Per-View are gave us great recognition. We came here to implant Jiu-Jitsu and it has been a great success in the United States. I feel like a pioneer of Jiu-Jitsu who has been very successful.

Q: What is most important for you: success, recognition, or money?

A: I've breathed Jiu-Jitsu since the day I began to understand myself as a person. Jiu-Jitsu has given me everything I need: not only recognition, not only money, not only health and dignity, but everything I need as a man. Naturally, one thing is linked to the other-if you really like something and are interested in developing whatever you do to the highest level, money comes as a consequence.

Q: Was it the money that brought you to the United States? Were you feeling difficulties, or was it the desire to expand your Jiu-Jitsu throughout the world?

A: I had reached all of my goals in Brazil. It was a routine for me to win all of the competitions. My academy was full of students. With the inflation and political problems of the country, with the difficulty of actually getting money together, I thought it was the best option. Not only to expand the art, but also for my personal benefit I would come to the United States. It was said and done.

Q: What about challenging well-known sports figures, like Mike Tyson?

A: I believe that each one has his sport. For example, Mike Tyson: I think that he was the best boxer in the world. Understand? I do not see anyone who could in his prime face him in the world of boxing. But one day I picked on him for having said he was the best fighter. Since that day I began to look for him, saying I wanted to fight with him in all my interviews. He has to prove that he is the best fighter if he truly feels that he is, because I believe he is not. Mike Tyson would not last three minutes in my hands. In relation to this, Jiu-Jitsu mixes all of the arts in an event that combines everything.

Q: Do you have a personal code of bushido?

A: Yes, I have it. For me, this is something very clear in my mind. I always try to do my best and I always believe everybody has value. I respect everyone; my honor is more important than my body. If I feel I must do something and I might die, I don't care about my physical body. My spiritual body is more important. I just believe one hundred percent in keeping my dignity. I can't be bought, and nobody can change my ideas. My philosophy is also to always support the people who stay with me. I never turn my back on a friend.

Q: Are you a religious man?

A: I believe in God and in a Higher energy. I believe in energy. I believe in good vibrations. But I do not go to church. I do not see a connection between God and church.

Q: A long time ago during a press conference in Denver, Colorado they asked your age and you responded that you were "ageless." What did you mean by this?

A: What happens is that people are very labeled by their age. I have a philosophy of life that compensates my age, not by the fact of being afraid of getting old, but because I think that people have to live the moment intensely. With time, you can lose resistance but gain experience, so you gain energy.

Q: In your opinion, what role does fear play in a real fight?

A: Fear is always present. For me that's good. You must be afraid. If you're not afraid, you're not intelligent. It's very important that you respect your opponent and be afraid of what he can do. But this goes back to emotional control. Don't let the fear get strong. It's there, but you keep it in a shell. As soon as things start, you have to believe in what you know and in yourself, and turn on the automatic pilot. Just do it and don't think about it or your fear. Only the stupid don't feel fear.

Q: What is the most important aspect of Rickson Gracie Jiu-Jitsu in terms of the students?

A: Our Jiu-Jitsu is something you can do for your entire lifetime. My father ensured that our philosophy and techniques would work whether you are big and very strong or small and frail. It is all about leverage and feel. It is simple. You must be able to defend yourself at all times, under all physical conditions. Today you are feeling good, you are a large and strong man. Today you might get into a fight and be able to, if nothing else, simply overpower your opponent because of this. But what if next week you are sick with the flu? Then you would not be so strong, and your thinking might not be as clear. Still, you must defend yourself successfully. Kicks and punches when you are feeling good are easy, if you are in reasonable shape and have stamina and power. But if you are sick, all of this changes. In my Jiu-Jitsu you can still defeat most opponents quickly with little effort, no matter how you are feeling at that most important moment.

Q: Why is it so hard for anyone, regardless of style, to match up against a Gracie family member? Do you think you will ever be beaten?

A: You cannot practice grappling, or ground fighting, or Jiu-Jitsu for six months and believe that, because you can execute a few techniques very well, you will beat us on the mat. We have been studying our art for over 70 years. I began training when just a young boy. My family has fought in the dojo, in the ring, in the streets and on the beaches of Brazil. We are always training and always ready for the challenge. Yes, everyone can be beaten, and I know this. But as of yet, I have not been.

Q: What is the reason behind proposing or accepting challenges?

A: Every fighter, everyone who has spent his/her life searching and training deserves all my respect. But if you open any magazine, you're going to see some people claim, "I believe this is the best" or "I'm the best at what I do." So if they really believe 100% in what they do, then they should be always ready to prove it. So I'm open to fight anyone at anytime just to reinforce my beliefs. It doesn't make sense to say, "I believe in what I'm doing, but I'm not going to fight." So we are always accepting challenges and we are always ready to fight (in order) to prove we believe 100% in what we do.

Q: What would happen if you ever lost a challenge match?

A: It's hard to say. But if I lose, I'm not going to relate this to the techniques; it's going to be a personal mistake. It's going to be something I should have done and I didn't. I think at that point my opponent would deserve to win. I don't have any pressure on my back because the only commitment I have is to do my best. So I am very serious, very professional, and I try to prepare myself the best I can mentally and physically by putting everything in God's hands. I surrender to God. If it is my time to lose or even to die, then it's a good time. Every day I wake up, thinking it's an excellent day to enjoy a day on the beach, an excellent day to fight, or an excellent day to die. So I'm always prepared for whatever happens. I don't feel pressure, ever. No matter how many fights I did before, I'm willing to do it over again.

Q: How do you see Jiu-Jitsu in the future?

A: I believe Jiu-Jitsu will unify all martial arts. For a fighter to really feel complete, he/she needs to have the vision that a Jiu-Jitsu fighter has: of being able to live with whatever problem, whatever surprise. He/she has to be able to adapt to any situation that may appear. The Jiu-Jitsu fighter is always ready in this way. A boxer and a karate fighter cannot adapt to variation.

Q: Define the qualities and attributes (both mental and physical) of the "complete fighter"?

A: The bottom line is that complete fighter got to have a well balance between the mental, physical and spiritual aspects. It's a combination of heart and skill.

Q: When do you know you were fully prepared for a fight?

A: It's impossible to know when you are "fully" prepared for a fight. That's something that you never know. All what you can do is to have a complete approach to your training and preparation where you cover all the basic, both physical and mental, and put yourself fully into it. My personal training involves the physical part (including the conditioning and Jiu-Jitsu techniques) and the spiritual or mental. I have been always mentally prepared to fight so the spiritual aspect is not something that takes me a long time. I can get into that mood in a very short time. The physical although I always try to be in top shape, it would take me around three months to be in at the level I consider appropriate to face a well-prepared opponent in the ring. A major aspect of my preparation is my diet. I follow my family diet and depending how close is the fight I eat more protein or carbohydrate. The food you eat id the fuel of your body, so you should pay attention to your nutrition. Depending of how well you eat, you'll perform not only during the fight but during the training for the event. Personally I love to eat fresh fruits, vegetable and white meat and I try to avoid heavy foods and pork.

> **"It's impossible to know when you are "fully" prepared for a fight. That's something that you never know."**

Q: Would you elaborate more on your diet?

A: You shouldn't be eating all the time because this takes energy away from you. If your body is constantly digesting, you are wasting energy. It's that simple. One important aspect is how you combine the food you take. If you don't know the right combinations you may suffer of headaches, joint problems, insomnia. If you combine them incorrectly you may create a chemical imbalance which brings other major problems later on. The idea is to eat light but getting all the important nutrients. I try not to eat at least three hours before going to bed. I do eat red meat although my family doesn't. As a fighter I think is important, I do it twice a month, which is not a lot though.

Q: Let's talk about some technical aspects of a fight. What is your main strategy in the ring?

A: The final goal is to win. I don't need to punch my opponent into pulp to feed my ego. It's a sport. I will do whatever it takes to win but no more. I don't need to hurt anyone to prove that I can win a fight. My main strategy is to protect myself and avoid to get hit. After I covered that aspect, then I try to adapt to what my opponent gives me. Jiu-Jitsu is based on exploit the opponent's weaknesses. Sometimes I faced really big opponents, then I have to do things accordingly. Once you have an understanding of what your opponent can do the idea is to limit the elements he can use. By doing this, his possibilities of attack and defense are restricted. It's here when he's in trouble. At that moment I already have my answers ready to whatever he does. I believe in one-hundred-percent defense. I use the counter. I'm not an aggressor. I use the opponent's mistakes, and believe that I can get him just as soon as he tries something against me. I always give him the first option. In other words, he will choose how he's going to be beaten. It takes patience to do that. When you're fighting you shouldn't go after your opponent at full speed. Physical training is not the only part of the equation to be a good fighter.

Q: To do the minimum damage to an opponent requires a lot of skill, right?

A: Unfortunately, we all see these events where the fighters try to destroy the opponent instead of winning. For me destroying someone is not a victory. This boils down to respect and sportsmanship. Fighting is something violent, but we are athletes who practice a combat sport. We are there to test our skills, with regulations and sportsmanship. I like the Japanese approach. They organizations are not interested in brutal, brawling kind of fights. We don't need to make it brutal and bloody. We can leave that for street fights where our lives are at stake. That's a whole different story.

Q: Why do you think that is?

A: Maybe because of the Bushido, the "code of the warrior." In Japan they respect you if you win but to gain their deepest respect you must behave as a real warrior, like a samurai. You need to display class in all your acts. And I like that.

Q: How important do you think it is for a specialist in grappling to learn how to use his hands and feet for striking?

A: If you are strictly a jiu-jitsu or wrestling competitor, adding punches and kicks to your arsenal won't do any good because you are not going to need it. On the contrary, if you are a Vale Tudo fighter then you need punching and kicking skills to complement your grappling skills. To be a well-rounded fighter you need both components of the equation. This is the only way a grappler will be fully prepared for a no-holds-barred or Vale Tudo competition.

Although your main goal is still take your opponent down and defeat him on the ground, you need an understanding of the punching and kicking techniques because you need to know how to counters these aspects of combat. To counter these techniques you must understand how they work and what their timing is. Otherwise, you are going to be surprised by them. Your understanding of how they work will allow you to shoot in for that takedown and to avoid the punishment your striking opponent will try to inflict as he is fighting to avoid being taken down.

In my fights, I use punching and kicking but if you look closely I don't use these elements as the final tool to finish my opponent. I punch and kick so these techniques open a way to use my jiu-jitsu. If I punch the guy too much my hands will be damaged and that's not what I want. I look for a better way to defeat my opponent without unnecessary violence. I'd rather use jiu-jitsu to do that than punch the guy until the end. From a technical point of view, I use punching and kicking in such a way they work for my jiu-jitsu, and from a moral point of view you could say that I try to be as gentle as possible.

Q: Once you are on the ground, what position you prefer?

A: My technique is based on my opponent. I try to stay in what I call the "zero zone." From there, I'm ready to read what the opponent gives me to react. It takes a very strange balance to fight that way, but in the very end you don't know what you are going to do; you simply wait to see what the opponent gives you and then you take it. I go with the flow of the movements and actions my opponent gives me.

It's true that I like to keep my opponent in my guard. The reason is that sooner or later he is going to make a move to try to escape, and that action will open a door for me to counter. It's like having an answer for everything he may try to do. You just have to control and wait for him to move. Of course, it sounds simpler that it is in real action, but the underlying principle is to stay in that "zero zone," control your opponent so you are safe and wait for his move. Then, react to it in the best possible way.

Q: There are the differences of fighting with a gi (sport jiu-jitsu) and without gi (vale tudo)? How does the whole strategy change?

A: Yes, there are differences and a good fighter needs to know what these are. Training with a gi gives you more possibilities as far as techniques are concerned. You have more choices for choking, getting an armlock or controlling your opponent. In any grappling activity, getting a good grip is a relevant part of the fight and with gi it is easier than when your opponent isn't wearing one. When your opponent has no gi, the fight becomes a little more physical due to the fact that you have to control his body in a different way. You have to look for the major limbs and areas that you can hold consistently like his head, trunk, etc. If you compete in sport jiu-jitsu (gi), you'll need to know all the variables because your opponent can use many different grips that will end up putting you in a very difficult position. There are more techniques, more variables; therefore, it takes more time to become skilled in the art. Fighting without a gi cuts the number of possibilities down so the basics can be mastered in a shorter period of time. Don't get me wrong; it doesn't mean it's easier. Unfortunately, I have seen some good jiu-jitsu fighters enter in Vale Tudo events and lose due to the fact they used the wrong approach to the no gi situation. When you go from gi to no gi, you need to know how to change and adapt your guard, your controls, your clinch, etc., otherwise you are going to be defeated.

There are several considerations for each type of situation but in Vale Tudo I don't like to use the gi because that would give my opponent the advantage of more options to control me. I might use it in some special conditions, though. But basically if I don't have a gi on, I limit my opponent's possibilities of holding on to it and the "stalling" factor can be very important in a fight. Of course, I'd love all my opponents to wear a gi, but they are smart guys too!

Q: How do you approach your jiu-jitsu when teaching a women's class?

A: Well, things are changing these days. In the past you didn't have too many women competing in jiu-jitsu so the classes were focused more on self-defense aspects than in competition techniques. I truly believe that everybody can get benefits from training in the arts and I try to focus my classes so women develop self-confidence and self-esteem by training in jiu-jitsu. My programs are designed to give women specific ways of defending themselves in dangerous situations. The main idea for a women being attacked is to create space and run. A woman doesn't want to stay there and trade blows with her attacker. The bottom line in teaching a class is not whether the student is a man or a woman but his/her level of ability to perform the techniques. If a woman student has previous jiu-jitsu experience then I can put more pressure and go at full speed. Not with the intention of hurting but to make her feel the pressure of a consistent attack. This is the same thing I would do with a man.

Through my years teaching the art, I have found that sometimes it's beneficial for a woman to learn and train jiu-jitsu from another woman. They feel more "in tune" for obvious reason. Because of that, my wife Kim often help me with the instruction, which makes the student feel more comfortable and confident. What is very important is to incorporate training with men so the female student has the opportunity to experience the power and strength of a man doing the attack. In women's self-defense the goal is not to get the aggressor in a choke or arm lock. The idea is to protect yourself and escape safely. Don't stay there trying to overpower the attacker. Use common sense and you'll be safe.

Q: You are an exceptional fighter but you are also considered an excellent teacher. What do you think is the secret of a successful transition from fighter to teacher?

A: Competition is something good, especially when you are young. After years of competition the main reason for me doing jiu-jitsu slightly changed. I had nothing to prove anymore. Winning trophies was not an important issue and I truly began to enjoy the art in a deeper way. I matured and my overall approach and perception of the art did too.

The main difference between a fighter and a teacher is that a fighter does it for himself and a teacher is able to change people's lives through his teachings. As a teacher you influence your students' lives in many ways. The goal is different and more relevant. As far as I'm concerned, having been a fighter first allowed me to understand things first hand and have real experience to pass onto my students. It's my responsibility now to transmit these experiences and knowledge to my students in the proper way.

I know some excellent fighters are not good teachers but I guess this is because the love for sharing what they know is not inside of them. It boils down to the individual's personality. But the opposite is also true. I have seen people that weren't fighters but they have an exceptional ability to teach and share the art. They know all the little details, the angles, the positioning, the correct application of strength, the knowledge of why and how the technique and the movement works, etc. And they are capable of creating champions as well. Being a good teacher has to do with your passion to live the art and share your knowledge with others. You need patience and understanding. The approach is totally different and in some way the fighter must transform himself to become a teacher. If he doesn't know how to switch the mode, then he will end up either hurting the students or not having good disciples.

> **"If you don't have the passion to share and spend time taking care of people, then teaching is not for you. It's that simple."**

Q: Should the teacher have a different philosophical approach as well?

A: Yes, of course. The main objective is not yourself but your student. As a teacher you must be connected to the overall philosophy of incorporating martial arts into your life and not necessarily with the fighting aspects or elements of competition. It's not about what you can do in front of your students to impress them but what you can do to make the students good. If you don't have the passion to share and spend time taking care of people, then teaching is not for you. It's that simple. As teacher you have to give the student everything you have: your experience, your knowledge and you time. You can't give him your talent or your feeling for the art because this is very personal and something that he has to develop on his own. You do your half and the rest is on the student's shoulders.

Q: How much pressure is involved in being a Gracie?

A: Although the Gracie family didn't create the art of jiu-jitsu, the Gracie name has become a symbol of effectiveness using the art. Because of the reputation of many members of my family, past and present, there is definitely a responsibility. To a certain extent every member of the family has the obligation to meet those expectations and this is a hard task. To answer your question, yes, there is a pressure being a Gracie but at the same time I can't conceive my life without that pressure. I've had to live with it since the day I was born so I can't imagine my existence without having the name "Gracie," and all that goes with it, attached to my daily life. My philosophy of life is to respect everybody and everything, trying to do my best in whatever I'm involved at that particular time. Any human being, if he is responsible and tries to maintain high expectations for himself, has that kind of pressure, regardless of his name. Any high level athlete has a pressure every time he performs. Being a Gracie is the only way I have to live my life. There is no way out for me!

Q: Have you ever gotten bored of Jiu-Jitsu?

A: No never. It's true that, like everybody else, I need a change in the direction to keep myself motivated. It's normal and human. Teaching provides me with that "direction" within the same field. When I teach, for me it's something very special. I do it with love. I'm sharing an art created by my family so in a way I'm sharing one of my family assets. And I want to do it in the right way. I believe that main reason why I don't get bored or lose motivation in what I do is because I don't put pressure on myself about what I must do. My workout must to be fun not a torture. If it's fun I can truly enjoy it and don't get burnt. The key is doing it in a enjoyable way.

Q: Whom would you like to fight?

A: I know a lot of people would like to fight me. I fight those who the promoters think are good for the business. It's not about me saying whom I want to fight. People think that I choose my fights. That's not sense. Who you fight is based on many different factors, most of them out of my hands.

Q: When are you planning to retire?

A: I don't plan. I live in the present so as long as I can feel my body working in the way it is now, I won't retire from fighting in life. But I knew one day I was not going feel the same and I was not going take the chances to get hurt. I only concentrate on today. Age is not a factor to me, the determining factor is my body. I don't think how old I am because it's irrelevant to me. If I want to do something, I just do it. I don't think about my age. We all are aware that one day we'll start feeling physical limitations but as human being what it's really important is not to have mental limitations. That's what I strive for.

❝The Jiu Jitsu I created was designed to give the weak ones a chance to face the heavy and strong.❞

~ Helio Gracie ~

RIGAN MACHADO

The Force of Submission

BORN IN RIO DE JANEIRO, RIGAN MACHADO IS ONE OF BRAZILIAN JIU JITSU'S MOST STORIED FIGURES. A CHAMPION IN BRAZIL, RIGAN WAS ONE OF THE FIRST BLACK BELTS TO COME TO THE UNITED STATES AND INTRODUCE AN ENTIRE GENERATION TO THE LOST ART OF GROUND FIGHTING. IN SO DOING HE HELPED CHANGE AMERICAN MARTIAL ARTS FOREVER. THE FACT THAT HE IS ONE OF THE MOST FAMOUS AND RESPECTED INSTRUCTORS IN THE WORLD KEEPS HIM EXTREMELY BUSY TEACHING IN SOUTHERN CALIFORNIA OR TRAVELING TO SPREAD THE ART AND PHILOSOPHY OF THE MACHADO JIU-JITSU. HIS EASY-GOING ATTITUDE REFLECTS HIS RELAXED APPROACH TO THE ART DEVELOPED BY HIS UNCLE CARLOS GRACIE. A PERPETUAL STUDENT OF ANY KIND OF SUBJECT RELATED TO HIS LOVED ART, RIGAN MACHADO ALWAYS STRIVES TO BE BETTER AT WHATEVER HE DOES. AND THE BEST IS YET TO COME.

Q: You've been considered one of the top submission fighters in the world for many years but yet have refused to do MMA events. Why is that?

A: You see, I only like to do things that are fun for me - that I enjoy and get pleasure from. I love Jiu-Jitsu and I love to compete in Jiu-Jitsu so that is what I have done. Professional fighting is a much different step. You have to love, 100 percent, the fighting game. I feel like I still have a lot to accomplish as a grappler. A professional fight does not give me the same feelings that I get from Brazilian Jiu-Jitsu. For me, it is going to be more something that I want to do to see the other side. The reason I didn't do the MMA fights is because I didn't have enough hunger to be in any competition like that. To fight MMA I want to have the same hunger as when I compete in grappling or Brazilian Jiu-Jitsu.

Q: So have you trained punching and kicking?

A: Yes, but that's a complete different aspect of my personal training. I'm from a different world that uses takedowns, clinches, and finishing holds my approach has to be different. And everything I learn has to fit into my scheme. I'm not going to change the things I like just for the money.

Q: What kind of rules do you like the most?

A: It's hard to say. There are many styles or grappling. But when you step onto the mat it is just going to be one style-grappling. The people who have more grappling skills are the ones who will have the best chance in the fight. It doesn't matter if the guy is a sambo player, or a judo fighter, or this or that. The good grapplers will do fine. But I still believe the Jiu-Jitsu fighters own the ground. Some of the other styles are not as used to being on the ground.

Q: So you feel that the style is more important that the person?

A: No. How you fight is still based on the individual-how hard he trains, how hungry he is. That is what makes the fighter. In Brazil you see many good fighters, but hunger and determination is what makes a champion. But it is not only the mind. There are many pieces to the puzzle: speed, strength, flexibility, endurance, and attitude. They all work together but it is based on personal motivation, which cannot be taught. You have it inside or you don't.

Q: Are the Brazilians still as dominant as they used to be?

A: No. Brazil was just the beginning of the modern grappling movement. I believe from there that seeds have been spread all around the world. I believe that in the future it will be more and more difficult for Brazil to dominate so much, due to how many Brazilians are teaching around the world. But that is how it should be. For me, I want to be the best teacher I can be. I want to build a good school, good students, and a good environment for everyone, regardless of where they're from. That's my job. If a student is not from Brazil and he becomes good, then that makes me a good coach and makes me happy. That is my future goal - to train more champions.

Q: So you're more focused on your students that yourself?

A: In life you have many different goals. My goals right now are to concentrate 50 percent on myself and 50 percent on my students. But in the future I will be concentrating almost 100 percent on the students. I want to build up many great fighters for many types of events: for professional fights or for Brazilian Jiu-Jitsu, or submission, or for anything. But right now, to do that, I have to concentrate a lot on myself. What's hard for me is that I have to work very hard teaching, doing seminars, and shooting movies. So to be focused I have to stop teaching, I have to stop movies, and other things to try and concentrate on my training. When I'm training I like to only focus on myself and use all my energy to try to improve my skills and to get the mental and physical sides of myself at 100 percent. What used to be better for me in Brazil is that I only used to train. I never had to work or do anything like that because my work was my training. But now, in the United States, I have to teach a lot and do a lot of classes and a lot of travel for the seminar. So that bugs me more than anything as far as making my training harder. When I'm getting ready for a fight, I wish I only had to train.

> "A proper submission, whether it is an arm lock, knee bar, or whatever, is all a result of a proper opening and that is where the gi is most helpful."

Q: Do you think it's possible to train submission and MMA at the same time?

A: To begin with, you have to train in two different worlds and keep them separate, because both are so technical. But later, then you can put them together but it depends a lot on your personal ability and level of understanding of what you're doing. So when I teach students then I will teach the things that I am good at. Then I can bring in others who are good at punching or whatever, to teach the students to be a complete fighter. Kind of like the way Dan Inosanto does.

Q: What is the difference between training with or without the gi?

A: The difference is that with the gi, the submission game is much more technical. When you wear the gi, you have many more chances to catch your opponent. You have a chance to use the gi to your advantage. You have a much better control for your opening moves. You can tighten up different points on your opponent's body, which set him up for the move to follow. A proper submission, whether it is an arm lock, knee bar, or whatever, is all a result of a proper opening and that is where the gi is most helpful. When you don't have the gi, you have to use a lot of speed and strength. It is not so much a technical match as it is a physical match-many of the techniques are either limited or completely eliminated. The number of chokes you can attempt are greatly reduced; arm locks are harder to get, because you lose so much leverage that you have to get much tighter to your opponent. So there are negatives to not having a gi. However, depending on your strategy, there are also potential advantages to both.

I believe today that it is very important to train both with and without a gi. The way I train is the way I like to teach. I have trained with the gi most of my life. But I like sometimes to challenge myself by adapting the techniques I learned with the gi to grappling without the gi. In this way, I keep myself from getting too comfortable with one way of training-because then you stop learning.

Q: But don't most top MMA fighters train exclusively without the gi?

A: Yes, that's true I suppose. But in my academy, for example, I have 200 students, but maybe only 10 percent of them want to go into professional fighting. The rest, 90 percent, want to learn Jiu-Jitsu for fun, for fitness, for self-defense, or to compete in sport tournaments. That's why the sport rules were invented - it's a way to give the students goals for their training. Tournaments are something to shoot that aren't as violent or intense as professional fighting. And the gi is better for tournaments because it creates more options for the students who are competing in them.

Q: Do you use different grips when you're using or not using the gi?

A: Sure. With the gi, sometimes you can do a lot of different set-ups in order to expose your opponent to a submission. You can keep a comfortable distance from your opponent, stay loose, and still grab the lapel, or the material around the elbow, or even the gi at the hip or the knee, and still control him. But with no gi, the game is much different, you can't control your opponent from a distance and still set him up for a finishing hold. Because a grip that would work with a gi, will be quickly broken with one. There is no lapel to grab, for example, and if you try to hold the neck, the opponent just has to turn his head a little and you slip off. So instead of grabbing for specific points on the body, you have to think about controlling entire regions of the body. For example, instead of controlling the lapel from a distance, you have to get close and control his entire upper body by circling your arms around his body, or by trapping his arm under your arm.

But in either situation, you have to think like a grappler. You have to change your approaches to a move, but you should still be trying to hit the move. In other words, don't let the fact that you have or don't have a gi throw you off your grappling strategy-don't let it take you out of your game. Control the situation rather than letting the situation control you. You must adapt the details, but keep the big picture the same. Use all the same tools, just in different ways.

Q: So chokes are easier to apply with the gi?

A: Actually, it really depends on the situation. For example, to do the basic rear naked choke, or the back choke, is much easier without the gi, because your arms get real slippery in a match because of the sweat and you can slide your arm in much easier and get deeper penetration with less effort. When you have the gi it is sometimes more difficult because the material adds a lot of friction and the arm won't slide in as easily. The gi actually stops the back choke many times. With the gi, when you have the back, I think the collar choke is a much better technique to use. So you have to adapt your entry while keeping the ultimate goal the same-to give your opponent a little nap. It's just with the gi, there are more options.

Q: So you learn more techniques with the gi?

A: There are more techniques because there are more options for each move. For example, with I'm practicing take-downs, you have a chance to try a judo throw, to use the gi to block when someone tries to sweep you, or to open someone up for you to sweep them. But when you take away the gi, you pretty much take away all the judo throws-or at the very least they are severely limited. It's much easier for you to slip in, go low, and shoot for the legs with a Freestyle wrestling technique than it is to try a judo hip throw. So right there you're eliminated the option of the judo throw.

But this is a very relative thing, and it goes both ways depending on what art you've been practicing. When you put a wrestler in a gi, for example, they can easily get lost because they have no idea what to do when someone grabs them by the clothes instead of the body. So a Jiu-Jitsu man can use that to his advantage. The guard is another example where I use the gi to keep him close to me. Without the gi, a wrestler will have a lot more room to operate. But with the gi I can control him by controlling the gi with my arms, without having to clinch. I can keep him from going to the side more effectively, or in the mount I can keep him from escaping from the bottom. There is much less chance to slip away.

So when I train with the gi, I practice those types of moves that would be to my advantage, and then training without the gi I also focus on those things that will help me the most. However, the key thing to remember is that the angles are always the same. The only thing that changes is the grip-the way you control your opponent for the entry. But everything else is the same.

Q: In the past we didn't see a lot of leg locks in Jiu-Jitsu tournaments? Does Brazilian Jiu-Jitsu have many leg locks?

A: For a long time you didn't see a lot of leg locks because of the rules. In the tournaments in Brazil, 10 or 20 years ago, those things were not allowed. Now, though, they are legal and you see a lot more knee bars, heel hooks, and foot locks. The heel hook, though, which puts so much pressure on the knee and the hip, and can cause very serious damage, is the one that Jiu-Jitsu schools in general, I think, don't like to see in day-to-day training. No one wants to get their ligaments torn up and their knee destroyed. A lot of people just do Jiu-Jitsu for fun or self-defense, so I think not letting students use that move is a way of protecting them and keeping the training safe. That's the big advantage of Jiu-Jitsu, after all, over other martial arts-you can train really, really hard and not get hurt. So I think that Jiu-Jitsu teachers want to preserve that concept.

But little by little you see more different types of leg locks added to the Jiu-Jitsu arsenal. Jiu-Jitsu has four different belt levels: blue, purple, brown, and black. People at the brown and the black belt level are those that have started to use more leg techniques. And that is spreading to the lower belts now.

> "You can train a martial art, or a martial sport, such as Jiu-Jitsu, which is both, for sportive uses. But while you're doing this you always have to think about reality"

I believe Jiu-Jitsu grows a little every day. The real purpose of grappling, in the Brazilian Jiu-Jitsu way, is to be able to apply the moves in a real situation. So you have to use moves that can cause damage. But you don't have to damage other students to practice them. So even non-leg-lock moves, such as neck cranks, are not things that I like to see students use on each other. If I see someone doing excessively dangerous moves to other students then I will tell them to stop. If they continue, then I will ask them to leave the school before anyone gets hurt.

Q: What is your overall philosophy of training?

A: You can train a martial art, or a martial sport, such as Jiu-Jitsu, which is both, for sportive uses. But while you're doing this you always have to think about reality. You have to train the sportive methods, but then always keep adapting them and yourself to be able to use them in real situations. You can't lose sight of that or you lose sight of Jiu-Jitsu itself. That is the base idea of Brazilian Jiu-Jitsu-practice for sport, but be able to apply it for real.

Q: How did you usually train for an event like Abu Dhabi or a Jiu-Jitsu Championship?

A: I tried to focus on my Jiu-Jitsu skills by doing a lot of drills with my students and my brothers. I also did a lot of cardio workouts and also a lot of wrestling training for my stamina. The techniques of wrestling are different but they help a lot. Because the Jiu-Jitsu skill are training a lot of techniques with your back on the ground, passing the guard, side control-things like that. When you train standing, you're training takedowns. Things like tie-ups, shoot the legs-single and double. You need to learn a game-plan to develop your balance, skills, and posture. For me it's like two different worlds I'm trying to put together.

Q: Are there any fighters you look up to?

A: I admired, when I was growing up, a coach I used to have who has since died. This coach, for me, is my biggest motivation I have in my whole life. My dream is to come close to being like him. His name was Rolls Gracie. He died a long time ago in a hang-gliding accident. He is the person that I really admire and who still inspires me to train hard.

Q: You must consider him one of the all-time best fighters.

A: I do-but I also admire many other fighters. Not only from Jiu-Jitsu but also many different styles from many different generations. Rolls, in his time, used to just be unbelievable. But I also admire Rickson Gracie. Rickson is a little bit older than me and I used to watch him fight when I was a purple belt and he was already a black belt. He inspired me to train. I have great respect for Carlson Gracie-he was a truly amazing fighter. I admire even wrestlers such as Dan Gable - he's the technician of coaching. Dave Schultz is another guy. When I came to the United States, I really admired. Mike Tyson and Sugar Ray in boxing were other guys who inspired me to become an athlete.

Q: You have a close relationship with Chuck Norris and have appeared on his show, "Walker, Texas Ranger." What is he like?

A: I look upon Chuck Norris as a brother. I don't look at him and see a movie star-I look at him and see a friend. When he invited me and my brothers to work on his TV show we had a great time. He made us feel very relaxed and very welcome. He is just a real nice guy. He helped us to come to United States and has supported us 100 percent. He is one of the best things you have in the United States. He's also a real tough fighter. He's still hungry. He wants to train morning, noon, and night-any chance he has. He wants to train very hard. That proves why he is Chuck Norris. He trains hard, even when he works every day. He always come up to me and asks me to train. He's an amazing guy.

Q: Where do you see yourself in the future?

A: I just want to be a good fighter, a good person, and to be respected by people. What makes me real sad, sometimes, is when people play politics and say bad things about you. That doesn't make sense to me, because how can you talk about people who have done so much to promote the sport and make it better. People say things because they're jealous, or just to make themselves look better in comparison.

RODRIGO MEDEIROS

Going for the Kill!

ONE OF THE MOST DRIVEN AND TENACIOUS OF ALL OF CARLSON GRACIE'S WORLD CHAMPIONSHIP FIGHTERS, RODRIGO MEDEIROS TRAINED IN RIO FOR 14 YEARS BEFORE BEING AWARDED THE COVETED BLACK BELT FROM MASTER CARLSON HIMSELF. TRAINING DAILY WITH THE TOP JIU-JITSU FIGHTERS IN THE PLANET, MEDEIROS DEVELOPED AN ATTACKING STYLE THAT CLOSELY MIRRORS THAT OF CARLSON HIMSELF. BUT JUST AS HE ALWAYS GOES FOR THE KILL IN TOURNAMENT COMPETITION, MEDEIROS ALSO GOES FOR THE KILL WHEN EVALUATING THE PRESENT STATE OF WORLD JIU-JITSU AND ITS POTENTIAL FOR FUTURE GROWTH.

NOW OPERATING TWO SCHOOLS UNDER THE CARLSON GRACIE FLAG, MEDEIROS HAS PLANS FOR FUTURE EXPANSION AND FEELS THAT JIU-JITSU WILL ONLY GET BIGGER. WITH CHAMPIONSHIP STUDENTS OF HIS OWN, IN BOTH JIU-JITSU AND NO-HOLDS-BARRED FIGHTING, MEDEIROS GENERATES THE SAME LOYALTY AND ADMIRATION THAT CARLSON GENERATED IN HIM DURING THEIR MANY YEARS TOGETHER. AND TO THOSE WHO SAY THAT BRAZILIAN JIU-JITSU IS NOT AS EFFECTIVE AS IT ONCE WAS, MEDEIROS HAS A TYPICALLY STRONG REPLY: "ONE HUNDRED PERCENT OF ALL MMA FIGHTERS TRAIN IN BJJ. IF THEY DIDN'T THEY WOULDN'T EVEN KNOW THE GUARD OR THE MOUNT – BUT THEY ALL DO. IN ADCC, 99 PERCENT OF FINALISTS ARE ALSO BJJ FIGHTERS. SO TO SAY BJJ IS NOT EFFECTIVE AS IT ONCE WAS IS JUST PLAIN SILLY AND IGNORES THE FACTS." ENOUGH SAID!

Q: How long have you been practicing jiu-jitsu?

A: Since 1982, so over 22 years. I actually started martial arts before that in judo, when I was 5. I went through it to the brown belt level, but when I discovered jiu-jitsu I focused myself more on ground training and just stayed with that. When I moved to U.S. in 1996 I did start to train in other styles such as boxing, kickboxing and wrestling, just to help round out my complete fight game. I started training with Maneco, a Carlson Gracie black belt, and then after that I studied with Carlson when I was 16 and already had a blue belt. Carlson's academy was a like boot camp! The eliminations inside the academy for the right to compete was harder than the actual tournaments themselves!

Q: So was Maneco good at jiu-jitsu?

A: Maneco was one of the best black belts in the '80s in sport jiu-jitsu. Judo had a little bit on the ground but nothing like jiu-jitsu, and I really liked the ground. In 1996 I came to the U.S. to compete in the Pan American Games. I won my division and after I was going to leave I spent a week here on vacation. I went to San Diego and I went to Hawaii. And when I got back, on my last few days, I stayed in Carlson's house. And he was ready to open his academy and he invited me to teach with him. He helped me out my entire life. So he said he needed an instructor and asked me to stay though the end of the year. I called my father and told him. I had a pretty good life back in Brazil. I had an academy, I had a girlfriend, I had a nice apartment. But I told my father that I was going to be here through the end of the year and I thought it would be a good chance to meet people and to learn English. But then I just ended up staying. For me it was a great experience.

Q: What happened to the school?

A: It went away. When that happened he was ready to leave the school and close the building and I was ready to go also. But one of my students said, "I have a nice place where you can open your own school, so why don't you stay?" So I agreed. Brazil is a great place and a lot of fun, but I don't really stand out there. Here, people respect you as an athlete and a jiu-jitsu teacher. In Brazil, that respect is mainly reserved for the soccer players. Now, in Brazil, a lot of jiu-jitsu players are getting a lot of respect. But back then 1996 – 1997 they weren't getting that respect. Even no-rules fighters weren't that big then. The tournaments, you know, were very small and no magazines really covered it. Now it is getting to be a big sport.

Q: What is the difference between the American and Brazilian style of jiu-jitsu?

A: I think the best teachers are here. Rickson Gracie, the Machados, and a lot of other good teachers are here now. The only difference is that in Brazil jiu-jitsu is more popular. And right now they have more magazines and more fight wear and better organization. In America, jiu-jitsu is still growing. I think in few more years that jiu-jitsu here will be like it is there. In Brazil you don't have a lot to do. So a kid will go to the academy at nine o' clock in the morning and leave at nine o' clock at night. But here the kids have to study, have to work, have to pay all the bills. He lives by himself. So you have to find time to train and it's hard. So the people in Brazil train more. They train much more, that's the difference. They have more options to train and more tournaments they can go to in a lot of different places.

Q: It seems like there are a lot of Brazilian blacks belts, but yet not that many top teachers. What makes a black belt a good teacher?

A: In the United States, potential students have to be very careful who they train with. You have a lot of people who leave Brazil with a blue or purple belt, but when they get here they magically have a black belt. They give themselves a black belt and they start teaching. My opinion is that you have to have a background in every belt, like I did. I spent 4 or 5 years in each belt I earned. I competed in every tournament in each belt. When I was a brown belt, I already had about 15 years of experience in jiu-jitsu. So that is very important. If you want to teach, if you want to have a team, you have to have that experience. You have to be able to relate to each belt, because you spent a lot of time at that belt level.

Q: What are the actual qualities that make a good teacher?

A: I think that you have to be very patient with everyone. You have to know how to divide the players. Some guys you can't press hard, because they are just doing it for a hobby and for fun. Other guys train to be competitors or fighters – so these guys you can push harder. But you can't treat everyone the same. I think the methodology you use to teach is very important. You have to stress the basics and always keep going back to the basics – the mount, the guard, passing the guard, defense against knee on the belly. All the basic positions are where everything comes from. So I make my guys learn the base well. The simple things are very hard to teach and to learn. For example, how you move the hips. You think it is easy but it's very hard. You have to visualize every student. A student might come into my class and check out the school and right away I can tell if that person is going to be a good student or not. I can just tell.

Q: It seems that in no-holds-barred at least, that wrestlers have caught up with jiu-jitsu fighters on the ground. Do you think that jiu-jitsu is still enough to win no-holds-barred matches today?

A: No. In Royce's time, for example, no one knew jiu-jitsu. So it was very easy to fight against opponents who had no idea what was coming. But today, everyone knows jiu-jitsu. People have a background in boxing, muay Thai, and also wrestling – and they also train jiu-jitsu. So they have more skills in the no-rules fights. So today jiu-jitsu fighters have to learn takedowns and also defenses against takedown, and they have to learn how to punch and kick and to defend that also. If not, they are going to lose. Before it was a martial art against another martial art. But that day is gone. Today it is fighter versus fighter. It is hard to find a pure jiu-jitsu guy beating everyone, or a pure wrestler beating everyone or a pure puncher and kicker. Everyone cross-trains. You have to be complete or you are going to lose.

Q: From your many years of judo, do you incorporate some of its techniques?

A: Yes, I teach some judo too. I have been training judo since I was 5 years old. I don't train anymore but I took it for 20 years before I just got tired of it. But I still teach it. And also since I've been here I've been teaching wrestling. So I mix a lot of things up. So when you have a little distance between your opponent then I like to see people shoot in with a wrestling takedown. When you are in grappling range with no distance, then I try to use judo because I think it is more simple.

Q: What kind of overall training schedule would you recommend to someone who is just starting in jiu-jitsu.

A: For guys starting out, I tell them to study at least three time a week in a two-hour group class if they really want to learn it. They I tell them to stretch every day, and also do some cardio like bike, or swim, or run twice a week. That is just for starts. Of course, if you're going to compete you have to increase all the training amounts. But it is very important to tell people that what I think makes jiu-jitsu so great and what attracts people, is that every martial art except jiu-jitsu has a limit. After five years in judo, for example, you have learned all the techniques there are. The same way with muay Thai of kickboxing. There are only certain amounts of techniques they possess. Not true with jiu-jitsu. You always have new techniques. That what's amazing about jiu-jitsu. Jiu-jitsu is infinite – anyone can teach you a new move. A white belt of two months can teach you a new move they've seen or learned. They can show you a new situation and you have to study it. So if anyone says he is a master and has learned it all, he's lying. In jiu-jitsu you have to die learning.

Q: So if someone stops learning then they are not doing jiu-jitsu?

A: I think that if you are a black belt, and you stop training jiu-jitsu and stop learning, then in three or four years when you try to come back all your techniques are going to be old and out of date. Some new move is always coming, and if you don't keep learning you're going to be obsolete.

Q: Do you pay a lot of attention to your diet?

A: I think that diet is very important, not just for jiu-jitsu but for you entire life. You are what you eat. The way you eat is connected to your success. As a jiu-jitsu fighter you eat, you train, and then you rest. Everything is connected. If you train, train, train, and then afterwards go get a burger and then sleep to 2 p.m. and then try to train again, you've never going to be at your full potential. You have to have the right diet. You have to mix the right amounts of protein, carbs, and fiber.

Q: Aside from the physical aspects of jiu-jitsu, have you gained any mental benefits from it?

A: I always tell all my students that if you're just taking jiu-jitsu in order to just beat someone in a fight, then you're thinking small. Jiu-jitsu is for life – it teaches how to treat people. Because you're so confident in yourself after taking jiu-jitsu that you naturally become more calm and respectful without realizing it. Also, in martial arts in general, you make very good friends. When I was young I was a really hyper kid. I was born and raised in the streets of Rio. You have to be tough to be born there and to survive there. So today I can tell you that it is something very important because it made me a different person. I've traveled to Europe, to Saudi Arabia, and Japan, and I've always made good friends through jiu-jitsu.

Q: So you feel jiu-jitsu helps to make you a complete person?

A: I see people who don't attend any academy and you can see that they have no confidence and no self-image and have a lot of stress. I also see guys that are very violent. But over time I see all these people change for the better. All the time I had students come to me and say, "Thanks a lot for changing my life." They didn't have any direction or purpose or guidelines for living and jiu-jitsu gave them that.

Q: Did jiu-jitsu come easy to you?

A: It came very natural to me. I never had a hard time with any technique or situation. I fell comfortable in any position. It's funny, in jiu-jitsu you always change. Every different time you have a certain position that you do well in and is your favorite move, your opponents will eventually notice that and learn to block it. So you have to constantly change your game and develop new parts to it. When you're a competitor you always want always to come up with a surprise to gain an advantage. But the basic parts of jiu-jitsu are always the same, so you never really feel lost.

Q: Is there a point where you can ever stop learning?

A: I don't think so. Jiu-jitsu is the only martial art that you'll die still learning about it. When you get the black belt, if you think that you know everything you are wrong. This martial art is infinite. That's why you always want to learn more and more. I think learned more after I got my black belt than before

Q: What are the keys to continuous learning?

A: Be focused and learn the basics very well – everything will come from there. It is like the root of a tree. It is also important to learn in stages – don't step longer than your leg.

Q: Has jiu-jitsu changed since you started?

A: Right now it is a lot more organized than it used to be. There is the World Championships, the Pan Americans, and magazines that cover it them all – everybody knows what jiu-jitsu is now. When I started competing, just your family and the other athletes were really interested in it. But now a major tournament is a big event. I think that the Confederation of Brazilian Jiu-Jitsu (CBJJ) has helped to take jiu-jitsu to a higher level in Brazil. I hope the U.S. can also get organized in the same way.

Q: Who would you like to have trained with that you haven't?

A: Rickson Gracie, but not just for technique alone. BJJ will give you a lot more than just the ability to fight. It will also give you discipline, confidence, self-esteem, and respect for others. There are many things Rickson teaches that go beyond his techniques. But if you're talking about technique only, leave your ego at the door and be ready to tap for the rest of your life. No matter how good you are, Rickson can elevate his game to the next level and keep pushing you to become better. This is the same for white belts or for world champions.

Q: What keeps you motivated after all these years?

A: The fact that I'm still learning something every day. It also makes me very happy to change people's lives teaching this phenomenal art. To hear a student say "thank you" always makes my day. To be able to teach jiu-jitsu is a privilege that not many people have. I never forget that.

Q: Do you have any particular preparation method before a big tournament?

A: I just train hard, Carlson always said that he prepares his students to fight against a lion – then if a kitty cat comes along it will be no problem. So when I know I'm well-prepared I feel very confident. I don't fight if I don't feel that I've prepared myself well enough. I have also done transcendental meditation for more than 10 years and that has helped my concentration a lot.

Q: Is it possible for a grappler to learn every move there is?

A: You have to find what your strong points are and then emphasize those. Personally, I mainly train positions I can effectively adapt to my game. Of course, I try to learn everything and experiment a lot for fun, but when I'm training for a competition I concentrate on putting my opponent into my game and don't get drawn into his.

Q: What do you remember most about training in Rio?

A: I grew up watching the best guys train for no rules and BJJ. In the '80s, jiu-jitsu had more rivalry between academies, but at the same time more union against other styles. I will never forget when we had the challenge match between jiu-jitsu and luta livre in Rio. I was about 18 years old then and all the top BJJ fighters of that day guys on that time train together in Carlson Academy, Murillo Bustamante, Marcelo Behring, Rosado, Pinduka, Fabio Gurgel, Amaury, Wallid and others. I was there everyday to watch them and sometimes train when Carlson let me.

Q: Is jiu-jitsu more than just a sport to you?

A: For me, jiu-jitsu is a way of life and it changed me. When I started to train and compete I felt more confident, healthy, and ready for the tough streets of Rio and anywhere in this crazy world. Jiu-jitsu for me is more than a martial art and more than my work – it is my hobby and my life!

Q: What are the most important qualities of a successful BJJ fighter?

A: More than the technical skills, it is your attitude, your loyalty, and your respect. Jiu-jitsu is natural, so you shouldn't do anything artificial. You can have good results in a short time but only if you pay the physical price, eat healthy, don't use steroids, and do a lot of natural exercises such as yoga or swimming, and don't think in the next month and yes in all you life time. I respect the art more than everything, so I know that if you close a lock on me you will hurt me – whatever belt you are. Respect in training and for the art means not hurting your classmates. That is an important thing that new students sometimes forget.

Q: What are the main areas an instructor should focus on?

A: I usually train together with my students and not just give them coaching from the sidelines. Right now, I have a very good quality of training at my school – the same level as the top academies in Brazil. When I first started teaching here in 1996, I had to create training methods that would push me, since there were no high belts that I had trained yet. I put the students on my back and let them get in the choke and let them started mounted or in cross-side control. Now I have very good students and I can't go easy anymore. If I slack off they will make me pay! Overall, I focus on making the students learn the basics very well, and then after that help them to develop their own style and adjust it for their own body style. For vale tudo fights I think cross-training is good, but for the basic skills it is always BJJ with the gi.

Q: Do you feel that BJJ is no longer as effective as it once was?

A: I hope people still realize that the Gracie family was the first to start this kind of event, back in 1930 in Brazil. Today what I see is people just trying beat the BJJ guys and then saying that BJJ doesn't work anymore. What I see a lot of people who just start training without the gi, and have a small knowledge of jiu-jitsu and a background in something else, and open academes and invent names for it like submission wrestling, freestyle grappling, submission grappling, luta livre, etcetera. But they are all the same thing – BJJ without the gi. It is a part jiu-jitsu just as judo is a part of jiu-jitsu. I honestly don't know why they do this. Maybe to be able to open a school and make money even though they are not qualified to teach. I believe these people are trying to make BJJ loose its reputation for their own personal gain. So to say BJJ is not effective is just plain silly and ignores the facts.

ROYCE GRACIE

The First Cut Is the Deepest

THIS RIO DE JANEIRO NATIVE SHOCKED THE MARTIAL ARTS WORLD ON NOVEMBER 12, 1993, WHEN HE RAN OVER ALL HIS OPPONENTS IN THE FIRST ULTIMATE FIGHTING CHAMPIONSHIP. WHILE FIGHTING FLAWLESSLY IN THE OCTAGON, HE IMPECCABLY REPRESENTED THE LEGENDARY TRADITION OF THE GRACIE FAMILY TO ALL THOSE VIEWING THE EVENT ON TV. MANY THINGS HAVE HAPPENED SINCE THAT COLD NIGHT IN DENVER, COLORADO, AND ROYCE GRACIE'S LIFE HAS DRASTICALLY CHANGED. AFTER MANY YEARS OF TEACHING OUT OF THE GRACIE ACADEMY IN TORRANCE, CALIFORNIA, ROYCE RECENTLY DECIDED IT WAS TIME TO PURSUE HIS DREAM OF TAKING JIU-JITSU TO A NEW LEVEL. THUS, NOT ONLY DID HE BEGIN CONDUCTING CLASSES ON A MORE INTERNATIONAL LEVEL AND TRAVELING MORE AND MORE, HE BEGAN TO DEVELOP WHAT IS NOW KNOWN AS THE "ROYCE GRACIE NETWORK."

MARRIED AND WITH CHILDREN OF HIS OWN, THAT YOUNG KID WHO IMPRESSED THE WORLD WITH THE GRAPPLING TECHNIQUES DEVELOPED BY HIS FATHER, HELIO GRACIE, IS AS BUSY AS IT GETS. AFTER A FEW YEARS OF OBSERVING MMA AND NO-HOLD-BARRED EVENTS PROGRESS IN DIFFERENT DIRECTIONS, ROYCE DECIDED TO GO BACK TO FIGHTING. WHEN HE WAS READY, HE CHOSE JAPAN. EXPERTS MEASURE THE SIZE OF A MAN'S BODY – NOT THE SIZE OF HIS HEART, SPIRIT AND SOUL. IF THEY DID THAT, HE WOULD BE A SUPER HEAVYWEIGHT. THIS IS ROYCE GRACIE, A TRUE LIVING LEGEND WHO CHANGED THE WORLD OF MARTIAL ARTS FOREVER. AFTER HIM, NOTHING HAS BEEN THE SAME. THE FIRST CUT IS ALWAYS THE DEEPEST.

Q: How was it growing up in Brazil in a jiu-jitsu environment?

A: It was fun and something very natural. My father never wanted us to do weird things so we studied, went to school, trained in jiu-jitsu, played on the beach, etc. It was very relaxing and nice. My jiu-jitsu training was always with my father, my brothers – Rickson and Rorion – and also with Rolls Gracie. For me, training jiu-jitsu was a normal thing in my life. I never felt pressure because my father understood that kids don't like to learn…they like to play. So training in jiu-jitsu was play for me. That's what I'm trying to pass onto my kids. When they go to the Academy, it will be like going to the playground.

Q: You have been an icon, especially for those people who believed that size was relevant in a self-defense situation. How do you feel about it?

A: Many people, when they saw me winning the UFC against bigger and stronger guys, realized that there was hope for them. If they knew the necessary techniques, they realized that they could actually protect themselves against bigger opponents. I probably opened doors for some other people and brought hope for those who didn't know that it wasn't necessary to be a monster with huge muscles to defend yourself effectively.

Q: The Gracie family started a tradition with the vale tudo fights against practitioners of other styles. Why do you think some people never liked that approach?

A: Well, to begin with, most people don't want to match what they know with what others know. The reason for that is they don't really believe in what they practice. The only reason the Gracie family had to do these kind of matches was to put to test what we were developing and to prove to others that what we have works against an uncooperative opponent, regardless of the style he practices. The UFC brought that to the rest of the world, but the Gracies were doing it in Brazil for more than 65 years. That's the reason why I got into the UFC. I believed in the art.

Q: In the first UFC, you were skinnier and lighter than all the fighters. Nevertheless, you beat them all using pure technique and not brute strength. It is true that jiu-jitsu works without using brute force?

A: It is true if the opponent doesn't know how to defend himself. In that case, you don't really need to use strength. Instead, you use leverage and positioning. If you face an opponent who knows jiu-jitsu, then the physical characteristics could make a difference. Even if the other person knows jiu-jitsu you should look for the right technique based on leverage and correct principles instead of relying on your strength. The key is, as my father, Helio Gracie, likes to say, "We don't apply the technique, we ask for it." By this, he means we prepare the situation for that technique to happen. Don't force it. Create an environment in which the technique will be there naturally.

GRACIE

Q: In the very beginning, some members of the Gracie family entered judo tournaments but then they stopped. Why?

A: Well, it was a good way of proving a point. Many of the techniques and maneuvers we do in jiu-jitsu are not allowed in judo competition. Judo is mostly a game these days, and our approach to fighting is different. jiu-jitsu is not about sport, and we are not judo players.

Q: After you stopped fighting in the UFC, many people said that you were afraid because things were different and people knew how to fight. How do your respond to that?

A: People talk sometimes because they don't have enough important things to do. Of course, everybody is entitled to express an opinion, regardless if that opinion is based on facts or a stupid affirmation. I have never been afraid of fighting. Things in the UFC changed, and I realized that the way the event was going was putting me at a big disadvantage against all the big guys because they (organizers) were reformatting the event to fit the TV audiences. And that was fine with me, but I was not going to enter an arena in which everything was against me. I only ask for fair rules and regulations. After the UFC, I went and fought in Japan because they did accommodate the weight difference in a much better way. They were fair and square, and I had no problem fighting other people. At no moment have I ever been afraid of fighting.

> **"After the UFC, I went and fought in Japan because they did accommodate the weight difference in a much better way. They were fair and square, and I had no problem fighting other people."**

On the other hand, promoters and fans want me to fight every other month, and that can't happen. How many times does the boxing world champion fight in a year? Once, maybe twice. That's it. I can't be fighting all the people who want to fight me. It doesn't go that way. Things don't happen that way in any sport. So people should think before talking. Some of those things they were asking for at that time were very unreasonable.

Q: Do you realize that you have changed the martial arts forever?

A: I was simply a vehicle for that. Rorion was the mastermind behind the UFC and the Gracie revolution
in the United States. I simply did what I have been doing all my life.
I stepped into the ring and fought.

Q: Your loss to Ismael Wallid was one of the major upsets in the history of martial arts.

A: I know. I give all the credit in the world to Wallid for what he did, but I wasn't focused enough or angry enough. And that was my mistake. I wasn't sharp enough. The three-year layoff from fighting dulled my blade, and I paid the price. I was teaching and sparring with people but not with a goal in my mind. Wallid beat me clean and square. I learned a lesson that day. If you are not 100% prepared and focused, don't fight.

Q: Your father was there with you. What did he say?

A: He made technical comments on my performance and told me to be totally focused next time.

Q: Did Wallid say anything to you?

A: Yes, he came to me the day before and said, "You are a very nice guy. I don't really want to fight you." I said, "Thank you and good luck tomorrow." He is a tough guy and very respectful. I still believe he was very lucky that day.

Q: What was your most memorable moment in the UFC?

A: I would say winning UFC IV. The first one was a surprise because people didn't really know what was happening and hadn't seen jiu-jitsu. In the second one, people were saying that it was a set-up and a fake, even though I had to win four fights in one night, which was very tough. When I didn't complete the third tournament – even though I didn't lose – that opened a lot of people's eyes. At that point, they didn't question the reality of it and didn't think that it was arranged for me to win, which it never was. The fourth one is when I can back and beat Dan Severn, who at that time was just terrifying everyone with his power. That was when I got back to the top and validated myself in front of the whole world. That was my most satisfying win in the UFC.

Q: What was your toughest fight?

A: Probably with Kimo, because I fought the wrong way and gave him a lot of chances that I shouldn't have. I fought totally wrong. I tried to use strength and push him back and beat him with power instead of using his own power against him. He's a very strong fighter, and you're not going to beat him that way. I did get the submission, but it took a lot out of me. I got dehydrated after that match and passed out right before I came back for my next fight. I still got into the Octagon hoping that I would recover, but then I lost my vision and couldn't see. The referee asked me if I was ready, and I said I was. Then I turned around and told my brother, "Do something. I can't see a thing." That was tough.

Q: What happened in the locker room that night? Did you pass out?

A: To be honest, I never had the chance! My father and my brother Relson had me up and moving all the time. I took a shower to cool down, and they tried to keep me loose for the next fight. The heat and humidity were terrible, and all the fighters took oxygen back there. I was trying to rest as much as I could to get ready, but there wasn't enough time. The fights back then did not have time limits and there were no rounds. It was a whole different ballgame, to say the least.

Q: Did you accept that as a defeat in your record?

A: The old rules in the UFC said that if your corner throws the towel, you lose. So yes, I accept that fact. It is true though that Harold Howard never beat me because we never got into the fight. Technically, however, I lost. I only have respect for Howard because he said that my attempt to fight – considering how I felt – was one of the classiest gestures he'd ever seen in his martial arts career. I have to thank him for these words. He came to compete and there is a lot of respect in that. I truly appreciated his words. He could have reacted another way because I didn't fight him, but he didn't.

Q: Why did you leave the UFC? Was it because of the rule changes?

A: Yes. It was the rules and mostly the time limit. Bigger and bigger guys were coming into the UFC and limiting the time really hurt me. I thought it created a huge disadvantage for me. People who know me know that I don't fight in weight divisions. Size doesn't matter to me. My opponent's have mainly always been bigger than me.

Q: Was it tougher then?

A: Back then it was style against style – not fighter against fighter. But with the tournament format you had to fight three or four times in one night. You would always get injured during the first match and then have to fight hurt for the rest of the night. You never knew who you were going to face in the next round so you couldn't just train for one person like you can now. From a purely technical and physical perspective, it was much more challenging. Today, because everyone knows so much more, each individual fight is probably tougher. Back then the format was much more difficult.

Q: Why have you always fought with the gi?

A: I trained with the gi all my life. I'm comfortable with it. Plus, the gi always helps you grab your opponents better when they get sweaty and slippery. It helps to control your opponent and to keep your position. Plus, you can circle your arms or legs around him and then grab the gi. That helps to reduce fatigue in long fights. Because I've trained with the gi all my life, why would I take it off the day of the fight? It doesn't make sense to me. So I'm used to it, but it doesn't mean that if I use the gi that I'm a sport fighter only. My father and uncles always fought with the gi in their vale tudo matches. I don't think that I'm doing anything differently than them. It's just something that we use everyday in training and teaching and so we use it when we fight.

Q: Did your father encourage you to wear it?

A: Oh, yes. He was always in favor of me wearing the gi. He thought that it gave me advantage over people who didn't wear it. It worked for him so he thought that it would work for me. It wasn't so much tradition as much as he thinks it is good strategy.

Q: In your UFC years, did you ever feel that the gi was a disadvantage?

A: No, because my opponents didn't know how to use the gi against me. For it to be a disadvantage, they would have had to have known a lot of strategies that just weren't common when the UFC started. Now, perhaps, that might be different because so many people know jiu-jitsu. Back then the knowledge just wasn't out there.

You don't want to suddenly change the strategy that got you there and won a championship for you. When I won the first UFC with the gi, I just naturally left it on and kept going with it. Someone had to give me a reason to take it off in a fight. I never felt that happened.

Q: Is it harder to fight a grappler or a striker when you're wearing the gi?

A: It's just a matter of different strategies. There's no such thing as an easy fight, regardless of what you're wearing. A grappler might use the gi to hold you, stall the fight, choke you or use it for his own advantage in some way. A striker won't know how to do that. He just doesn't think in those terms because all he wants to do is to land a big bomb and end the fight. But he can always hold onto the gi with one hand to keep me away and then try to hit me with the other hand. If the guy knows what he's doing in either case, it can be tough. So it's mainly a matter of who you're fighting, not so much if he's a grappler or a striker. Every opponent is different and presents different challenges. It matters more who they are and what their tendencies are in the ring. Each shirt has to be custom made to fit whomever your opponent is. Strategy is always a matter of a lot of different factors. Even when you don't know who you're fighting or what they like to do, you will find out quickly when you press an attack. They will sprawl against a takedown, tie-up with you, try to knee you, go for a takedown and/or force you to react. Even in a match your strategy will change depending on what your opponent does.

> "Strategy is always a matter of a lot of different factors. Even when you don't know who you're fighting or what they like to do, you will find out quickly when you press an attack."

Q: What about submissions? Is it harder to get one when you are wearing the gi?

A: No, it's always hard… no matter what! Wearing the gi or not wearing the gi is less of a factor than what your opponent gives you. Jiu-jitsu is a very adaptable art and there are no pre-set moves against specific attacks. There are sets of options that you learn to consider from certain positions, but what really matters is how quickly you can evaluate those options and then change and react. That is always what gives jiu-jitsu an advantage over other martial arts that have pre-set moves and kata or whatever. Jiu-jitsu is built around learning to react – not just learning certain moves.

Although you need both, mental agility is probably more important than physical agility. All the time on the mat sparring teaches your mind to work quickly as well as your body. Once you become instinctive in your reactions and don't have to think about your counters or your attacks, then you're getting the true essence of jiu-jitsu. This can take years to get to that point. Once you get there, you definitely know it. I like to train against really big and strong guys, because most of the people I fought were bigger than me. So I wanted to feel weight, strength and power during my preparation. Some of my training matches were harder than my actual UFC matches. I would rather train hard and have the fight seem easy to me, rather than to do the opposite and be shocked and overpowered.

Q: Royce, you got injured and took some time off. Some people speculated that you weren't really hurt. What really happened to you?

A: One day I started to feel numbness in the fingers of my right hand. This [sensation] went all the way down to my right leg. After doing some exams, the doctors said that I had a pinched nerve and a bulging disk, and he said I shouldn't be doing any kind of exercise, let alone jiu-jitsu. The problem with these kind of injuries is that you never know what caused them. Simply by sleeping wrong you may get it. I could have gotten it from lifting weights, running or simply by practicing jiu-jitsu. I had to carefully resume training. You simply can't rush these things.

Q: Some people said it was an excuse to not fight Mark Kerr.

A: People always say things. I really don't care what they were saying because I was extremely busy and concerned about how to heal myself. When you are dealing with something serious in your health, do you really think I pay attention to those comments? No way.

Q: When did you leave the Gracie Academy?

A: I left the academy in September 2001, after 16 years with Rorion. It was a very difficult decision for me to make, but I was teaching at the school from 9 a.m. to 1 p.m. and from 4 p.m. to 9 p.m. Monday through Saturday. It wasn't a bad schedule, but I was also doing seminars. If there wasn't a seminar, I'd teach Monday through Saturday. If there was a seminar, I'd only teach until Thursday night. I would leave town on Friday morning, teach the seminar on Saturday and Sunday and return home late Sunday night. On Monday morning at 9 a.m., I'd be back at the academy to start all over again. It was a comfortable schedule, but I simply wasn't able to see my family! Every day I was able to give breakfast, lunch and dinner to my kids, but we couldn't spend any time together. Whatever time I had with them, I was in such a rush that I really couldn't enjoy it. In order to do that, I needed to have a schedule that I could fit around my seminars and my family. My family is very important to me. What good is it if I gain 10,000 students but lose my own kids?

Q: Was it hard to be on your own?

A: There were many opportunities coming my way when I was at the academy, but I never paid attention to them. I simply let Rorion take care of everything. So it was difficult for a short while to adjust to all the details. But I started to pay attention to things. I started reading more and learning more about business. I also started to spend more time with my family. In a way it was hard but in another way it wasn't.

In the past, the father taught his children how to survive. In modern times, it became the mother who taught the kids. Actually, sometimes in the modern days it is not even the mother who can do that; it is the babysitter who teaches the kids how to become adults. I wanted to teach my own kids. Any free time I have I want to spend with them. I don't want to be just a fictitious father; I want to be there for them. I want to teach them about life, and I want to teach them how to become adults. When I was growing up, I spent a lot more time with my mother than with my dad because my father was always at the academy. For all my school functions – my homework and personal duties – it was my mother who helped me. I really missed having my father around, so I want to be there for my kids. But I also wanted to have time to pursue my personal vision of an international jiu-jitsu organization.

Q: In the seminars, you're mainly teaching sport moves?

A: Not by a long shot. The primary reason that people learn a martial art – any martial art – is to be able to protect themselves. After the UFC, a lot of people started learning Brazilian jiu-jitsu for self-defense. What they actually got when they went to classes was how to win a sports tournament with rules. They learned how to do a sweep and get two points, then a half-guard move and a reversal for two more points. They didn't learn how to defend themselves in a real situation.

Don't get me wrong. I am all for sports jiu-jitsu, but we need to remember why people started to learn martial arts in the first place! If you don't know how to escape from a bear hug or a headlock on the ground, a new half-guard move won't help you at all! Brazilian jiu-jitsu was developed by my family as a way for a small person to defend himself against larger opponents. I went to the UFC to show that those techniques worked and everyone saw that they did. I didn't go there to show my spider-guard! So I wanted to bring everyone's attention back to the essence of the art, which is the self-defense aspect. I think I've really hit a nerve, because the response has been overwhelming!

Q: Tell me about your first fight against Yoshida, the Japanese judo gold medalist.

A: I wanted to fight him for the challenge. Everyone said that he was the best grappler in the world, but I wanted him to prove it to me. Fighting is something that gives me real focus. I like the training, the strategy, the preparation... the whole thing. In the fight itself, I got robbed. Very simple, Yoshida looked at the referee and said, "Royce is out. Stop the fight." Since when do you talk to a referee and tell him what to do… and then he does it? You can't do that in boxing or in any other type of competition. That's not right. They worst part is that he did not have a thing; he did not have a choke. I've lost before. I know how to lose, but don't rob me.

Q: Did you tap?

A: I didn't tap at all. Why should I when he didn't have a choke? There was no reason for me to tap.

Q: Why did you decide to fight him again?

A: I was disgusted by what happened in that fight. If it can happen to me, then it can happen to anyone. When they ask me if I wanted to fight again, the only person I had in mind was him. I had unfinished business because the first never really ended. This time I was satisfied.

Q: When did you get the idea that you would take off the gi?

A: As soon as I got the word that we were going to fight, I talked to my father, Royler and Rickson. I asked them all what they thought, and they all agreed with it. But we also kept the strategy secret. Royler worked on the technical part of the fight and Rickson worked with me on the mental part. Rickson told me to always keep my opponent uncomfortable in every position. This will make the opponent think that he cannot win.

Q: Were you worried about the outcome of the second fight?

A: If you don't go into a fight knowing that you will win, then you have already lost. It's a reality of life that men are competitive. And the most competitive game draws the most competitive men – and that's no-holds-barred fighting. That's why they are there. They know the rules, they know the score. The object is to win. Winning is not a sometimes thing, it's an all-the-time thing. You don't win once in a while, you don't do things right once in a while. You do then right all the time. Winning is a habit, but unfortunately so is losing. So you have to keep focused on a positive outcome and not get distracted or have self-doubt. But you have to pay the price in training in order to be No. 1. I really wanted to surprise Yoshida. He said the fight would be a war, so I decided to treat the training as a war, too. So I totally kept it quiet. Didn't say a thing about what I was doing… just a few people who I trusted. If there were media or people I didn't trust present when I trained in public in the U.S., I would train with the gi on. In Japan, we didn't go to the training place they gave us to use. We got some mats and got a room at the hotel and trained there.

Q: Were you nervous or angry right before the fight?

A: Not angry or nervous. I was very calm and totally under control. I was prepared. First, he didn't show up in the line-up when they introduced all the fighters. So I knew he was coming in by himself. During the introduction to our fight, I knew that Yoshida was behind me. But I didn't give him the pleasure of turning around and seeing me. When I finally turned around, I saw him and went right to his back and breathed on his neck… just so he could get used to me being on his back.

Q: What was the look on Yoshida's face when you climbed into the ring and took off the gi?

A: He gave me a double look like he couldn't believe what he was seeing. It was like he was thinking, "This isn't part of the plan." It was total surprise. He said the fight would be a war, and I had the element of surprise. From that point on, I knew that it was going to be my night. Everything was on track, and I was in control.

Q: Were you looking more to hit him or to submit him?

A: I was looking more to embarrass him.

Q: Do you think vale tudo fighters have to cross-train now because jiu-jitsu isn't enough?

A: To fight vale tudo, everybody has to cross-train. That's a plain fact. There is no other way now. I've been doing kickboxing for more than 10 years. So this wasn't anything new for me. How I fought was different but not the tools that I knew.

Q: Everyone is saying that the Yoshida match was your best fight ever. What did you change mentally to fight so well?

A: Like Rickson said, "Take a step back and look at your first UFC. Then play that kind of game. Don't try to hype yourself up as a mean fighter because you're not a mean fighter. That will just drain you and make you weak. Play a cool game and deliver what you know."

> **"Over the years, I have learned that you can't change people that much from how they naturally are. You can't turn a leopard into a lion."**

Q: How has no-holds-barred changed from the first UFC until now?

A: It used to be style against style. Now it is fighter against fighter. It's man against man. The fighter who wins will have done the best cross-training, prepared the best strategy, trained the hardest and had the best day. It isn't so much the style any more but rather the fighter.

Q: What is your approach to training and teaching?

A: Over the years, I have learned that you can't change people that much from how they naturally are. You can't turn a leopard into a lion. What you have to do is to take what they do best, improve on it and find their weakest points. Then you can help them find alternatives so the weak point gets stronger. I can't tell you to fight the way I fight because you are not me. You have your own style so I have to take your characteristics and make you better. To do that, I don't need that much time, because I am not trying to reinvent the wheel; I am just trying to improve it. To be able to fight, you need to stay within your style. I won't try to change it; I'll just make the right adjustments. I have a lot of experience in fights and people know that I talk from personal knowledge – not from something that I have just heard or read about.

Q: You mentioned once that you try to do everything naturally and in a very relaxed way. How do you apply this approach to your training?

A: For all the supplementary training besides jiu-jitsu, I try to keep my own pace. If I'm running, even if I do it with someone, I follow my own rhythm, my own pace. I don't think that I have to beat a world record or anything like that. Depending on how I feel is how I train. I don't like to have anyone clocking me when I run because I like to monitor my own running session. I use this specific approach for my cardiovascular training. When I train with weights, I do it a little bit different. I try not to miss one single day. If I'm sick, I'm sick… so I rest. Sometimes I feel that I'm pushing too much. Before I overtrain, I intentionally slow down and do the same activities but with no pressure on my mind. When you are using a trainer, it is easier to overtrain because he will push you hard every single session. You have to be careful with what kind of personal trainer you have. If I feel I need to stop, I stop for a day or two. It won't be the end of the world because of that. You should learn to listen to your body and take care of it. More sometimes is not better. Especially when you are feeling tired. If you keep pushing, you may end up hurting yourself. It is better to take a day off and come back stronger and more motivated than before. As far as jiu-jitsu is concerned, that is more of a technical training, although the intensity of my sparring depends on how I feel on a given day.

Q: What keeps you so motivated to fight and to test yourself after all these years?

A: I just don't like it when people try to tell me what I cannot do. I love a challenge, and I love jiu-jitsu. When people tell me that I can't fight again, that makes me want to do it. I think fighting should be fun… a fun challenge that you take seriously.

Q: Today everybody seems to learn from everybody. Have you incorporated elements from other grappling arts into your jiu-jitsu repertoire?

A: Not really. But I think that a wrestler's takedown and counter is something that a lot of people have absorbed. I think this is a very interesting element for a grappler, regardless of his style. I definitely looked into it and picked up some tricks here and there.

Q: What has changed from the Royce Gracie who stepped into the Octagon for the first time to the Royce Gracie of today?

A: I'd like to say that nothing has changed, but it is not true. I was single and now I'm married with children. I was teaching and working out of the Gracie Academy and now I'm on my own traveling around the world teaching seminars and spreading the art my father developed to every possible corner of the world. Inside of me, I'm still the same person. I enjoy the same things, and I haven't changed much. I don't have too much time to do other things, but I'm the same Royce Gracie who fought in the first UFC that night in November 1993.

Q: You have published several books on various topics, such as Brazilian jiu-jitsu, physical conditioning and nutrition. Why did you do that?

A: First, I wanted to leave a printed legacy, and I think these books are a good example of that. Then I realized that it was an excellent way of answering many of the questions that students ask me every time I teach. The idea came from the necessity of answering the students' questions. And I think these books have accomplished that mission. The information is great and the quality of the work is indisputable.

Q: Who do you think is your toughest opponent?

A: Always... my toughest opponent is always the one I imagine inside of my head.

Q: Do you have any regrets about your career or life?

A: I don't. Everything happens for a reason. Good or bad you can use everything to your advantage – just like in fighting. If you have the right attitude, then there is no bad in life. There are just different opportunities to do well and to become better. Happiness and success is within us all, regardless of outside influences. Each of us can choose how we want to feel. Attitude is everything.

Q: What does it mean to be a Gracie?

A: It's a very heavy name to carry. Being a Gracie doesn't just mean being a family member, it also means being a student and a member of the world jiu-jitsu community. All my students are members of the Gracie family – not just myself or my cousins or my brothers. To a certain extent, we all share common values and goals. For us all, it is just like my father says: "Everything that I am is jiu-jitsu. I will uphold the honor of jiu-jitsu in my everyday life with proper actions and morals, and I will defend the family name with my sweat and blood." That's what being a Gracie means.

"Jiu-jitsu is personal efficiency to protect the weaker, which anyone can do. It is the force of leverage against brute force."

~ Helio Gracie ~

RORION GRACIE

Testing Reactions

You may like him or dislike him, hate him or love him, agree or disagree with him-but there is no middle ground when it comes to Rorion Grace. The truth of the matter is that this eldest son of jiu-jitsu legend Helio Gracie is one of the most influential figures in the world of martial arts in the modern era. He took martial arts by storm when he created the Ultimate Fighting Championship in 1993, broadcast it on television, and opened the doors for a horde of his countrymen to teach the art his father created and developed over the past 70 years. Rorion brought a new approach to martial arts and changed the worldwide scene forever. The modern history of martial arts is written before and after the UFC-and before and after Rorion Gracie. He created a new way of looking at reality fighting, and his vision and way of doing things brought him into the spotlight.

There is something about Rorion Gracie that places him head and shoulders above any other jiu jitsu teacher. Not only is Rorion an expert in the art his father taught, but he also combines his technical knowledge with a charismatic personality and a professional attitude in business as well. For Rorion Gracie, however, whatever he has accomplished in the past, stays in the past. He has no time to look back because for him, the best is always yet to come.

Q: When did you begin your training?

A: I was practically born on the mat. I can't think of any period of my life when I was not training or teaching jiu-jitsu. The oldest recollection I have of my involvement with jiu-jitsu is a demo I did with my father. I was so little that the backs of the chairs were taller than me as I walked down the aisle towards the stage where he stood. The most significant memories I have, however, are those of my father teaching. His ability to explain with passion and dedication was unique and entertaining. When I began teaching, although I was very young, I knew I couldn't go wrong if I followed his footsteps. So I used his words and told his stories-and sure enough my students loved it. As I grew up, I started adding my own stories and experiences. By then I had learned the perfect way to teach.

Q: You earned a law degree in Brazil. Why did you quit law and come to the United States?

A: Well, first and foremost I am a jiu-jitsu teacher. When I decided to go to law school, I was not searching for a new profession. I simply believed that going through college would be a way to expand my possibilities. I teach jiu-jitsu because I love it, not because I can't do anything else. Besides, I'd rather wear the belt around my waist instead of around my neck! The reason I came to America is that the Gracie name was extremely popular in Brazil, and because of my A+ personality I didn't want to stay there and live off my father's accomplishments. I wanted to build upon them. So I set out to spread the word of the Gracie legend. After all, if you want something to happen and the world to see you-you have to do it in America.

Q: What was it like in the beginning?

A: A little rough. There was a time I found myself panhandling and sleeping on the streets. Not for a moment, however, did I have any doubt that I would reach my goal of convincing the martial arts community that they all needed jiu-jitsu. Groundfighting was too important to be ignored! Then there were those challenge matches in the garage during the early days, which would convince one non-believer at a time. Month-after-month, and year-after-year I endured, until finally starting the UFC. After that everyone understood what I was talking about. It took me 25 years but I accomplished my goal.

Q: What made you issue the famous Gracie Challenge?

A: There has always been a lot of talk about how a certain style will teach you how to destroy someone with one hand-and this other style will enable you to pulverize three people with one finger, et cetera. Although there were instructors who knew their styles well, there were some who would capitalize on the mystic aspect of the martial arts and claim to be able to do some unbelievable things-some of them so deadly they could not be shown!

To know how to punch and kick is great, but we can't close our eyes to the most crucial aspect of a real fight-which is that 95 percent of all fights end up on the ground. The Gracie Challenge had the objective of demonstrating the effectiveness of what we teach. I owed it to all my students. It was the only way to prove my point.

Q: Why is it so important to be effective? Doesn't this produce bullies?

A: If you teach any subject you should be able to demonstrate your knowledge. In the world of martial arts, knowledge equals effectiveness-which in turn gives you confidence. For example, what if a three-year-old child came up to you and said, "I want to beat you up." Since he represents no threat, you would smile and say, "How cute! Now go play, baby." But if his father, a big and strong guy, came at you and said the same thing, you may get worried because you are not sure that you can handle him. Gracie jiu-jitsu enables you look at that big guy as if he were the child. The only reason why a person takes on the attitude of a bully is because deep down they are an insecure individual. Aggressiveness is used to try to intimidate the other party. If you lock that bully in a room with someone who he knows can beat him up, that bully will change into a really nice guy. When you reach a certain level of effectiveness, it changes your prospective. You start trusting yourself. That is the confidence that will make you more tolerant and even-tempered. It was this quest for genuine effectiveness that motivated my father to improve his fighting system and which has been the inspiration for the whole Gracie family.

> **"If you teach any subject you should be able to demonstrate your knowledge. In the world of martial arts, knowledge equals effectiveness- which in turn gives you confidence."**

Q: How did your father Helio became involved in jiu-jitsu?

A: The Gracie family was first exposed to it almost 100 years ago when a Japanese jiu-jitsu instructor came to Brazil to aid a Japanese immigration colony. It was then that my uncle, Carlos Gracie, had his first taste of this martial art. Carlos, the oldest, taught his brothers the traditional Japanese jiu-jitsu he had learned. Helio's frail health, caused regular fainting spasms and kept him off the mat. But it did not prevent him from watching the classes day-in and day-out and eventually learn the stuff. One day, Carlos was not around for a class and Helio, then 16, offered to step on the mat and teach the class. The student liked it. When Carlos showed up very apologetic, the student said, "No problem but I would like to have classes with Helio from now on." On that day, the history of jiu-jitsu changed forever. Due to his small stature and light bodyweight, Helio could not make some of the moves work. So he found himself modifying them little-by-little to fit his needs, figuring out ways to use more leverage and less strength. As he got more and more into it, Helio developed new ways of controlling bigger opponents and getting them into submissions. Amazingly enough, to this date, he is still studying jiu-jitsu.

Q: What is the difference between Gracie and Brazilian jiu-jitsu?

A: When I arrived in America in the late '70s, I began teaching in my garage and decided to call it Gracie jiu-jitsu to differentiate from the Japanese jiu-jitsu some people here had heard about. I always told the same story: "Uncle Carlos was the first Gracie to learn jiu-jitsu and Helio perfected it." Fifteen years later, I created the UFC which was the turning point for establishing Gracie jiu-jitsu on top of the world. That brought a lot of attention and value to the Gracie name. Some of my cousins felt that if they could convince the people that Uncle Carlos, their father, was the one who had perfected the system and that they were the "keepers of the flame." As such, they could make easy and quick money selling instructor's certifications of Gracie jiu-jitsu to anyone.. However, I owned the registration on the trademark, "Gracie jiu-jitsu." This is why the term "Brazilian jiu-jitsu" came into the scene. It was the next best thing. They are not different styles and they don't teach you different techniques. The arm-locks, chokes and foot-locks are exactly the same. Only recently did the U.S. Trademark Office determine that based on the huge and highly successful marketing campaign I have been doing all these years, Gracie jiu-jitsu became a generic term. It cannot be registered now and is therefore a style of martial art, just like judo or karate. Now my relatives and their affiliates have a dilemma-should they keep calling their style "Brazilian jiu-jitsu" because they have been using it for a while, or start calling it "Gracie jiu-jitsu" since that is what they learned and is its true name? Time will tell.

> **"Orientals bow to each other as a cultural habit. I don't teach Oriental culture, I teach Gracie jiu-jitsu, and a simple hand-shake is good enough."**

Q: But some people in the family insist that Carlos not Helio was the one responsible for your family's system.

A: I loved and admired my Uncle Carlos. He was the man who managed Helio's career and was the spiritual leader of the family, leaving us the priceless legacy of his life's work-his knowledge in the field of nutrition. However, let's be reasonable. Uncle Carlos did not wake up one morning and say, "I am going to perfect a whole new style of fighting for a couple of years before I spend the next 70 years of my life developing the Gracie Diet." Give me a break! The credit for the refinement of the traditional Japanese system, which gave birth to what is known today as Gracie or Brazilian jiu-jitsu goes to the one-and-only Helio Gracie. Newspaper clippings, photographs and other priceless memorabilia, now on display at the Gracie Jiu-Jitsu Museum in Torrance, California, will take you back in time and put you ringside at some of his incredible fights. This will clear any doubts and answer all questions. Furthermore, let me remind you that those who today wrongly insist that it was Carlos who perfected the style were not even born at that time. It is obvious that jealousy has affected their reasoning.

As if all that was not enough, take a look at Helio Gracie, who did nothing but jiu-jitsu his entire life. Today at age 90 he is as ready, as always, to step on the mat and demonstrate to anybody, a simpler and more technical way to apply a move. Let's face it - Helio Gracie is the embodiment of jiu-jitsu!

Q: Your father challenged the great boxer Joe Louis, right?

A: Yes, but Joe Louis declined! Joe Louis was on tour in Brazil and my father issued a challenge to pit boxing against jiu-jitsu. Joe Louis was to fight without gloves, just tape to protect the knuckles. It is true that a good punch from Joe Louis would have knocked my father out-but he was confident that he could get into a clinch. Of course with both men in a clinch, the fight would very much favor my father. Anyway, Joe Louis' manager, Marshall Miles, sent a letter declining the offer. He also challenged Primo Carnera and Ezzard Charles. It is all at the Gracie Museum.

Q: Years later you issued the same challenge to Mike Tyson, right?

A: Yes. The idea was to demonstrate that being the boxing champion of the world doesn't make you the best fighter. People always had that misconception until the UFC. Everybody knows that the only chance a boxer has in a NHB fight is that one punch. The boxer can't afford to miss or get caught in a clinch. With the odds of 95 percent of all fights ending on the ground, pure boxers better stay out of the NHB arena.

Q: You don't bow in the traditional way of martial arts, why is that?

A: It is not necessary. Orientals bow to each other as a cultural habit. I don't teach Oriental culture, I teach Gracie jiu-jitsu, and a simple handshake is good enough.

Q: You drastically changed the face of martial arts when started the Ultimate Fighting Championship. Why did you start it?

A: I grew up with the certainty that most real fights end up on the ground. The knowledge of jiu-jitsu has enabled me to protect myself effectively even against bigger and stronger adversaries. That is a priceless feeling. I have also seen thousands of people grow in confidence and improve their self-esteem when they were introduced to this wonderful art. Since my arrival in America a quarter-of-a-century ago, my primary goal has been to alert people to the importance of groundfighting. I wanted everyone to learn the art that did so much for me, the entire Gracie family, and thousands of students in my homeland of Brazil. I saw in the UFC an opportunity to expose to the world the truths and fallacies inherent in contemporary martial arts theory. Prior to the UFC, striking reigned supreme.

With victory after victory, jiu-jitsu as a grappling art has dominated the editorial and technical articles of every major martial art magazine in the world. More importantly, everyone is doing it, just like I hoped for.

Q: Why are you against time limits?

A: When you impose a time limit, you are in effect giving a fighter a psychological "safety net." You are saying to him, "No matter how bad it gets, if you can hang on for X minutes you will be OK." The existence of this "light at the end of the tunnel" completely changes the physiological and emotional state of mind of the fighter. They can't help but alter their strategy to include an imposed time limit into their chances of victory. With the security of a scheduled conclusion ticking in the back of his head, a fighter's level of anxiety is greatly reduced.

Q: So you think the time limit affects the fighter's state of mind and mental approach to the fight?

A: Definitely. Take two men to separate but identical remote, desert locations. To the first man you say, "I know this is difficult, but all you have to do is last 24 hours until we pick you up again. If you play it safe, if you don't expend too much energy, or take any risks, you should make it." This doesn't sound like anyone's idea of a great vacation, but I think most of us-secure in the knowledge of rescue-could manage to hang on. Fair enough.

Then go to the second man and tell him, "You are on your own. No one is coming to save you-ever! Your only hope lies in your own skill and ingenuity. Survive or perish-it's up to you. No playing it safe." The way the second man is going to act is totally different to the first one. That's why I tried to prevent eliminating the time limits in the UFC. Stripping away the pretenses, the judges, the scores, and the games. Two men enter-one man leaves. Let's find out what works and what doesn't. It's that simple.

Q: At your academy you encourage private classes. Why?

A: The effectiveness of our system is due to its simplicity-and it's far better to learn them one-on-one where we can coach the student individually instead of telling a whole class to play follow the leader and hope they can keep up. We want them to practice with us, to ensure the development of the proper reflexes. We don't want the students to memorize the moves. We teach their subconscious to react, which is faster than the conscious mind. It's like when you are driving down the street and a kid runs out in front of your car-your reflexes make your foot hit the brake. If you had to think about what to do with your conscious mind, there might be a tragedy. It's a simple matter of developing strong basics-the kind of foundation that eventually allows the student to become really efficient.

Q; What attributes and qualities makes a good teacher?

A: He must know the subject very well. He must have a genuine interest in helping the student improve. He must love teaching. The motto here at the Gracie Academy is there is no such a thing as a good or a bad student.

All the students are the same. There is such a thing as a good or a bad teacher. All teachers are not the same. We only have great teachers. Here, everyone learns"

Properly performed, revealing knowledge to another is a deeply involving, almost symbiotic exercise. A sincere teacher, a devoted teacher, does not stand aloof and in judgment as his pupil struggles along his path. The sincere teacher walks shoulder-to-shoulder with his charge, traveling the same path, sharing its difficulties and challenges. The genuine teacher is there to help the student identify obstacles; discuss possible solutions. He shouldn't be comfortably perched upon some distant pedestal. True teachers are very rare.

Q: Are all the members of the Gracie family teaching the art in the same format and methodology developed by Helio Gracie?

A: Although we all learned from the same source, not everybody in the Gracie family follows my father's guidelines. His teaching method is focused on self-defense, which involves the little known but extremely demanding stand-up aspects of jiu-jitsu. It is a tough act to follow because it requires lots of: falling, getting choked and having your limbs turned and twisted in all directions countless times and then some. It is hard work on the teacher's part. If the motivation is money, no one will keep it up, regardless of how much they are making. You have to do it for love. It is much easier to let the students to roll with each other, and push the sparring for competition approach which is OK, I guess. But here at the Gracie Academy our primary goal is to increase the student's effectiveness in self-defense. That means that the teacher will be on the receiving end of every technique so he can give feedback to the student on the execution of each move. There is no doubt that many people are happy with the sportive angle. However I know my father's intention was not to develop a sport but a method of self-defense. That is why we do it his way.

> "A sincere teacher, a devoted teacher, does not stand aloof and in judgment as his pupil struggles along his path."

Q: What's your opinion about mixing styles. Does the practice of one nullify the effectiveness of the other or can it be beneficial?

A: Of course, I think it would be important to have a strong base in jiu-jitsu because most fights will end up on the ground. It is not a bad thing to learn the other aspects of combat to help you to better apply your main art. What I have seen sometimes is people who have been training in jiu-jitsu for 20 years, start training in a striking art for a couple of years and when they fight they put their 20 years of jiu-jitsu in the back burner and rely on punches and kicks against a fighter who has been practicing strikes for 15 years. This is not smart and they are digging their own graves.

Q: You are the man who started it all with the creation of the UFC. What are your thoughts on the future of Mixed Martial Arts events what do you think should be done to improve the sport?

A: I don't think it will ever go back to what it was before. My idea at the time I created the UFC was to compare styles. Today everybody does the same style of fighting-punching and kicking with some variation of jiu-jitsu. Now is not about the style, but about the athlete. As far as the events go, the current rules are making it too sanitized. I would take the gloves off and the put time limits out of the game. When that happens I will tell you the rest (laughs).

> **"There is no reason why jiu-jitsu can't be an Olympic sport-but for that to happen there must be a complete overhaul within the worldwide jiu-jitsu community"**

Q: What do you see in the future of jiu-jitsu and the Gracie family?

A: There is no reason why jiu-jitsu can't be an Olympic sport-but for that to happen there must be a complete overhaul within the worldwide jiu-jitsu community. And this must start with the rules currently used in jiu-jitsu tournaments. These rules are not bringing out the best in the sport. They are subjective, hard to understand, and encourage stalling. The Gracie family started the jiu-jitsu revolution and through their associates and students continues to be a major influence in the way the sport grows. The International Gracie Jiu-Jitsu Federation is being created with my father's blessing to organize events with a new set of rules that will revolutionize the practice of jiu-jitsu. As for future competitors, there is a new generation of Gracie family members growing tall and strong - so the best is yet to come.

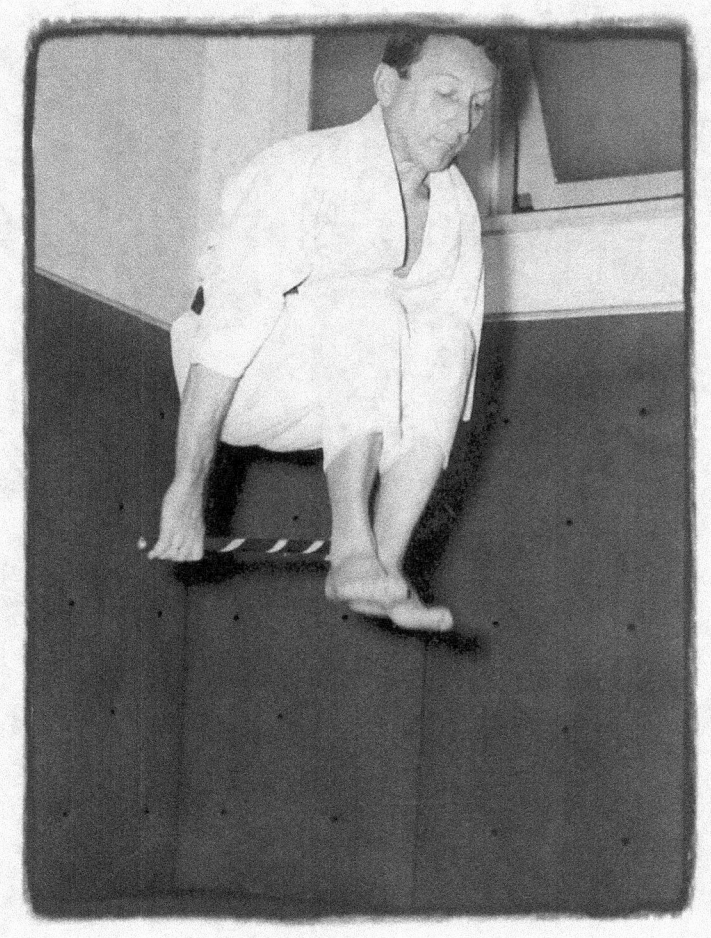

❝**Be as just and enthusiastic about others victories as you are with yours.**❞

~ Carlos Gracie Sr. ~

ROYLER GRACIE

The Heart of a Champion

ONE OF BRAZILIAN JIU-JITSU'S MOST ENDURING CHAMPIONS, ROYLER GRACIE HAS NEVER RESTED ON THE LAURELS OF HIS FAMOUS FAMILY, BUT HAS LET HIS FIGHTING RECORD AND RING ACCOMPLISHMENTS SPEAK FOR THEMSELVES.

HE HAS BEEN INVOLVED IN MARTIAL ARTS HIS ENTIRE LIFE AND HAS BEEN COMPETING CONSTANTLY SINCE HE WAS 7 YEARS OLD. HAVING FOUGHT IN MORE JIU-JITSU EVENTS THAN PERHAPS ANY OTHER BRAZILIAN JIU-JITSU FIGHTER IN HISTORY, ROYLER HAS ATTAINED THE STATUS OF BEST IN THE WORLD. HIS CAREER HAS SPANNED OVER 28 YEARS AND THREE GENERATIONS. DURING THAT STRETCH HE HAS BEEN A FOUR-TIME BJJ WORLD CHAMPION, A TWO-TIME ABU DHABI COMBAT CLUB (ADCC) WORLD SUBMISSION WRESTLING CHAMPION, A PAN AMERICAN GAMES CHAMPION, A BRAZILIAN NATIONAL CHAMPION, AND RIO DE JANEIRO STATE CHAMPION. HE ALSO MANAGED TO FIGHT IN SEVERAL MEMORABLE MMA MATCHES ALONG THE WAY, SOME AGAINST MUCH BIGGER MEN. UNDISPUTEDLY, ONE OF THE MOST SCIENTIFIC FIGHTERS IN THE WORLD, ROYLER WON THE MOST TECHNICAL AWARD AT BOTH THE 1997 BJJ WORLD CHAMPIONSHIPS AND AT ADCC 2000, MAKING HIM THE ONLY MAN TO HAVE EVER CAPTURED BOTH PRESTIGIOUS AWARDS.

IN AN ERA IN WHICH MOST FIGHTERS ARE WORRIED ABOUT THEIR RECORDS AND WON'T FIGHT OUTSIDE THEIR WEIGHT DIVISION, ROYLER HAS OFTEN TAKEN ON MUCH HEAVIER OPPONENTS. HIS REASONING IS SIMPLE AND SPEAKS VOLUMES ABOUT THE MAN HIMSELF: "I JUST WANT TO SEE HOW THE MATCH WILL TURN OUT AND HOW I WILL DO. MORE THAN ANYTHING ELSE I WANT TO LEARN MORE ABOUT JIU-JITSU, AND IN ORDER TO DO THAT I HAVE TO CHALLENGE MYSELF."

Q: Tell us a little bit about yourself?

A: I started to train BJJ when I was 3. At the time I really didn't know what I was doing, I'd go to the academy to play soccer dressed in a gi. It was fun, Brazil is the land of soccer and you generally give your kids a soccer ball, but I was given a gi. So my father and my brother Rolls, in order to get me and the other kids interested in coming to class and to the academy, made us play soccer dressed in a gi. It was really fun then. All my brothers where at the academy also, so it was the gathering place. We practically ate, slept, and breathed jiu-jitsu then, so the sport took over my life very early on, but very naturally because all the other kids in the family did it too.

Q: When did you start to fight?

A: For my first competition I was only 7 years old. My dad came to me and said, "I want you to go there and have fun. If you win I am going to give you five dollars-but if you lose I am going to give you ten dollars." So I thought, "What a deal, if I win I make a little money and get the medal, and if I lose I get even more money." So I always looked forward to competitions because it was always a win-win situation. Now I see the wisdom of this, because no one enters a competition or a fight to lose; everyone wants to win. So in order to take away the pressure from me, he devised this reward. Because when you think about it, being that my family had many champions, the pressure for us to win was naturally stronger than for other kids. I believe it had a great effect on me and is why I still look forward to competing and why I thrive during pressure situations. In my mind I just need to do my best-before and after the competition. I mention before the competition because if, for some reason, I didn't prepare myself correctly, I would feel bad. But that's never happened before and I hope it never will.

Q: How many times did you fight?

A: I started at 7 years old, but I have lost count of how many times I have fought in tournaments. But just as a black belt I have approximately 300 fights recorded on video and film. But I didn't record all my fights as a lower belt so that number is much higher.

Q: Who where the big names when you started to compete?

A: I fought many people: Peixotinho, Marcio Simas, Marcio "Macarrao", Carlson Gracie Jr., Ricardo de La Riva, Amauri Bitteti, and so forth.

Q: So you have crossed several generations?

A: I believe that I have fought three generations of fighters.

Q: You also have fought several fights, including underground fights, like the time you fought Eugenio Tadeu. How old where you then.

A: I was 21.

Q: Was that your first vale tudo match?

A: Yes. That fight happened at our academy and it sort of happened without warning. I was teaching at the academy and my brother Rickson called and said, "Hey, Royler, tomorrow you have a vale tudo against a luta livre (free fighting) guy." At the time, jiu-jitsu and luta livre fighters had a real strong rivalry going so I accepted. Rickson called late in the afternoon and when I asked when, he answered, "Noon!" I then asked him if it was OK, if I took the rest of the evening off and rested, and he agreed. So it was on the spur of the moment, at least for me, with no preparation.

So I showed up the next day to do a "fight-train" as Rickson called it, with Eugenio Tadeu, who at the time weighed about 25 lbs more than me. We fought for 46 minutes with kicks and punches, all done for free, because at that time there was no money in vale tudo fights-so we fought just to see who was the better fighter. There were six people from my team watching and six people from his team. I left the fight feeling great because I had never done a vale tudo before and it was a new experience in my life.

Q: Tadeu already had a few matches prior to that, right?

A: He had a few fights, was used to street fighting, and he really liked fighting.

Q: Then after that you had a series of vale tudo matches?

A: Over a period of time. I fought one in Brazil, then I fought in Japan Vale Tudo 1996 against Noburo Asahi who was ranked number one in the Shooto organization at the time. Then I fought in Pride 2 against Yuhi Sano in 1998. After that I did the fight with Sakuraba in October 1999 and just recently in Deep 2001 against Japanese fighter Murahama. During that same time I was also fighting the world BJJ tournaments. I was the champion four years running in 1996 through 1999. I also fought in the ADCC championships and won both in 1999 and 2900. I fought in a few Brasileiros (Brazilian national tournaments). I also did a few special events like the Copa Pele. The Copa Pele had special jiu-jitsu matches in an outdoor arena that was set up every summer on the beach in Rio.

> "The person with the least amount of endurance would prefer a shorter fight, and the person who is more technical prefers a longer match."

Q: Describe the Deep 2001 match.

A: During the first round I was able to get Murahama's back right away, I believe by the third minute I was on his back. He was, however, an experienced fighter with many professional stand-up matches and he knew how to protect himself. The fact that he was only 5'2" made it easier for him to protect his neck. I spent about six minutes of the first round on his back trying to submit him. Around the ninth minute I decided to try an arm attack but we ended up too close to the ropes and his arm was wrapped around the ropes and the more I tried the harder it got.

In the second round he was feeling more confident and we exchanged some punches while standing up. I got a little tired and I started to have a harder time taking him down. I finally took him down and attempted a foot lock but it was quickly defended by him. I believe that the fight was pretty even-he is a good striker and only needs to connect with one good shot to end the fight. Because the fight is never over until it's over, one mistake with a good striker can be fatal. A grappler, however, has to work a lot harder to get the precise moment to sink in the submission. The draw was a fair result. I have no complaints. I think that we both deserved the draw, but I also believe that the rules favored a draw.

Q: Why was your fight two rounds of 10 minutes each?

A: Well, my fight was the main event so I believe that the promoters decided to make it longer. I think this would have been better for the other fights also, because it gives the fighters more time to develop a strategy and positioning. The person with the least amount of endurance would prefer a shorter fight, and the person who is more technical prefers a longer match. I am not talking about a three-hour fight, but I prefer two ten-minute rounds or even three rounds of that length. I believe anything longer than one hour makes for a boring fight. To my way of thinking, if a fighter who is my size draws with me after 20 or 30 minutes, then it is fair to say that we are even. Of course, if you go another round then anything can happen, but they can happen just as much to me as to him, so it goes both ways. I do not believe in saying that if a fight had gone longer I would have won. I believe that from a promotion and entertainment standpoint you have to limit the matches to under one hour-and my preference is 30 minutes.

Q: It seems that the Gracie family is always accused of going to an event and changing the rules at the last minute. Is there any truth to this?

A: I really don't understand that criticism. I always leave for an event with the rules already agreed to by both parties far in advance. As a matter of fact, when I arrived in Japan for Deep 2001 a reporter asked me that same question and I turned around to him and said that I didn't know of any changes and asked him to tell me what had changed. He couldn't answer. I remember the time I fought with Sakuraba, who was 40 pounds heavier than me, and all that I asked was for longer rounds-two rounds of 15 minutes instead of 10 minutes. I don't think that that was an unreasonable request. I have never had the chance to fight someone who was 40 pounds lighter than me. But if that ever happens and he asks for three rounds of 20 minutes each, I am going to agree. If he asks for 20 rounds of three minutes each I'll also agree! The fact of the matter is that the contracts are drawn way in advance and the rules are set before anyone signs a contract; so I don't know where these stories about last-minute changes come from.

Q: What motivated you to keep fighting?

A: I have always loved fighting. After a while it becomes a natural part of your life. I live exclusively from fighting and teaching jiu-jitsu, grappling, and MMA. So I ate, slept and breathe it. I looked at it as a way to measure myself and to make a living at the same time. I focused on my work which involved teaching at academies that I had in Rio, doing seminars that I conducted everywhere in the world, and then fighting. The fights gave me an extra income. So I saw MMA as a way to broaden my career, while at the same time making extra income. I don't believe that anyone will tell you that they love to fight MMA. People may love the attention and the exposure and the perks, but no one in his right mind likes to hit someone or to get hit in a fight. You may love the challenge that is fighting but I don't believe that you can love to fight MMA. Fighting is something that traumatizes the body and it not something that I believe anyone would realistically do just for the pleasure of it.

Q: You are known for your ability to think and adjust your strategy during a fight. How did you develop that mental skill?

A: I have read the book, The Art of War, at least 50 times. It has influenced me a lot. One of the things that it says is, "If you know yourself but don't know your enemy, for each victory you will have a defeat. If you don't know your enemy and you don't know yourself then you will lose every battle. If you know yourself and your enemy then you don't have to fear the result of 100 battles." I was also lucky to have been born into a family of fighters and was fortunate enough to have grown-up around fighting. So I learned from watching and absorbing the experience of many champions-and not just those from my own family.

Q: What do you think of the evolution of submission grappling? Since the early days of Brazilian jiu-jitsu, when you taught out a garage in L.A., it has become an established sport with a huge number of followers. Are you surprised?

A: Not really. Think about it. Years ago there wasn't a magazine dedicated to grappling or MMA alone; nowadays you have several publications. I think this whole thing has been because of the success that BJJ had in MMA. I believe that BJJ had a tremendous influence in the media in turning public attention to the idea of wrestling and submission styles being a legitimate combat art. All of a sudden, out of nowhere, there was something very different and fresh and very effective that changed the way people viewed fighting. There is not a top-level fighter today who doesn't have BJJ knowledge. Likewise the world of stand-up fighting has made BJJ practitioners look to develop skills that complement their style as well. But when BJJ came into the scene it really created a revolution. Judo is very important, luta livre is very important, wrestling is very important, and sambo is very important-but it was BJJ that initially showed that ground fighting is at least as important as stand-up striking in a fight.

Q: How you approach the different elements (cardiovascular, strength and technical) in your training program?

A: Training for me is part of my life, the thing that I try to do is to adapt my lifestyle depending on what I am training for. I strongly believe that you have to be extremely fit to be ready for battle. So I had different routines depending if I was going to fight a BJJ tournament, a no-gi grappling event like ADCC, or an MMA match. The only common ground in my training was the aerobic part. I believe that you have to have strong endurance in order to perform at high level. For that I did a lot of running and biking. I like biking a lot because you get to see a lot of things and the exercise is more fun. If I was going to be in an MMA match, then I did lift weights according to a specific routine set up for me by my trainer Jayme Rousso and also took supplements according to the advice of my ortho-molecular nutrition advisor Dr. Osvino Pena. I also trained boxing with Professor Claudio Coelho.

If I was going to compete in BJJ, which means fighting with a gi, then I will do a lot of judo and did a different series of weight training than I could do for MMA. The emphasis was more on endurance rather than strength, so I did focus more on repetitions with lighter weights rather than fewer reps with heavier weights. Also I used to train more the auxiliary muscle groups rather than just the main muscle groups of the chest, arts, legs, et cetera. I find that combination strength, where you are working several muscle group together at the same time, is more realistic to how the body will work during a fight. This is especially true with the gi, because of the unlimited positions that can result from the grabbing of the gi. I also believe in focusing mentally in order to truly achieve peak performance. The mental aspect is at least as important as the physical. I sometimes focused so hard that I got cranky and irritable. So after the training was done and the event was over I sometimes had to apologize to a lot of people! I used to rent an apartment and left my house so that I could concentrate 100 percent on training for events. That of course is really hard because I love my family and I missed them. But becoming a champion requires personal sacrifice. I am very lucky to have a very understanding and supportive wife who has made my life easier rather than make it harder.

> **"Grappling is a much more slippery fight than BJJ, because of the fact you don't wear a gi, and the need is for quick explosive motion rather than slow and methodical techniques."**

Q: Did you approach the training differently if you were going to fight a vale tudo o straight grappling tournament without gi?

A: If I was training for a grappling event then the training was similar to what I used to do for a BJJ tournament but the emphasis was once again different. Grappling is a much more slippery fight than BJJ, because of the fact you don't wear a gi, and the need is for quick explosive motion rather than slow and methodical techniques. Because of this, I adjusted my weight training and my cardio exercise accordingly. I did explosive repetitions with heavier weights and other things like that. As far as techniques go I used to concentrate more on takedowns and on getting to the back for a choke, as arm bars are harder to get without a gi. I also tried to avoid practicing the guard, because in grappling you don't want to be laying on your back waiting to react to your opponent, but rather attacking him and forcing him to react to you. In grappling without a gi, you need to be very active and be constantly on the move - so I trained for this by constantly shifting positions with my training partners. The important thing to keep in mind is that you need to do your homework and find something that works for you and then keep improving it. I truly believe that fights are won or lost outside of the limelight, way before you step into the arena. That is what I kept in mind and that is what motivated me to keep pushing in training.

Q: Finally, did you ever think when you fought Eugenio Tadeu for free, that MMA would become so well-established and popular?

A: Vale-Tudo or MMA has become a money-making machine for an elite few. However, there are many athletes that are fighting for very little. There are many people that are not getting what they deserve. Fighters need to be able to get a fair payment; but for various reasons, some of which are the fighters' own fault, they will fight for any amount. I believe that anyone that fights deserves to get more than they are getting now. Luckily, the events are getting more popular and the new promoters are people who love the sport and who are visionaries. They are making big strides to fairly compensate the fighters. That will be very good for the sport. ○

BELFORT
TRAINING CENTER

JESUS

VITOR BELFORT

A Force of One

VITOR BELFORT IS ONE OF MMA'S PREMIER ATTRACTIONS. "THE PHENOM" AS HE IS RIGHTLY CALLED, BURST ONTO THE MMA SCENE IN 1996 AT THE AGE OF 18 WITH A 12 SECOND KO OVER JON HESS IN SUPERBRAWL 2. HE FOLLOWED THAT UP WITH THREE STRAIGHT KO'S IN THE UFC BEFORE LOSING TO RANDY COUTURE IN UFC 13. AFTER A SUBMISSION VICTORY OVER JOE CHARLES IN THE UFCJ, MANY FELT THAT BELFORT HAD PERHAPS LOST HIS EXPLOSIVE PUNCHING POWER. IN HIS NEXT FIGHT AGAINST THE "UNBEATABLE" VANDERLEI SILVA IN BRAZIL, HE WAS CONSIDERED "WASHED UP" AT THE AGE OF 19 AND WAS WIDELY EXPECTED TO BE CRUSHED. SOMEONE WAS CRUSHED THAT NIGHT IN RIO-BUT IT WASN'T BELFORT. IN A SHOCKING TURN OF EVENTS, BELFORT DESTROYED SILVA IN ONLY 44 SECONDS IN ONE OF MMA MOST FAMOUS UPSETS. WITH THIS VICTORY, THE PHENOM PROVED THAT HE WAS MORE DANGEROUS THAN EVER AND THAT REPORTS OF HIS DEMISE HAD BEEN GREATLY EXAGGERATED-HE HASN'T LOST SINCE.

WITH HIS SCULPTURED PHYSIQUE AND INTENSE FIGHTING STYLE, MANY HAVE THE IMPRESSION THAT BELFORT IS NOTHING MORE THAN A MINDLESS AUTOMATON OF DESTRUCTION. NOTHING COULD BE FURTHER FROM THE TRUTH. WHILE POSSESSING A CONFIDENCE THAT A TOP ATHLETE MUST HAVE IN ORDER TO COMPETE AT THE HIGHEST LEVEL OF ANY SPORT, BELFORT IS WELL AWARE OF THE EPHEMERAL NATURE OF FAME AND KNOWS THAT ANYONE, ON ANY GIVEN NIGHT, CAN BE BEATEN. THIS FEELING OF VULNERABILITY HAS LED BELFORT TO TRAIN FURIOUSLY IN BOXING, WRESTLING, JIU-JITSU, AND JUDO. WITH SUCH A DIVERSE MIX OF SKILLS, BELFORT BECAME UNPREDICTABLE AND VIRTUALLY IMPOSSIBLE TO FORMULATE AN EFFECTIVE FIGHT PLAN AGAINST.

Q: How did you get involved in martial arts?

A: I got involved when I was 8 years old. I started fighting judo. Martial arts in Brazil was big all the time. Then I started learning jiu-jitsu with Jacare when I was 10 years old. I studied with him for a year then I left to train with one of Carlson Gracie's students because his school was closer to my house. But when I didn't do well in school, my mother took me out of jiu-jitsu and I started training in boxing. There used to be a stamp the teacher would give you to show that you had gone to school that day. I stole it so I could stamp myself, and I just went to the gym and trained boxing for a year. When my father found out he said, "Let's sit down and talk. If you want to be a fighter you have to behave in school, and if you don't then I'm going to punish you and you're not going to be able to do sports."

At that time I did a lot of sports as well as martial arts. My father was a volleyball player and my mother was also athletic. They always thought that I should do sports to keep me out of drugs and gangs and trouble. They wanted me to have sports idols instead of following bad influences. So then when I started back in jiu-jitsu and wrestling, after my father told me to behave myself, I started to do very well. I think that God just blessed me with natural ability. I was just 18 years old for my first fight in Hawaii. Then I went to the UFC right after that and won the UFC tournament. From then on my life has just been blessed by a higher power.

Q: You have trained in judo, boxing, jiu-jitsu, and wrestling. Which of those do you enjoy the most?

A: I like jiu-jitsu the best, followed by wrestling, and then boxing. I like judo the least because it has too many rules. The first three are all fun because you can personally express yourself without being limited by excess rules. It really just depends on the moment as to which one I like the best. Sometimes I feel like I want to box, sometimes I feel like wrestling, and sometimes I want to do jiu-jitsu.

Q: How did your first fight happen?

A: I was working out and training at a fitness center, and a friend who managed the club was one of the sponsors of the fighting event. His name is Donny Bender. I was supposed to fight in Battlecade, in Extreme Fighting, but I was so young that I couldn't fight because I was not yet 18. So when I turned 18 Donny knew I wanted to fight and asked me, so I said yeah. He said they were going to put up an appearance fee for me to fight. But I said instead of an appearance fee why didn't they just make the purse winner take all. So that's what they did and I was successful in that fight against John Hess in just a few seconds. I thank the Lord for the victory, and from that day my life just went up. Hess was a veteran fighter at that time, and I was just a kid. But I really punished him. I took him down, I put my knee on his belly, and then I knocked him out.

Q: When you went into the UFC did you have any idea you would become an overnight sensation?

A: I knew that I had a lot of skills that people in the sport didn't have at that time, because I could punch and also grapple. A lot of people came at me to take me down because they thought I was just a puncher. You never know what is going to happen, of course, but I had a feeling that I would do well. I always say that tomorrow is a promissory note, yesterday is a cancelled check, and today is cash on hand. That is the way that we should all live our lives. When I put myself into a fight-and I really concentrate on it-I know that I can do well. But when my mind is not there, that is when I don't do as well as I should and have a bad time.

Q: You're generally considered to have the most natural talent of any fighter. But some also say that you don't live up to that talent. Is that because you lose focus?

A: The problem is that I get bored with the sport sometimes. That is what happened to me in the past. I'm not going to blame other people for what I've done or haven't done. I'm guilty. If I don't want anything to happen in my life that distracts me, then I have that choice-I decide. But when I had my loss to Randy Couture, I was totally out of focus and totally mixed up. I had a girlfriend at the time who caused a lot of confusion in my life and I was very young and I didn't know how to deal with it in a mature way. Also, I was still very young and things had happened very fast for me-too fast. Sometimes in our lives we make mistakes. And when we recognize that mistakes were made then we can correct them. God gives us free will so we can do what we want. And sometimes we forget to ask God what we should be doing. I think it is important to keep in mind that somebody, someplace, somewhere is better than you-more talented, wealthier, whatever. You have to be humble and not think that you're the best. A true champion is one who doesn't think he is the best, but yet others do. So when my mind is not there for a fight, then Vitor is not there and anything can happen. And that is what happened in the Randy Couture fight and also the Sakuraba fight.

Q: Many feel that when you're truly focused that you're nearly unbeatable. Do you feel that way?

A: Nobody is unbeatable-that is the thing that I know for sure and that I remind myself of. But I think that for a guy to beat me, he really has to on his game that day and that God has to want him to win. But it will be a brawl. But when I'm not in shape-when I'm not 100 percent-then I could have trouble. The thing is that I've only fought good guys, you know. Most all of the guys I've fought have been the best and the guys I've lost to have been the best-Randy and Sakuraba. So when you fight the best, and you're not all there, then you can't expect to do well.

Q: When you fought Sakuraba it seemed like you dominated the fight in the early going, then you just stopped fighting. What happened?

A: A lot of people don't know that two weeks before the fight I had knee surgery. But I had made a commitment that I was going to fight and I thought that it would look bad for my career if I didn't. So I decided that I would step into the ring no matter what. A couple of months before that fight I was supposed to fight in the UFC, and I dropped out of that because of another health problem. So I felt that if I dropped out of two fights in a row that people would think badly of me. So I felt that I had to do it, even though I probably shouldn't. But people don't know what goes on in my life day to day. They only see the headlines. So I just decided to try to do my best. I didn't have time for my knee to really heal, I didn't have time to train, and I was really out of shape. I knew all that but I still went in to try to win.

But to make it even worse, at the last minute Pride made me lose 20 pounds. That was not in the contract, but they made me do it anyway because Sakuraba was afraid to fight me heavy. He respects me a lot and so he would only fight me if I went to 199 pounds. They weighed me at 6pm the day before the fight and then they told me that if I wasn't 199 by the next day the fight was off. I was scared because I had flown all the way from Brazil and I needed the money. So even though the weight limit wasn't in the contract I signed, I decided to do it. In that way I felt that they set me up. When Sakuraba fought Royler Gracie, Pride didn't make Sakuraba lose 20 or 30 pounds the night before the fight. But I didn't want to disappoint my fans. So I lost the weight mainly just from sitting in a sauna and sweating.

Then in the first three minutes of the fight I broke my hand so badly that the bone was sticking out and I couldn't punch for the rest of the fight. But I still didn't quit and tried to grapple him. But he didn't want to grapple, all he wanted to do was to score points and that's what he did. He was scared to grapple me but he fought smart and just scored points-that's how he fights. I tried to get a rematch after that fight so I could get in shape and train at the correct weight, but they would never give me a rematch.

Q: It seems funny that he would fight Royler Gracie who was 50 pounds lighter.

A: I have a lot of respect for Royler for doing that. Royler is a warrior. He didn't care how much Sakuraba outweighed him. But Sakuraba didn't want to fight me without making me lose 20 pounds. I was there with him and his manager, you know? A lot of people who were there saw it. I went to the sauna with a jacket and just sat there. But I had to lose the weight or else I would not have gotten paid and I would have disappointed my fans. So I just wanted to be professional. To be fair to Sakuraba I don't know if this came from him. He doesn't speak English so the demand for me to drop the weight could have come from his manager. Sakuraba has fought big guys before in the Grand Prix-so you never know. But I know that whatever the reason he didn't want to step into the ring with a weight difference-but I have a lot of respect for Royler for getting into the ring with him.

Sakuraba is a good fighter and I do respect his fighting ability-but I want my rematch with him. I deserve my rematch with him. They should promote that fight but they never talk about it. But I know the mentality of the Japanese and they want Sakuraba to look good all the time, and I think that I would make him look bad. They want him to keep winning. But I think this is not fair to me. I think that I deserve this rematch. I don't know for a fact that I would win against him, but I know that if I step into the ring 100 percent that I wouldn't bet against me. People have made that mistake before.

Q: It seems like every time people give up on you, you come back and surprise them.

A: When I'm ready, I'm ready-I feel that I can take anyone. I show a lot of things. But you know, no matter what you do people will still not be satisfied. Every time there will be someone saying, "Vitor just got lucky." That's what fighting is all about. So I guess that I just got lucky 9 times in all my wins. I'm 22 years old and I have a lot more fights that most guys who are 32 years old. I'm just beginning my career. I want people to know that. But I think that I should get a little more respect. I respect all fighters-even the one who are just beginning. I respect them because the fighting business is just like having a job, you know? You have to be humble to every one who is involved-from the guy who puts up the ring to the promoters who put up the money. I respect everybody so I think that people should respect me. Some fighters are just too cocky. I don't see cockiness as a sign of confidence; I see cockiness as a sign of fear. When you have fear you're cocky, but when you're confident you're humble.

Q: Was there any fights in the UFC that you were afraid you were going to lose?

A: The first time I went into the UFC I was very young-I had just turned 19. I had to fight two fights in a row and so of course I was nervous. God just blessed me that day and I won. Of course, everybody gets nervous but sometimes you get more and sometimes you get less. In that first fight in the UFC I was nervous and then against Sakuraba I was nervous because I knew that I wasn't in shape. I knew I could dominate him, but when my hand broke and I couldn't punch that made me nervous.

Q: When you fought Vanderlei Silva did it shake your confidence that everyone thought you were going to lose?

A: I never lost confidence in myself but some people thought I did. My game is to sometimes play tricks on the other fighter. Sometimes I play like I think I will lose just so I can come out and surprise my opponent. But at the time I had a really bad headache because of a medicine I had taken. And people thought that because of that Vitor was scared. But I wasn't scared, I was just afraid to fight with the headache because I didn't know what was causing it. Anytime anything touched my head, it would make my brain throb-so of course that worried me. And people made a big thing about that. But the truth is that I was really confident about the fight itself and it showed in what I did to him. I walked through him. The day before the fight they asked Vanderlei what he thought and he said, "I'm going to knock Vitor out in 5 minutes." When they asked me though, I just said, "I think this is going to be a tough match so lets just see what happens." I didn't talk a lot with my mouth, but I just let my fists talk for me-I talk a lot through my fists. I don't need to talk outside the ring because what I do inside of it speaks for me. Talking trash is not my style, you know? I don't need to impress anyone. I have done a lot of things in the sport and people know what I can do. But some people always think that you have something more to prove. I don't have to prove anything to anyone. I just want to step into the ring, do my best for the fans and give a good show. I fight to put on a good show and I fight for myself.

Q: You're known as MMA's most exciting puncher. Have you always had fast hands?

A: Well, of course I train to have fast hands but a lot of it is a gift-and I thank God for that. There are a lot of fighters in the world, but not a lot of exciting fighters. That's what I train for-to put on an exciting fight. But a lot of my fighting tools I haven't even shown yet. People are still going to see a lot of new and exciting things from me in the years to come. My career is just beginning and I have so much more to show the NHB fans. It's just a matter of time, you know? When the time is right then you're going to see it.

Q: Most people think of you as a pure striker. How do you think of yourself?

A: I take every fight one at a time. In Pride fights I've stayed in the guard and punched people out from there because that is how the fight went. I can dominate a fight from many positions and control it from beginning to the end. I just did that in my last two Pride fights to show that I could do that. Maybe in my next fight I will work submissions or maybe I will stand and punch. I like to be unpredictable so my opponents don't know what to expect from me. Just like Tyson. When he steps into the ring we don't know what can happen-he can even bite, you know? Anything from Tyson will be exciting. But some guys when they step into the ring we know what they're going to do and we know it is going to be boring. So with me, people don't know if I'm going to grapple, or wrestle, or box, or do jiu-jitsu. People don't know. Vitor Belfort is unpredictable. Right now, my mind is totally on business. I want to bring the sport up, make money for it and for myself, and help to bring in new fans. The most important thing is the fans. You can fight to win, but you had better fight for the fans, too. If you win the fight but yet lose the fans then you've lost everything. Better to lose the fight and win the fans. Winning the fans is what drives the sport forward. Of course, my goal is to win the fight and win the fans.

Q: Against Gilbert Yvel, many said you would lose. But yet you showed enough to win and to prove your doubters wrong.

A: I can say that I was only fighting one strategy in that fight because I knew that I could control him on the ground. So I did that from the beginning to the end. I knew that I was going to win that fight. You don't know you're going to win for sure, of course. You have to step into the ring and do your best. I'm ready for anything.

Q: Many people think of you as a pure jiu-jitsu and MMA fighter. But didn't you concentrate on boxing for a while?

A: I always loved MMA but at that time the sport was going so bad, people were treating the sport like garbage. Using it just as a way to make money and then get out. I don't think that way. I think we've got to make money of course, but first of all make our fans and the people that love the sport happy. Too many promoters were not thinking that way; they were not treating the fighters right. They just pick-up a fighter and say, "Hey, man, wanna make some money? Just come here and fight." The rules were so nasty, so bloody, so bad and I didn't like that. I said, "Hey, that's not what I want for life and that's not what I want for the sport." What I want for the sport is for it to get big again. When I decided to go to the Olympics, one week before the trails I was hurt and I couldn't go to the trials. So I missed my chance. Then Pride offered me a fight right around that time. So I said OK. So I trained for two weeks and I went to fight. And I was so happy because Pride has good rules. Now I have the chance to go professional boxing. You see, I want to prove that I can do both. I know I can.

Q: What is your training like now at this moment in your life?

A: I train Monday though Saturday. We mix it up with kicking, punching, grappling, wrestling. We put it all together. I try to do a little bit of everything everyday. Some days we do guard, kicks, and punches. Other days we do passing the guard, takedowns, and arm bars. I think that if you mix it up every day then you don't get bored and it keeps the training fun.

Q: Do you train with any one person in particular?

A: Just whoever is there. It depends on the day. When I am in the U.S. I try to improve my skills in many different areas because there are a lot of good guys outside jiu-jitsu. So I train boxing, wrestling, and whatever. I don't limit myself. Some schools only want you to train at their school, but I am not like that. I like to learn from everybody in order to improve. The key of training is that you can't have too many rules. You can't say don't train here, or don't train there. Of course, I'm not going to train my opponent, or the opponent of someone on my team. But I can train with other guys. I don't have rules like that.

In the group of people I train with, we don't compete that way when we train. We think more about technique than about not tapping. On a certain day I might tap to a white belt if I'm in a certain position and want to put myself in danger and see if I can get out of it. We want to learn from each other so we don't have a lot of ego in the school.

Q: How many hours total do you train each day?

A: Four, six, or eight hours depending on what I'm training for-submission or vale tudo or boxing or whatever. It varies according to how close my fight is also. There are a lot of variable. Like I say, I train hard but I try to be smart and flexible. I control my training, I don't let my training control me. If I'm hurt I take it easy. If I'm tired I rest. If I'm sick I don't push it. But if I'm healthy and feeling good then I will train like a madman. I like to train with Paulo Caruso for my overall physical training. A lot of the fighters there train with him for strength, fitness, endurance, balance, and agility. Everyone who trains with him improves. I trust what he tells me 100 percent. He is the most important of all my trainers. With him I do specific training for fighting. We don't just lift weights, for example, we do specific types of training that works individual motions that you would use in the ring. He was a black belt in jiu-jitsu, then he got degrees in physical training-so he really understands the fight game and what fighters need.

Q: Do you follow a special diet?

A: I try to eat healthy but I do eat my junk food, too. I'm young so I don't worry about that so much. A lot of the fighters are older than me and so they worry about their diet because they need every advantage. When I'm older I will probably start to worry about it. I'm a regular person so I eat normal. The only thing I avoid is a lot of sugar and a lot of fat. I don't take a lot of supplements. Because I have a strong body a lot of people assume that I lift weights. But I don't lift anymore than I do anything else. I just try to train what I need to be a good fighter, not just to look good.

Q: Which fighters do you enjoyed to watch?

A: I liked to watch Igor Vovchanchyn, Gilbert Yvel, Sakuraba, Vanderlei Silva, Tito Ortiz, Frank Shamrock, Coleman, Renzo Gracie, Pedro Rizzo-I like a lot of fighters. I'm a fan of the sport as well as someone who competes. They are all so good. When I was a kid growing up I really liked Liborio, and Murillo and a lot of people I used to train with who were black belts when I was not. I still like them a lot. When I was a kid I saw them as an inspiration. And not just them. I liked Rickson Gracie at that time, who was training and fighting a lot. Everyone looked up to him. I learned a lot from watching all the top fighters. Royce, of course, was a big inspiration when the UFC first started. For me, Renzo Gracie is great. He always fights the tough guys-the top guys-and he doesn't care who he fights. He'll fight anyone. I really like him. He doesn't lie about his record and he doesn't make excuses when he loses. He just does his thing like everyone else.

Q: Did you feel a little like a Gracie, from being with Carlson so long?

A: Of course, a little. I was training with him before vale tudo really took off. But I think the mentality of some of the Gracie family is wrong. Some don't like to show all the techniques, they don't like you to train hard with them, they don't want you to train with anyone else or they'll kick you out of their school-that is not right. Jiu-jitsu should be shared not hidden. Otherwise how can it improve? Just because someone is from another school, why is it wrong to train with them? So what if he is a wrestler or a sambo player and you are a guy who does jiu-jitsu. So what? Let's train hard, fight hard, and let the best guy win. Afterwards, lets have a drink. They are my opponents, not my enemies. I like that they are good because they give me someone to fight who helps me to make money. They let me enjoy my life. I have to love my opponent for what he does for me. They support my family and my needs. I want to win but I don't want to hurt anyone.

Q: Is it difficult to live up to your reputation?

A: I know people expected me to get a 10 second knockout every time I fought, but I tried not to think about that. Everybody has an ego but I don't like to think that I'm great or wonderful or unbeatable. I like to remind myself that I'm just beginning-that I have a lot to learn still. I try to think of myself as a regular person and to live like one. I don't want to believe my own press. I want to fight and to not be part of the hype about myself. I'll leave that to other people-to the promoters and the writers. I'm just a guy who wants to live simply, enjoy life, and prove I can do good.

Q: Where would you like to be in five years?

A: In five years I would like to be regarded as someone who increased his learning in life and helped others to realize they could also achieve their goals. I think that we're here in life to learn. We learn until the day that we go out of this planet and move on. I want to enjoy and learn and I want people to look at me and say, "That guy, you know, he was a great fighter and also a great person." You don't need to be rich or famous to live good. Sometimes the rich live worse than the poor. If you're rich inside with family and friends then it doesn't matter how much money you have. I want to help people in ways that money cannot buy. Maybe by seeing what I do, they can see that they can achieve their goals also. I just want to live a good life. Just don't forget that tomorrow is a promissory note, yesterday is a cancelled check, and today is cash on hand.

WALLID ISMAEL

The Desire to Win

YOU MIGHT NOT LOVE WALLID ISMAEL, YOU MIGHT NOT CARE ABOUT HIM, OR YOU MIGHT JUST PLAIN DISLIKE HIM. BUT WHATEVER YOUR FEELINGS ABOUT HIM, YOU HAVE TO RESPECT HIM. BORN IN THE AMAZON RAIN FOREST, ISMAEL, THROUGH THE SHEER FORCE OF HIS DESIRE TO BETTER HIMSELF, WORKED HIMSELF INTO A POSITION WHERE HE COULD PULL-OFF ONE OF THE GREATEST UPSETS IN THE MARTIAL ARTS HISTORY. IN BEATING ROYCE GRACIE, A TRULY GREAT FIGHTER IN HIS OWN RIGHT, WALLID PROVED THAT DESIRE AND HARD WORK COUNT FOR AT LEAST AS MUCH, IF NOT MORE, THAN NATURAL TALENT OR PHYSICAL STATURE. THE BIGGEST THINGS ABOUT THIS WORLD JIU-JITSU CHAMPION ARE HIS HEART AND HIS FIERCE DESIRE TO WIN. WITH THE KIND OF WORK ETHIC THAT SURROUNDS HIS LIFE IT IS NO WONDER THAT HE FEELS SO CONFIDENT EVERY TIME HE STEPS ONTO THE MAT. ALL WHAT HE HAS ACHIEVED, HAS NOTHING TO DO WITH LUCK. HE SIMPLY BELIEVES IN HIMSELF. THERE IS A LESSON THERE FOR ALL OF US.

Q: How old are you and how long have you been training Jiu-Jitsu?

A: I am thirty-years old and have trained Jiu-Jitsu for twenty years.

Q: Do you believe Jiu-Jitsu to be superior to the other martial arts?

A: Let me tell you this: Jiu-Jitsu is an exceptional art. I respect all arts, but if you don't know Jiu-Jitsu, your art is not complete. Everyone who fights standing needs to know some of it, the same way a Jiu-Jitsu fighter also needs to know some boxing, some taekwondo or karate. I can box, I can wrestle a little and I've studied taekwondo. One art complements the other. I love martial arts and I love to fight! But every fight ends up body against body. Nowadays lots of people are training Jiu-Jitsu. Do you know Frank Shamrock's arm lock? That's Jiu-Jitsu! Mark Kerr can defend the arm-lock because he also trains Jiu-Jitsu. If a fighter doesn't know Jiu-Jitsu he is like a defenseless child. Why? Because, like I said before, every combat ends body against body. You see this in boxing matches, don't you? They clinch. Every fight will end on the floor.

Q: Would you describe your training routine?

A: I train vigorously. I run three-times a week for 45 minutes. I train eight-hours a day: four hours of Jiu-Jitsu and four hours of working out. It used to be that a Jiu-Jitsu fighter did not need to work out a lot since no one knew Jiu-Jitsu and it was easy to win any fight. Nowadays, everyone is training Jiu-Jitsu. Without good physical conditioning the defeat will be certain! And that's true for sport Jiu-Jitsu and Vale Tudo as well. I also practice yoga. That's a very important part of my training. I do it for relaxation and breathing, since I am by nature a very agitated individual.

Q: What about your diet?

A: For a while I did the Gracie diet but mine is a little more radical. I keep a vegetarian diet. For protein supplements I use protein shakes and a lot of egg whites and soy. I've followed this diet for fifteen years.

Q: What are your best Jiu-Jitsu techniques?

A: I am good at passing people's guard, and I train how to defend my guard a lot. Sometimes people say I only like the game from the top. At the academy, Carlson makes me train the guard all the time. My trainers and Bebeu, always make me do the guard. But when the fight is on I go right to the top. It's a warrior's thing, you know?

Q: What are your best submissions?

A: The side arm-lock and the back submission are my best. That's how I finished Royce.

Q: Why do you do so well fighting the Gracies when they are feared by so many?

A: I don't just do well fighting the Gracies, I do well fighting anyone. The Gracies are just like any others for me. I do well because I train and study Jiu-Jitsu a lot. It is the chess of the body for the very intelligent. I do five or six fights a year. My best fights were not even against the Gracies. I've been world champion at the IBF, the Ultimate Japan Superfight and the Luta Livre. I've always been a champion. I've lost a few, but that's normal.

Q: Did you ever thought that your defeat of Royce Gracie was going to mean the end of the Gracies?

A: Absolutely not! A few defeats will not end seventy-five years of tradition. Hopefully what I did was to end the myth that you have to be a Gracie to be a great Jiu-Jitsu fighter. That is an absurd idea. I believe as a result of this last fight, Jiu-Jitsu will grow in popularity in America because it showed Americans that they can be as good as a Gracie without being one. The Gracies still have their place, but I also wanted mine. I've always thought it to be wrong when they boasted to be the only ones who could teach Jiu-Jitsu. This is the greatest lie! I've shown them I can beat them, and will go on winning many other fights.

Q: Can you describe your classic fight with Royce?

A: The fight lasted almost five minutes. It was a tough fight. Royce has very good technique. We started standing, one trying to drop the other down. When I went for his legs he threw me down. I fell underneath but turned quickly, held his legs, and put him down. Tough fight. His technique is good. I tried to go behind his back and he placed me under his guard. He defended his guard and tried to get me in a triangle and to choke me, while I kept trying to go to one side then another. Suddenly, when I was trying to go to one side, I reversed direction and went the other way. I finally got to his side and he turned his back and stood up. I brought him down with a leg hook-I don't remember exactly-at one point he gave me his back. When he stood up I tried a hook to bring him down; I was on his back and fell with my hand reaching for his neck. I got hold of his neck with one hand on the collar, coming from underneath the arm, and the other hand on the collar on the neck. All I did was squeeze and squeeze. He tried to get away by doing everything right, everything by the book. However, it is part of the game: one wins, one loses. I went on and finalized it, but he never tapped out. He tried to fight it to the last minute and then fell quiet and fainted. I didn't realize that he had fainted, neither did the referee, until Rorion stormed into the mat and begged the referee to stop the fight.

> **"I think the hardest fight is the everyday fight of training. The fight to give up parties and the other bad temptations of life."**

Q: Did Carlson Gracie, Royce's cousin, teach you any specific techniques to beat him?

A: No, he did not teach me anything specific. It was all strategy. Royce had been invincible for so many years because he is a very intelligent, good, fighter. I was also invincible for 15 years. But we are, after all, human and sometimes we fail. I won the fight not because of luck. I won because my Jiu-Jitsu is a great deal superior to his.

Q: What were your expectations? Were you surprised at your swift victory?

A: I had no doubt I would win! I was well prepared. I train Jiu-Jitsu eight-hours a day. When Royce said at a press conference that this fight against me was just a training session I warned him: "Remember Ralph? Remember Renzo?

I am going to finish you up. You think you're leaving L.A.'s cold weather to warm up on Brazil's beaches, but you've got another thing coming. I am going to show you some bad weather, man." This is what I always say to my adversaries.

Q: What other Gracies have you fought and beaten?

A: Very few people know I defeated Ralph and Renzo Gracie before Royce. These were the three greatest Gracies. Listen, I love to fight. I am from the Amazon rain forest, which means I grew up with nothing. Everything I have came from Jiu-Jitsu. My home was at the Jiu-Jitsu school. There I slept at night and trained all day. All I wanted to do was to fight. I had been on a winning spree for a while which provoked some jealousy from the Gracies. They never want to see anyone do well but themselves. So they prepared Ralph to fight me. We had a ten-minute fight, which I won without much difficulty. Three years later Renzo came along. He was training a lot and winning many competitions. With all the titles he earned, the word went out that he was better than I was. They dared me to fight him and I took up the challenge. I am not one to be afraid. Renzo soon wanted to impose conditions. First he said he wanted a 30-minute match, to which I said yes. Then he changed his mind and wanted a one-hour match. I said, fine! I drive them crazy because I accept any condition they come up with.

> "I always see a fighter's career as a roller coaster: one day you may be at the top, the other at the bottom."

I fought him for an hour. It was an unbelievable match. Renzo remained under me like a child, not able to move! There were no rounds and I scored 12 and he nothing. So the one everyone expected to win spent one hour on the defensive. It was like I was fighting alone! Then my name exploded in Brazil and I became the most popular Jiu-Jitsu fighter. After that I won many Vale Tudos, and lost a few, but I kept on fighting.

Q: Do you feel a part of Gracie Jiu-Jitsu or do you feel like a traitor? After all, you defeated the most famous member of the Gracie family.

A: I am glad you asked that! I am a Jiu-Jitsu fighter and I fight for Carlson Gracie. While his family has tried to hide his name, I have always tried to bring the name Carlson Gracie to the forefront. But there is only one Jiu-Jitsu, Brazilian Jiu-Jitsu. There is no difference between Brazilian and

Gracie Jiu-Jitsu. This is all a marketing strategy invented by the Gracies. There are several excellent Jiu-Jitsu teachers in the U.S.-Carlson, Franco, and teachers from the Carlson team, to name just a few-who do not carry the Gracie last name. Bill Goupa once said, "Hey, Carlson, now is the time for Wallid Ismail Jiu-Jitsu! I said no! It is the time of the one and only Jiu-Jitsu, the one we all know, Brazilian Jiu-Jitsu! And I hope it will become the world's Jiu-Jitsu, because if we limit it we'll lose it. If the Americans, the French, or any others start to get good at it, it will just keep improving and growing. Only the incompetent, the ones who don't want to train a lot, want to keep it a secret.

Q: Some of the best Jiu-Jitsu fighters train with Carlson Gracie. Do you believe him to be the best teacher in the world?

A: I don't think there is any doubt about that. It has been proven again and again. Show me a good fight and you'll be see the Carlson team right there. The Carlson team doesn't pick fights, we just fight them!

Q: Which would you rather fight: Jiu-Jitsu or Vale Tudo?

A: I would rather just fight anything. But I love to fight in Vale Tudo because I love to punch. Funny thing about me, I love to punch. Sometimes I even cause my opponent to loose consciousness. The times I lost were because I wanted to punch where I should be using Jiu-Jitsu technique. Vale tudo is in my blood and I'm not afraid. A fighter is not the one who knows only how to hit, but knows also how to be hit.

Q: You have a reputation of winning the most difficult fights but loosing the easiest ones. What do you say to that?

A: I haven't lost many times, just twice. The first one, at the Ultimate Fighting, I thought it would be very easy. But what happened was my opponent held on to the fence and I got tired. I lost not because of inferior technique, but because of fatigue. The second one I also thought would be easy. Again I lost it because of fatigue, my technique being still superior. It is an interesting question because I realize I only lost when I was sure of the victory. But that's the way, that's just life. I have, though, challenged these same adversaries for a rematch but they did not want it. If I were given that opportunity I would then fight totally focused as I would on my more important fights.

Q: In your opinion, who are the five best Jiu-Jitsu fighters and the best Vale Tudo fighters in the world?

A: I don't want to answer that because I may leave somebody out. Besides, it's not a good idea to point to one or the other as being the best. I'll end up contradicting myself since I've always said the best is really God. There will always be fighters who are better than others at any given time, but to me the best will always be God.

Q: What was the hardest fight you've ever had?

A: I think the hardest fight is the everyday fight of training. The fight to give up parties and the other bad temptations of life. Especially for a successful fighter the opportunities for going the wrong way are always there: the parties, the alcohol, the drugs, and the women. A strong spirit is necessary to choose the right way and not the bad. I only believe in my success if I'm still training hard. I respect everybody who fights and doesn't run away from fights.

Q: What was the hardest time in your career as an athlete?

A: I always se a fighter's career as a roller coaster: one day you may be at the top, the other at the bottom. One needs to have a strong spirit not to be taken by the extremes: at the top not to let it go to your head and at the bottom not to let it defeat you. One needs to keep balanced. That is what I told my wife when, at my first defeat, people tried to put me down. People tried to denigrate my name, the way they are doing to Royce now. That's why I defend him today. These people are like hyenas. They don't attack the lion when it's healthy and strong. They lurk in the shadows, waiting for the day the lion has been hurt. I'm going to continue to train really hard, keeping my body in shape.

"**Believe strongly that the world is in your side, as long as you stay loyal to the best of yourself.**"

~ Carlos Gracie Sr. ~

WANDER BRAGA

Quietness and Confidence

THE ANCIENT PROPHET ISAIAH, SPEAKING IN THE OLD TESTAMENT, SAID TO HIS FOLLOWERS, "IN QUIETNESS AND CONFIDENCE SHALL BE YOUR STRENGTH." THOSE SAME WORDS DEFINITELY APPLY TO MODERN BRAZILIAN JIU-JITSU COMPETITOR AND INSTRUCTOR WANDER BRAGA. WITH A FIRM BELIEF IN FAMILY AND FRIENDS, AND A JIU-JITSU WORK ETHIC THAT HAS EARNED HIM NUMEROUS NATIONAL AND INTERNATIONAL UPPER ECHELON FINISHES, BRAGA IS LIVING PROOF THAT YOU DON'T HAVE TO BE LOUD TO BE TOUGH.

BORN AND RAISED IN BRAZIL, GAINED FANS AND STUDENTS ALIKE DRAWN TO HIS BALANCED AND FRIENDLY APPROACH TO TEACHING BRAZILIAN JIU-JITSU IN LOS ANGELES. BUT MAKE NO MISTAKE, THIS WINNER OF NUMEROUS BRAZILIAN VALE TUDO (MMA) MATCHES CAN BRING IT ON IF HE WANTS – BUT HE'LL BE LIKELY TO SHAKE YOUR HAND AFTER A FIGHT, REGARDLESS OF THE OUTCOME. HUMBLENESS, ACCORDING TO BRAGA, IS THE TRUE QUALITY OF CHAMPIONS: "BEING HUMBLE MEANS HAVING AN OPEN ATTITUDE TO LEARN AND GAIN KNOWLEDGE, AND TO ENDURE SWEAT AND PAIN WHILE TRYING TO IMPROVE YOUR SKILLS. IT MEANS THINKING THAT YOU ARE STILL A BEGINNER AND STILL HAVE A LOT TO LEARN. IF YOU HAVE THAT IMPORTANT QUALITY, EVERYTHING ELSE WILL BE POSSIBLE BECAUSE YOU'VE GOT A STRONG FOUNDATION TO BUILD ON."

Q: How long have you been practicing Brazilian jiu-jitsu?

A: Almost two decades – and I haven't lost any interest since the first day I stepped on the mat. It is a kind of love story. I can't think of my life without thinking of jiu-jitsu. What I am today is a direct product of the philosophy and teachings of the art. Because I started early, most of the influences that made me as a man came from my friends and teachers in jiu-jitsu. My first and only teacher is Jorge Pereira and I owe him a lot.

Q: Have you ever trained in other martial arts?

A: When I was very young I trained karate a little. Recently I have been practicing boxing since I teach jiu-jitsu at L.A. Boxing, one of the top gyms in the world. I believe boxing is a perfect compliment for jiu-jitsu because it teaches how to use hands effectively. I am seriously thinking about becoming a professional boxer. I really love it. It is a great sport and a very effective fighting method.

Q: Do you think it is good to learn many martial arts styles?

A: In general, if you learn 10 different martial arts styles you will just end up being confused. If you only want to practice self-defense then there is no reason to train in anything but Brazilian jiu-jitsu. But if you are serious about vale tudo then you should train boxing, muay Thai or other striking arts. You need to learn how to use punches and kicks as well as protect against them. If you are a jiu-jitsu man, though, don't step into the ring and try to kickbox with a kickboxer! Stick to what you know best and what you've been practicing. That's what you'll really have a feel for.

Q: What kind of training drills did Jorge Pereira do to help you get a "feel" for jiu-jitsu?

A: When I was yellow belt, Jorge used to turn off the lights and we would all start to slap each other. Imagine the situation – no lights and everybody slapping everybody! It was fun but also a very helpful drill for you to feel what is going on around you. Human beings rely too much on sight and once this is out of the equation the whole world changes. Your body needs to read the opponent's actions by feel. Keeping your eyes open gives you a sense of location – not only of your opponent but also of your own space and position. This is very important in both jiu-jitsu and in vale tudo.

Q: Do you remember your first vale tudo fight?

A: I was ready to fight in a vale tudo tournament but my opponent, a capoeira fighter, backed out and so I was going to get to go to the finals without fighting. I thought that was pretty cool. But for some reason it made Jorge mad and so he grabbed the microphone and challenged the whole capoeira team to find someone with enough guts to face me! The bad part was that the event was in their home town and I thought the whole team was going to go after me! So they finally found another guy to fight me – there went my free trip to the finals. Jorge came to me and said:

"If you don't beat this guy, we'll never be able to show our face in this town again." I fought the guy and after 15 minutes he gave up. I then won the final fight and the title. We managed to leave the town in one piece and I got my black belt from my teacher. To this day I'm not sure if Jorge did me a favor or not!

Q: Did jiu-jitsu movements come easy to you?

A: I believe I had some natural skill that helped me in the beginning – but if I wouldn't have trained every day I still wouldn't have progressed. Having talent and being gifted physically only means so much. You may have all the physical ability in the world, but if you don't sweat on the mat every day you won't become a champion. In the long run it is consistency and dedication that makes the difference. Strangely enough, those who quit in the early stages of training, after only a couple of years, are the ones who have the best natural ability for the sport!

Q: How has your jiu-jitsu evolved over the years?

A: In the past, every time I was competing I used to go for submissions. I was more aggressive and I wanted to be in active control the whole fight. Now, I like to play more of strategic game instead of going crazy for submissions. My game now is more tactical and quiet but at the same time more dangerous. I observe what my opponent does and then act accordingly. I don't rush but neither do I hesitate when I see an opportunity to finish. Scoring points is part of the game but I believe that submissions really exemplify the true essence of the art. But the rules of the game are the rules of the game and you have to know how to use them to your advantage. If you don't do it then your opponent will.

> "I look at jiu-jitsu as an extension of life. In life you don't stop growing and learning new things."

Q: Do you feel that you still have more to learn?

A: Definitely. I look at jiu-jitsu as an extension of life. In life you don't stop growing and learning new things. I believe that we always have something new to learn – I don't understand those who claim otherwise. Well, maybe if you're Helio Gracie there is nothing new and better, but it doesn't mean that you know everything he does. I like to read new books and watch videos whenever I can to absorb more information. That helps me to improve my technical level and better understand how the different aspects and elements of the art work together. I think it is very important to compete as much as possible because the art is evolving and there is always a new twist for an old technique. Competing gives you an edge that is impossible to have otherwise.

Q: What is the best way for beginning students to improve?

A: Set goals according to each level of your training and practice consistently. Beginners should learn the basics because they need to establish a solid foundation for the more advanced techniques. It is true, though, that many people get bored and discouraged so they start focusing more on different movements instead of working on the basics. This can be more appealing in the beginning but when the years pass by and you face an opponent who has a sound knowledge and skill of the basics, you'll find out that you are lacking something. Even if new techniques and movements appear, they all are based on the fundamentals and are simply a personal expression.

Q: As a black belt, is it hard to stay sharp in the U.S.?

A: In America, the fighters and top instructors coming from Brazil don't have many black belts to train with. This prevents Brazilian competitors from keeping the same competition level they had in Brazil. I'm confident things will change in the near future but still there is a big technical gap.

Q: Who do you admire in jiu-jitsu?

A: I have always admired Rickson Gracie and I'm lucky to have had the opportunity to train with him. Honestly, everything you hear about him is true and sometimes what people say doesn't truly describe how good he is. Not only he is an excellent technician but he also knows how to teach any kind of student from a white belt to an advanced instructor or to a world champion. His ability to relate to any kind of student is amazing.

Q: What would you say to someone who is interested in starting jiu-jitsu?

A: It is important for a student to know what they are looking for and what their priorities are. Do they want to learn self-defense or just be in good physical shape? Do they want to focus on sport competition, vale tudo, or both? Once the student has an idea then visit a school and watch the teacher. Observe how he relates to the students and how he breaks down the techniques. Talk to the teacher and get a feel for what kind of individual he is. Get a feel for the students and how they act. Jiu-jitsu is a great exercise and you'll be spending a lot of time at the school. You want to make sure that the people at the school are the kind of individuals that will bring positive things into your life.

> "It is important for a student to know what they are looking for and what their priorities are. Do they want to learn self-defense or just be in good physical shape?"

Q: What keeps you motivated after all these years?

A: Competition. Tournaments and competitions keep me going forward every day. Every competition is a new challenge and I train hard and give my best so I will perform at the level I expect. My students and my family are also a big motivational factor. I am a simple individual who loves simple things. In jiu-jitsu, stick to the basics and make sure you master those. In life, stick to the people that you love and who love you back and focus on things that make you grow. The important things are family, good friends, and health – put the rest aside. Good people bring good energy. And good energy brings success. Don't get me wrong, when I say "success" I don't necessarily mean money and fame! Having a family that supports you and loves you and having good friends that you can rely on is already a great success.

Q: How do you mentally prepare for a tournament?

A: I'm a quiet guy so I don't get out of control. Relaxation is very important before a match, and so I will visualize how things might happen and go through different scenarios. This makes me feel more confident and prepared. I also love to go to the beach and relax there. Jiu-jitsu it is an art where you need to be relaxed in order to give your best. Of course, this is very easy to say and very hard to accomplish. Everybody talks about relaxation but they don't explain how to achieve it.

Q: How do you achieve relaxation?

A: Number one is proper breathing. You need to keep your breathing pattern under control. The timing of the breath has to be steady and consistent under any circumstances. You also need to be confident of your technical ability. No confidence, no calmness. No calmness and you'll begin to gasp for air like crazy. In order to have confidence in your technique, you need to have proper training in the fundamentals so they become automatic reflexes. Only then can you be relaxed in a fight.

Q: Does jiu-jitsu have a spiritual side?

A: I think so. It definitely requires introspection. I have always tried to develop positive qualities such as humbleness, dedication, willpower and positive attitude. Don't give up when things get tough and always remember that there are many different way of achieving what you want. Don't think you are superior or better than anybody. Be realistic about your goals and your potential.

Q: Do people sometimes set goals they can't achieve?

A: We all have to be realistic about our own potential and abilities. We need to know our limitations so we can excel. Maybe a student doesn't have the potential to be a world champion – very few do. So the teacher needs to motivate the student and get the best out of him without making him believe impossible things. He needs to help the students to see their potential without creating false expectations. The same thing goes the other way, too. Teachers who constantly run students down also is bad. Be positive but be realistic. There is a big responsibility on the teacher's shoulders in this regard.

Q: What is the most important mental quality of a successful jiu-jitsu fighter?

A: Humbleness. This is a basic quality that everybody talks about but very few people have. Being humble means having an open attitude to learn and gain knowledge, and to endure sweat and pain while trying to improve your skills. It means thinking that you are still a beginner and still have a lot to learn. If you have that important quality, everything else will be possible because you've got a strong foundation to build on.

Q: What is the most important physical quality?

A: Try to be in good shape all the time. Keep your body clean and follow a good nutrition plan. Food is the fuel of your body. Be careful what kind of food you eat because it will directly effect the way you perform in competition and training. Keep your cardiovascular training up and eat a balanced diet.

Q: What do you think can be done to improve the sport?

A: I believe that Brazilian jiu-jitsu can become an Olympic sport. A lot of things need to be done to fulfill the requirements of the International Olympic Committee for the sport has to be practiced in each continent. It will take a lot of hard work to accomplish that but with the growing support from fans, practitioners, and governments around the world I don't see why can't become a reality. In mixed martial arts I believe that fighters should be taken into consideration much more than they are now. They should get paid bigger sums of money because they are the ones making everything possible. As the sport grows and the crowds get bigger in the U.S. I think it will happen.

Q: What does jiu-jitsu mean to you?

A: Jiu-jitsu is an extremely important part of my life. It gave me direction when I was young, and gave me the opportunity to meet great people that I have developed close ties and relationships with. Professionally, it is my job and I put myself into it as much as I can. All my existence evolves around jiu-jitsu and only my family is more important to me. I am truly grateful to the Gracie family for developing this great art and for working hard to spread it around the world.

"Jiu-jitsu is personal efficiency to protect the weaker, which anyone can do. It is the force of leverage against brute force."
~ Helio Gracie ~

GERSON SANGINITTO

Generation X-cellent

WHEN THE ART OF BRAZILIAN JIU-JITSU TOOK THE WORLD IN EARLY '90S, THE TWO MOST SIGNIFICANT FAMILIES TO SPREAD THE ART AND SERVE AS A SOURCE OF WORLDWIDE KNOWLEDGE WERE THE GRACIES AND THE MACHADOS. A DECADE AFTER ROYCE GRACIE WON THE FIRST UFC, HOWEVER, A SECOND GENERATION OF CAPABLE INSTRUCTORS HAS TAKEN ON THE RESPONSIBILITY OF SHARING AND UPDATING THE TECHNICAL ASPECTS OF THE ART. MANY THINGS HAVE CHANGED IN BRAZILIAN JIU-JITSU, DUE TO THE HIGHLY CHARGED COMPETITION ATMOSPHERE, AND NEW TECHNICAL DEVELOPMENTS HAVE MADE SOME OF THE TECHNIQUES USED AS RECENTLY AS TEN YEARS AGO OBSOLETE.

GERSON SANGINITTO IS ONE OF THE SECOND GENERATION OF BRAZILIAN JIU-JITSU INSTRUCTORS, AND HAS BEEN TEACHING IN THE UNITED STATES FOR MORE THAN FIVE YEARS. HIS KNOWLEDGE OF THE GRAPPLING ARTS IS NOT JUST LIMITED TO THE COVETED RANK OF FAIXA PRETA (BLACK BELT) IN BRAZILIAN JIU-JITSU, BUT ALSO HOLDS A BLACK BELT IN JAPANESE JUDO. THIS IS A COMBINATION THAT MANY TOP BRAZILIAN FIGHTERS AND INSTRUCTORS CONSIDER EXCEPTIONAL, DUE TO THE DIFFERENT EMPHASIS THE TWO ARTS PUT ONTO THROWING TECHNIQUES (JUDO) AND GROUND TECHNIQUES (BRAZILIAN JIU-JITSU).

A DIRECT STUDENT OF THE PRESIDENT OF THE BRAZILIAN JIU-JITSU FEDERATION, CARLOS GRACIE JR., SANGINITTO HAS SHARED MANY HOURS OF TRAINING WITH SOME OF THE TOP-NAMES OF JIU-JITSU, INCLUDING BOTH RIGAN MACHADO AND RENZO GRACIE. IN MANY WAYS, IT IS SAFE TO SAY THAT THE FUTURE OF THE BRAZILIAN ART IS IN THE HANDS OF THIS NEW GENERATION OF YOUNG TEACHERS WHO STILL HAVE THE PASSION AND DRIVE TO TEACH A FIRST-DAY WHITE BELT WITH THE SAME MOTIVATION THEY HAVE WHEN THEY IMPART KNOWLEDGE TO A CLASS FULL OF BLACK BELTS.

Q: How long have you been practicing martial arts?

A: I started in 1973 and I haven't stopped since. I haven't trained specifically in any other styles than grappling. I started judo first, and then began jiu-jitsu in 1984. As far as other martial arts systems like kung-fu, taekwondo, and karate, I never trained steadily, although through friends I have been exposed to them. My teacher is Carlos Gracie Jr. but there also are many people who have taught me a lot about jiu-jitsu. These include Paulo Cesar Mulatinho, Rigan Machado, Renzo Gracie, and Antonio Rodrigues.

Q: Have you ever had to use jiu-jitsu in a real fight?

A: Back in the '80s, in my early 2's, a friend of mine invited me to go to Ipanema to visit a karate academy and learn some of their moves. At first, we were only exchanging techniques in a friendly manner. But when it came to free training, things changed a little. I started to train with one of the instructors. He surprised me and came after me and really wanted to beat me up. I was thinking that this was going to be just an easy practice of the punches and kick I had just learned. But instead, the guy came at me right away and surprised me and gave me a fat lip. After his punch, I went after him to tap him out. I was not trying to punch him back, but I was enraged and wanted to prove that my technique was more effective than his. So I went for a double leg, took him down, mounted him, and then all of a sudden changed my mind and started to punch the guy in the face. I kept going until my friends finally made me stop. I guess that was my first vale tudo and the end of my karate training.

Q: Were you a natural at jiu-jitsu?

A: I don't know if I would say it that strongly, but I did learn the movements very easily. I remember that when I got my blue belt, I became an instructor for beginners because I always had a certain skill for teaching. It was probably because I always liked to teach, and I truly enjoy doing it. I guess the main reason why I was fast at learning jiu-jitsu was because of my judo training. I really think that my previous training in judo helped me a lot in my jiu-jitsu evolution. I was very comfortable with the idea of grabbing an opponent and grappling them on the ground. My transition to jiu-jitsu was very smooth and easy. Of course, there were aspects that were more difficult to absorb, but the idea of the grappling game was already in my body.

Q: Do you like vale tudo events such as UFC and Pride?

A: It's great exposure for jiu-jtsu fighters and for jiu-jitsu itself – these events demonstrate the effectiveness of Brazilian jiu-jitsu. Groundwork was something that nobody knew before the UFC. Royce Gracie opened doors for a lot of people because he showed martial artists from other styles how much it helped to have a knowledge of grappling. In general, I believe that all mixed martial arts events are positive. They bring publicity to all the martial arts and they help the sport of grappling to be recognized and to grow. When it comes to the athletes themselves, they acquire the added bonus of personal recognition and a little extra income. Fighters who participate in these events have to be extremely dedicated professionals. It is a job that requires hard training and full concentration. Besides building inner strength, the athletes learn different styles so they can understand and defend themselves against all attacks. So, I feel MMA helps the technical aspects of all martial arts to improve.

Q: Do you think that jiu-jitsu in America has caught up with jiu-jitsu in Brazil?

A: American students definitely are improving, but they are not quite there yet. Jiu-jitsu has been a mainstream martial art in Brazil since the early '80s and has been practiced since the early '20s. Also, the number of practitioners is a lot higher and the number of competitions is incredible – there are events every weekend. However, now there are many top Brazilian instructors living in the U.S. and they have American students who have a natural ability for the art. I'd say that pretty soon the Americans are going to get even with Brazil. But for now, Brazil still is number one.

Q: Do you feel that you have more to learn?

A: Definitely. A big part of jiu-jitsu is learning something every day – especially since jiu-jitsu is a growing and evolving art. It is in constant development. This is true not only in techniques, but also in regard to new strategies and tactics to use against different opponents. Skillful and creative fighters always are creating new positions and improving the game. So, we always are learning and implementing our knowledge with each other. As a practitioner and as an instructor, my schedules are different. As a practitioner, I use more time to build my physical conditioning, while as an instructor I have to dedicate time to planning out the best strategy for teaching a class. It is important that my students fully understand the principles of the art and consequently keep improving their game, endurance, and confidence. That takes planning on my part.

> **"Groundwork was something that nobody knew before the UFC. Royce Gracie opened doors for a lot of people."**

Q: What are the major changes in jiu-jitsu since you began training?

A: Brazilian jiu-jitsu has evolved a lot since the early '80s. Initially, BJJ was made up of just the Gracie family and their friends. Nowadays, the media has shown the world how great this martial art is. It started as a small community, but it now has become one of the greatest martial arts in the world. All this has happened without breaking or changing its principles, which proves its strength and effectiveness. A few years ago, the art of jiu-jitsu was more aggressive than it is today. The rules have changed a lot, so all practitioners, including myself, had to adjust our game accordingly. My game had to become extremely strategic and aggressive, since now a single mistake can be lethal. The level of the game is so high that any little mistake can cause you to lose a match. In the old days, for instance, there was a huge difference between a purple belt and a brown belt. Nowadays, you see purple belts giving a real hard time to both brown and black belts. The purple belts may lose in the end, but they give the top guys a run for their money. I think this is good for the art and the sport, because it means the technical level is going up.

Q: Who would you like to personally train with?

A: I would like to train with Rickson Gracie – or at least get on the mat with him just to feel his technique. Carlos Gracie Jr. took us to his academy a few times, but I never have trained with him personally. Everyone is a little different in jiu-jitsu, so it is good to train with all the top people. The strength of jiu-jitsu is in its differences. A person should find the style that best fits his/her aptitude and desire. It is very important for students to find a place where they feel comfortable. Only in the right environment can the right learning and improvement occur. Even now, my passion for the art and for teaching is what keeps me going. It brings me great fulfillment to see my students successfully applying a technique that I taught.

Q: Do you think it is necessary to fight on the street in order to try out jiu-jitsu self-defense techniques?

A: Not really, because nowadays a fighter can have specific training in his own academy and also test his skills in no-holds-barred events. However, if someone has fought a lot in the streets, this person does learn what he is capable of and might have an advantage over a person that does not have such experience. These real situations teach you how to deal effectively with the adrenaline rush, which can work in your favor or against you.

Q: What's your opinion about mixing styles?

A: I think it is good to know more than one style. The goal of an athlete should be to become a complete fighter. However, a person should specialize in one style and enhance his skill with some training in other styles. Brazilian jiu-jitsu requires great dedication and steady training. I don't believe that students should jump from art to art, because in the end they won't achieve full proficiency in any style.

Q: Has Brazilian jiu-jitsu been of personal benefit to you?

A: It brings me great joy and has brought me many new friends. I feel like I'm a part of a big family. It brings discipline, confidence, and attitude. Also, the challenge of competition helps to keep me fresh and excited about the sport. A successful competitor in Brazilian jiu-jitsu has discipline, dedication, persistence, and passion for what he or she does.

> **"Technique is the main thing everyone needs to develop and that only comes from mat time. Hours spent pumping iron won't improve your jiu-jitsu if your technique is not good."**

Natural ability is the start, and these qualities will keep you in the game. But you have to work hard. I guess these qualities are common not only in Brazilian jiu-jitsu, but in any serious competitor from any legitimate sport. It takes these qualities to become a good competitor.

Q: Is supplementary training important?

A: After grappling students have committed themselves to BJJ, they can complement their skills with other types of training. In particular, cardiovascular conditioning is crucial for the jiu-jitsu athlete. Weight training and stretching are also effective tools that with greatly help a fighter. But I always stress the fact that nothing replaces time on the mat. Technique is the main thing everyone needs to develop and that only comes from mat time. Hours spent pumping iron won't improve your jiu-jitsu if your technique is not good. Focus on technique first and then later move to supplementary aspects to enhance your technical skills.

Q: What are your plans for the future?

A: I want to keep teaching for as long as I can.

PEDRO SAUER

THE SILENT WARRIOR

TURN TO PAGE 1,229 OF "THE AMERICAN HERITAGE DICTIONARY" AND YOU'LL FIND THE WORD "SOLID." ONE OF THE DEFINITIONS IS "SUBSTANTIAL AND COMPLETE" AND IT ALSO MEANS "UPSTANDING AND DEPENDABLE, AS IN A SOLID CITIZEN."

SOLID IS AN APPROPRIATE WORD TO DESCRIBE PEDRO SAUER, WHETHER YOU'RE TALKING ABOUT HIS BJJ SKILLS OR HIS LIFE AWAY FROM THE MATS. NOT ONLY DID HE EARN HIS BLACK BELT FROM HELIO AND RICKSON [GRACIE] IN 1985, HE BEGAN HIS CAREER AS AN INSTRUCTOR IN 1986 WHEN ASKED TO TEACH WITH AN ORGANIZATION KNOWN IN BRAZIL AS CORPO/QUATRO (BODY OF FOUR), WHERE HE TAUGHT AND CONTINUED HIS TRAINING UNDER ALVARO BARRETO (A RED BELT UNDER HELIO GRACIE). AFTER MOVING TO UTAH IN 1990, HE TAUGHT AS ONE OF ONLY TWO NON-GRACIE BLACK BELTS UNDER THE GRACIE JIU-JITSU ACADEMY. IN OCTOBER OF 1996, HE BECAME AN OFFICIAL BLACK BELT INSTRUCTOR UNDER THE RICKSON GRACIE AMERICAN JIU-JITSU ASSOCIATION. CURRENTLY, SAUER RUNS HIS MAIN JIU-JITSU ACADEMY IN SALT LAKE CITY, UTAH, AND HE ALSO HAS SEVERAL AFFILIATED SCHOOLS ACROSS THE COUNTRY.

BUT THERE'S MORE TO PEDRO SAUER THAN A RICH JIU-JITSU HERITAGE AND INCREDIBLE PROFICIENCY ON THE MAT. IN COLLEGE, HE WORKED TOWARDS A DOUBLE MAJOR AND TOOK POST-GRADUATION COURSES AT FUNDACAO GETULIO VARGAS. HE WORKED IN BRAZIL AS A STOCKBROKER FOR 11 YEARS BEFORE DECIDING TO MOVE TO THE UNITED STATES AND PURSUE A CAREER TEACHING JIU-JITSU.

THIS IS A MAN WHO WOULD BE IN THE TOP OF HIS FIELD, REGARDLESS OF HIS PROFESSION. LUCKILY FOR US, HE CHOSE BJJ.

Q: How long have you been practicing jiu-jitsu?

A: I have been training in Gracie Jiu-Jitsu for more than 30 years. I have been practicing the martial arts since I was five. Before I discovered jiu-jitsu, I practiced boxing, judo, taekwondo and capoeira.

Q: Who were your jiu-jitsu teachers?

A: Rickson Gracie and Helio Gracie were my main instructors for 16 years. For six of those years, I was fortunate enough to train with Rickson privately. I remember the first time I saw Rickson fight. It was in front of my apartment. Rickson was 15 or 16, a skinny kid and the other guy was a Brazilian marine named Toto. He was 19. They squared off and Rickson took him down right away. He beat Toto so badly that we were all in shock. After the fight, three of Toto's friends (Fumaca, Don Ratao and Bileco) circled around Rickson and started threatening him. Rickson left and went home. After returning home, Helio put Rickson in the car — along with Rolls, Relson and Rorion — and went searching for these guys. Along the way they stopped and asked me where they would hang out, and I told them it was at a gas station on the corner of Marques de Abrantes. When they saw the three guys, Rickson started to chase them but they jumped behind a fence where Rickson could not get in. Three days later Rickson found the three guys in another building and beat up all of them. Rickson is relentless.

Q: Were you naturally skilled at jiu-jitsu?

A: No. I was a little guy who had no real physical abilities, so I had to work a lot harder than my classmates. I was kind of wild when I was young, and I was hanging out with the wrong crowd. Jiu-jitsu helped me mature.

Q: How has your personal jiu-jitsu style developed over the years?

A: I keep an open mind, and I've been on the mat seven days a week for more than 30 years now. I like to study the basics. When I think I know a lot, Helio, Rorion, Rickson, Royler, Rener and Ralek [Gracie] remind me of the little details that make all the difference in the world. The Gracie family is very intelligent and knowledgeable. They have had this "laboratory" for almost 80 years now, and Helio is the main "scientist." Some people say that the Gracies have an old school or conservative style, but many people don't realize that they have seen it all and have had three generations of perfecting their moves.

Q: Do you feel that you are still learning?

A: Of course, I do. Jiu-jitsu is a life-long learning process. Students see the immediate benefits in terms of self-defense, but this is just the beginning of the journey. The real benefits of Gracie Jiu-Jitsu come over time and can have a tremendous impact on anyone's life. I recommend that students continue to train for a lifetime. In order to do that, you must leave your ego outside and be ready to learn. Jiu-jitsu is a long and prosperous journey that will bring happiness to anyone's life. People who know me know that I strive for perfection in a move. I don't like settling for less than a perfect move. Maybe that's why I feel that I am still learning every day.

Q: What do you consider to be the major changes in the world of jiu-jitsu since you began your training?

A: Since the Gracies brought jiu-jitsu to the United States, we have a lot more people training. Our style is being adopted and incorporated in many other styles, changing the look and feel of it. I appreciate the beauty of good technique. The grappling I see lately is very rough and appears to require a lot of strength. But then again, I am spoiled because I was taught by the best.

> "Rickson Gracie and Helio Gracie were my main instructors for 16 years. For six of those years, I was fortunate enough to train with Rickson privately."

Q: What keeps you motivated after all these years?

A: To know that I still have a lot to learn, to see Helio Gracie at 92 on the mat with his sons and grandsons, and my passion for the real art of Gracie Jiu-Jitsu.

Q: Do you think it is necessary to engage in free-fighting to achieve good fighting skills in the street (self-defense)?

A: Testing your skills in the ring or on the mat will give you valuable experience, but I am against streetfighting. Jiu-jitsu should be used in the street only in self-defense.

Q: How do you teach your students to prepare for a fight?

A: Eat healthy, train hard and trust in the amazing art of Gracie Jiu-Jitsu.

Q: What is the philosophical basis for your jiu-jitsu training?

A: I teach my students never to hurt anyone. To hurt someone is to hurt yourself. The true art of Gracie Jiu-Jitsu is to control an opponent and make him submit without injury. That is why more and more law enforcement units are using Gracie Jiu-Jitsu.

Q: Do you have a particularly memorable experience that has remained with you as an inspiration for your training?

A: My constant inspiration is Helio Gracie, Rickson Gracie and the Gracie family.

Q: After all these years of training and experience, could you explain the meaning of the practice of jiu-jitsu for you?

A: To control violence without violence. Knowing how to get out of trouble without panicking and come home safely. Knowing how to stay calm under pressure, how to think fast and deal with bad situations.

Let me give you a funny example of staying calm. Three years ago my wife gave birth to my daughter on the bathroom floor. I saw the baby coming out and had no choice but to stay calm and take control of the situation. I delivered the baby, cleaned her nose and mouth and made sure she was breathing. And then I called 911. I was very proud of myself.

Q: What are the most important qualities of a successful BJJ competitor?

A: Technique is, by far, the most important factor. After that, stamina and physical conditioning.

Q: What advice would you give to students about supplementary training?

A: I would recommend introducing children to wrestling, judo and gymnastics. When they are older and can understand the fine points, teach them to train in slow motion and absorb details.

Q: Describe your personal training and workout system.

A: I have a series of four DVD's that we use as a foundation. Everyone should know this. I'm most happy with how they turned out. They show each move in great detail, as Helio and Rickson taught me. The moves will be new for some and advanced for others.

Q: How do you feel about fear affecting a fighter's performance?

A: Fear is a feeling that all intelligent people must have. It is the key to self-control and taking calculated chances. Gracie Jiu-Jitsu will teach a student self-control and how to be a better person. A confident soul is a peaceful soul. A jiu-jitsu practitioner doesn't feel the need to strike first, because he knows that he is not going to be beaten. This level of confidence allows a person to deal more effectively with the problems of everyday life.

Q: Do you have an association?

A: Yes, we have an association with more than 40 academies affiliated, and there are many real black belts in Gracie Jiu-Jitsu with knowledge in self-defense and, of course, ground work. I believe that many of the best academies in the USA are affiliates, like the Linxx Academy (Eddie Camden), Minnesota Martial Arts (Greg Nelson), Jeff Curram, Joe Gray, Alan Hopkins, Jorge Jimenez, Dave "Spaghetti" Bancroft, Dean Heileman (deceased), Shawn Weaver, John Shibonis, Henry Matamoros, Hal Faulkner, John Freeland, Tony Passos, John "One Eye" Carlquist, Sara Fairbanks, Nestor Bayot, Tim Wetlake, Scott Turner, Matt Strack, Chet Quint, Rick Lundell, Jake Johnston, Jeff Olsen, Eddie Edmunds, Jim Kelly, Reily, Ishamael Bentley, Chris Wells, Keith Owner, Dave Phillips and Jamie. Those are just a few of the brown and black belt affiliates.

Q: Do you have an instructor's certification program?

A: Yes, we do have a great instructor's program for people who have prior experience in martial arts and who would like to develop another part in their game (ground and self-defense). We take the instructor in two phases. The first phase is about 20 hours. The second phase is also about 20 hours and the instructor has to put in another 60 hours so he gets 100. He will receive an instructional DVD. After that, he can start an affiliation with all the members of our organization, and I advise every one to train at the Gracie Academy in Torrance, California, the Rickson Gracie Academy in Santa Monica, California, Renzo Gracie, Fabio Santos, Carlos Valente, Pedro Valente, Rodrigo Vahgi, Cleber Luciano, Claudio Franca, Rodrigo Medeiros in Brazil, Royler Gracie (Humaita), Alvaro Barreto (Copacabana), Renan Pitangui (Recreio), Tere and Jacare (Sao Paulo), Vitor Ribeiro Shaulin (Flamengo). Those are just a few of the people that I recommend that they train with. All the members of our group have total support and incentive to train in other's academies. This enables them to really evaluate with whom they want to be affiliated. When they get back, they share the moves with everyone else, so we never stop learning.

Q: Do you have a children's program?

A: Yes, we start with children at four years old. This system goes until the student reaches the age of 16 and then transfers over into the adult ranking system. We just signed four children into a grappling tournament, and we came home with four gold medals. These kids have no idea the benefits they are getting. In the future, the mind and body coordination they are getting will be a priceless asset. We believe that when a child learns how to control fear, he will become a very respectful adult.

Q: What are your hobbies?

A: I am a mechanic for German and American cars. One of my projects now is restoring a 1977 Porsche convertible, twin turbo with almost 600 horsepower. I am also finishing up restoring a 1960 Impala Nomad. Prior to that, I restored a 1968 Pontiac Firebird with a big block.

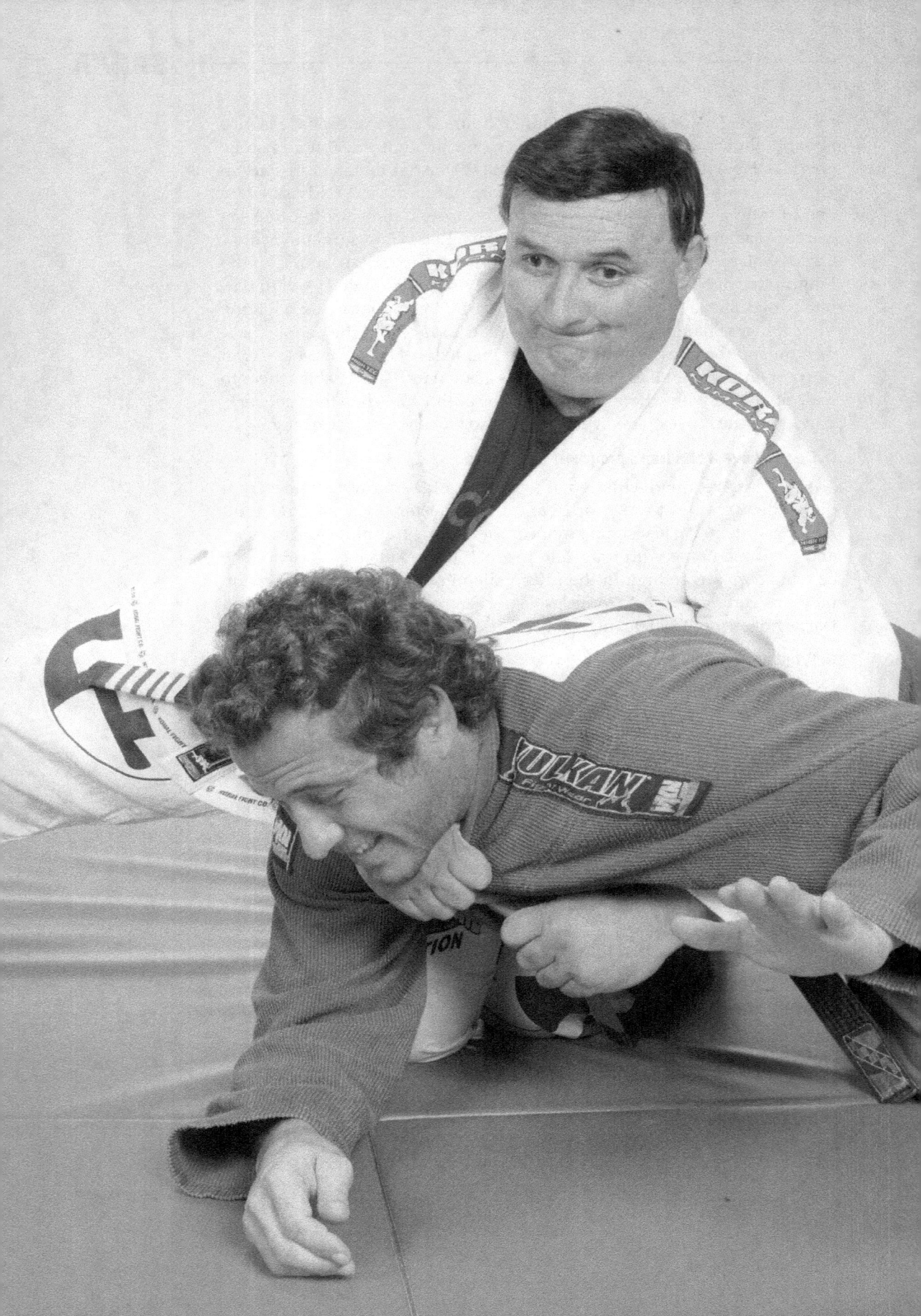

CARLOS VALENTE

Mentor and Professor

WHEN YOU LOOK IN RETROSPECT AT CARLOS VALENTE'S LIFE, YOU HAVE TO JUST SHAKE YOUR HEAD IN ADMIRATION. NOT ONLY DID HE START WITH ROLLS GRACIE, BUT HE SPENT YEARS TRAINING UNDER RICKSON GRACIE. THESE, FOR THE HANDFUL OF YOU WHO DO NOT KNOW, ARE TWO OF THE GREATEST JIU-JITSU STYLISTS EVER. THE INFLUENCE THEY HAD ON VALENTE HAS MOLDED HIM INTO ONE OF THE MOST KNOWLEDGEABLE, TALENTED AND CARING INSTRUCTORS TO EVER STEP ONTO A MAT. ANYWHERE..

IN THE FOLLOWING INTERVIEW, VALENTE DISCUSSES THE EARLY DAYS, THE GRACIES, THE UFCS, HIS CONSCIENTIOUSNESS AND A WHOLE LOT MORE.

Q: You were born in Rio. What was it like?

A: It was a tough neighborhood then. In the old days, Copacabana Beach was tough and famous. If you hung out there, you were sure to have a confrontation.

Q: Why did you start in BJJ?

A: Just like Andre [Galvao], I wanted to be a champion and be recognized as a champion. Then, when I had the belt and the titles, I said there has to be something else. And that turned out to be a mentor, a "psychologist" and a friend [to my students].

Q: When did you get started in Brazilian jiu-jitsu?

A: When I was six, I actually started in judo. By the time I turned eight, I was also doing jiu-jitsu, which happened to be at the first jiu-jitsu academy in Rio. That was in Copacabana Beach.

Q: At that time, how many jiu-jitsu schools were there?

A: In the early 1970s, there were not too many academies. The first academy was in downtown Rio, and Helio Gracie also had an academy downtown. At that time, karate and taekwondo were more popular.

Q: You trained with Rolls Gracie, who was Rickson's older brother. How did you hook up with Rolls?

A: My judo instructor knew the Gracie family. His father used to be a Helio Gracie student way back. Following a conversation between my instructor and father, I ended up in a Gracie school. As I mentioned, I did judo and jiu-jitsu together. When I went into the military (airborne), I was a purple belt in jiu-jitsu. The combination of judo and jiu-jitsu was so perfect. They went along well together.

Q: There were some challenges happening back then. What can you tell us about them?

A: Guys would visit the schools and make the challenge. You have to understand that the Gracie family exploded in the 1970s. This was also a surfer generation. Rolls was a surfer, and Relson and Rickson were surfers. Between surfing and the martial arts, this time in Rio (1970s to 1980s) was a most beautiful time. There was music and guys would hang around. When we finished training, we would go from the jiu-jitsu [mats] to a particular surf spot. Anyway, when a guy challenged the Gracie family, Rolls — who people did not know much about — took him outside and kicked his butt. He just played with him. [Pretty soon though] that Gracie name was getting all over the place. Rolls was the guy during my generation.

Q: You have described Rolls as an innovator. Why?

A: Because he was always searching. Not only did he beat everyone in jiu-jitsu, he used to go to judo tournaments and win everything. He was good in anything that he tried because [he was so] confident. He was good at surfing, he was good at judo. So, he decided to try hang gliding because he was always searching for a new challenge. His death, as a result of the hang gliding accident, was a tragedy.

In the early 1970s, he used to tell all of us that jiu-jitsu was going to grow, and he was going to move to America way before Rorion [Gracie] thought about moving here. Rolls' mom was a flight attendant in the States, so he was fluent in English.

Q: How did Rolls influence you?

A: He had desire, and he was driven by passion. He had so much passion to teach. The way he taught the black belts is the way he taught the white belts. To this day, I tell my students that he is the definition of an instructor. When he walked into a class, if everyone was joking around and talking, they would immediately quiet down. He had their respect, and he had charisma. They looked at him as if he were a guru, and I [always] wanted to be just like him.

He was also a philosopher, and the only one like him is Rickson. [In this respect], Rickson is way beyond everyone. He can touch your head, your emotions and your mind. There is a saying among old Brazilian jiu-jitsu instructors that if you spend time with Rickson that he will bless you for two or three years. Rolls was the same.

So, I want to affect their [my students'] lives every day. I want to teach and adjust the position just a little. But I [also] want to touch them and give them the support they need emotionally.

Q: When did you arrive in the United States?

A: I had been visiting, including going to Hawaii to surf, but I arrived to stay in 1982. I always had the desire to come here.

Q: You also trained under Rickson. How long were you with him?

A: Half of my whole life or maybe even 65 percent. I also learned the philosophy of life from him. For example, [he taught me that] a black belt is not just a belt and a gi is not just a gi. Rickson Gracie gave me my fulfillment as a fighter. In my personal life and business, he set me in the [correct] direction and jiu-jitsu is the thing or the tool that gives me the balance and the emotions to deal with every day life. I have had the opportunity to train with every Gracie member, and no one really has the energy that Rickson has shown. That is why he is ahead. [In my role as instructor], I have taken the tools that Rickson has used to get ahead.

Q: What makes Rickson so good?

A: I asked [his father] Helio [Gracie] why Rickson is better, and he said that Rickson is the one asking more questions [than anyone else]. I can remember the days when Rickson was a purple belt. He showed up and destroyed everyone.

Q: Tell us about Rickson.

A: Everyone has a different view of Rickson. Some think of Rickson Gracie, the fighter in Japan. That image is a powerful guy. When others have the opportunity to meet him, they are not sure how he is going to react. They do not know if he is he cocky or what. Actually, he is a most simple guy. Like the last time I took [Eduardo] Telles to his house. Rickson has done very well for himself and has a beautiful house along the coast. When we got there, he was doing his yard. I told him I had the boys with me, and he told me to bring them in. When we walked in, he made a joke. He's a very simple guy. It blows my mind. Of course, many may have the image of him as the samurai in the ring, but he is as simple as he can be. He will sit at the BBQ and get dirty, and he's the surfer kid. The perfect way to define him is the Rio kid. He's in shorts and surfing and sandals and he loves his kids. He is a regular guy. I credit all of my success to Rickson Gracie. Every time I see him he blows my mind more. I am older than him, but he makes me feel little and makes me feel like a kid. Rickson is the best.

Q: Is Rickson the best fighter of his time?

A: To this day, he still is for me. With the gi or without the gi. To this day, to anyone, to me, he is. He's got a science [to fighting]. It's not just the mental approach. People talk and say he's old or whatever, but people said the same thing about George Foreman. If you think he's old, think again. Rickson Gracie has the same body and is in the same physical condition that he was in 20 something years ago. You are not going to see one scratch or dent in his face. You are never going to see him breathe hard. I have never seen anything like it.

Q: What are the keys to being a quality instructor?

A: You must have respect and honesty. You must respect yourself and have the respect of your students. [For the most part], this new generation does not have respect and they do not have any mentors. This [phenomenon] has been growing and growing for the last 10 years. For me, getting or earning respect is more satisfying than [earning] money. I am more fulfilled with respect than with money. [Beyond that], I want to create an aura around myself. That is what I want. When we play around after we shot the pictures [for this story], that is what I love. Sometimes we'll do that at my house, and that is my fulfillment.

Q: Do you treat all students the same?

A: All students have to be treated the same, although everyone is on a different mission; everyone needs to feel important. With [Eduardo] Telles, I am like a father. I tell him to listen up. I need to show the exact same level of love and attention for everyone. Everyone has to be the same; otherwise, a student is going to feel dead.

Q: As an instructor, you also play different roles.

A: Yes, I may have to be the funny guy who breaks the ice. If someone is having a bad day, maybe I can bring something funny into the air. It is my obligation to be a comedian. My school is like therapy. I might be a doctor, a friend or a psychiatrist. If I miss [in my role as various functions], it can end up to be a big challenge for them to train every day. If you want a student to go beyond four years of training, he has to want to come to school and train because it's fun and the professor makes jokes and does something new. I need to be creative and take a guy under my wing if necessary. When they line up and I make a joke, they will forget about their problems. After 90 minutes of class, they will go away happy. My school is the hospital, but there is no need for Prozac or medicine. Besides, jiu-jitsu in America is expensive. I need to have the ability and sensibility to look in their faces and see what they need and keep them happy. I want to help them find their fulfillment. I also want to be their friend and listen to them.

> "I wanted to be a champion and be recognized as a champion. Then, when I had the belt and the titles, I said there has to be something else. And that turned out to be a mentor, a "psychologist" and a friend [to my students]."

Q: Do you enjoy being an instructor?

A: Oh, yes. It keeps me alive. There are times when I am tired when I have to teach. I look at the same gi that I have been wearing for 30 years, and I may [have to] drag myself to the car. But as soon as I see my students' eyes filled with respect and love ... that is my motivation.

Q: When your students do well in competition, you have to be ecstatic.

A: When I see the kids successful, that is way beyond the [happiness I could achieve if I had won the] lottery. If I win the lottery, that [fulfills a] material desire. I could then go buy a house, car or go around the world, but that [only provides] emptiness. For some, the only way they can get more fulfilled is through more money. Many coaches want to be successful and make money, but my fulfillment has to be more.

Q: Are you still learning?

A: I am still learning. To this day, it [my knowledge] keeps growing. For example, there are days when Andre [Galvao], Telles, Fernando [Terere] and Jacson Correia will want to show me something. In some cases, I have not even thought about this [type of technique]. So, that keeps me going, and this type of thing never stops.

Q: As an instructor, what is the greatest satisfaction you have?

A: When someone says that he is a student of Carlos Valente or "I'm from professor Carlos Valente." Someone came over to me during the Pan-

American Games and wanted to take a picture with me. He said, "I know who you are." That means more to me than money.

Q: Are you enjoying life and teaching?

A: Although I am at an old age, I am still having fun more than ever. I have got these names around me and they could be with anyone, but they chose me. That makes me young. They are 21, 28 and 29 and it makes me young to be around them every day. They have got some energy. Every day at the house we have a barbecue, we laugh and we go. Plus, they talk to me like I was their age. When they need to talk to an adult, they talk to me. This [way of life] is better than [living in] Beverly Hills. They saw me and they want to be here. When I visit Rickson, I walk in, and he gives a kiss. I got what I wanted. I have respect. I am recognized. It is not the money.

Q: Describe your personality.

A: When you meet me, I might be the funniest guy you have met. But I also have something to say. I could tell you stories to keep you occupied for one month or three months. I am also open-minded.

Q: How is it that you produce so many outstanding jiu-jitsu competitors?

A: Very simple. What makes these guys so good? They trust me. I have the ability [to get them to trust me]. When they trust me, the doors are open for them to listen to what I say and this gives me the opportunity to teach what I have to teach and to say what I have to say.

Q: You had a role in the UFC that some may not know about.

A: In 1993, I was an assistant director and helped to coordinate everything for the fighters.

Q: What impact has the UFC had on the grappling world?

A: It's just been incredible, and it has opened the door for all of us. It's enabled us to make a living in America. If we didn't have the UFC, we could not open a school and get a good reaction [from the public].

Q: What are some of the advantages of being an instructor?

A: First, let me say that this is a very unique profession. There are not many professions that give you so many connections or opportunities to meet people. It's like I have bridges [that take me to meet] many new people. As an instructor, it's almost like I'm a diplomat. I get to know people all over the world. I get to know police officers, dentists. It is tremendous.

Q: Would you change anything in your life?

A: Not at all. When I was young, I wanted to get into jiu-jitsu and then teach. I had that desire from an early age. Spending time in the military enabled me to get this far. It [the experience of being in the military] provided more discipline and boom. This is what I wanted.

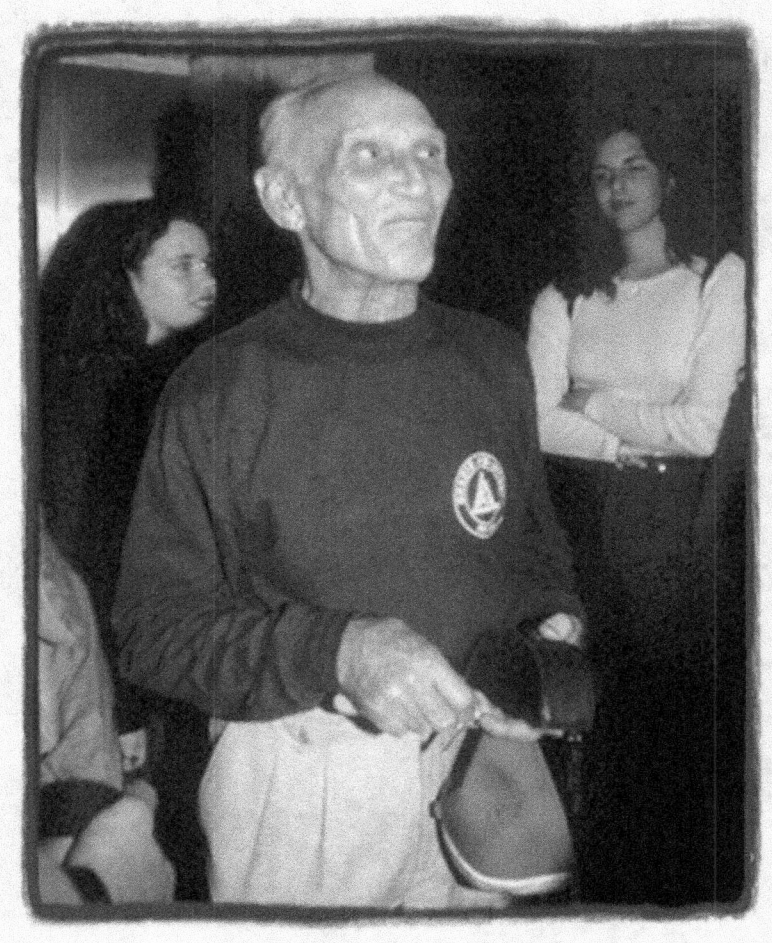

“Jiu-Jitsu is like a philosophy. It helps me learn how to face life.”
~ Helio Gracie ~

ANDRE GALVAO

HEART FOR THE FIGHT

BORN ON SEPTEMBER 29, 1982 IN SAO PAULO, BRAZIL, ANDRE GALVAO INITIATED HIS MARTIAL ARTS TRAINING WHILE STILL A CHILD. IT WAS THROUGH HIS OLDEST BROTHER THAT GALVAO GOT TO KNOW THE ART OF BRAZILIAN JIU JITSU WHEN HE WAS 16. HE STARTED HIS TRAINING WITH LUIS CARLOS DAGMAR "CARECA," A STUDENT OF THE ILLUSTRIOUS MASTER OSVALDO ALVES. IT WAS IN HIS SECOND YEAR OF TRAINING THAT HE MET THE ONE PERSON WHO WOULD BECOME HIS TRUE MASTER AND INSPIRATION, FERNANDO AUGUSTO, ALSO KNOWN IN THE BRAZILIAN JIU JITSU COMMUNITY AS "TERERÉ,"

GALVAO ALWAYS HAS BEEN A AVID COMPETITOR AND UNLIKE MOST BJJ FIGHTERS, HE DEDICATED HIMSELF TO FIGHTING IN ALL TOURNAMENTS, NOT JUST THE MAJOR ONES. HE RELIED ON THIS TO KEEP IMPROVING HIS SKILL SET. ANDRE WON FOUR WORLD CHAMPIONSHIPS IN A ROW, FROM BLUE BELT TO BLACK BELT (2002, 2003, 2004, 2005) WINING HIS WEIGHT AND THE OPEN WEIGHT CLASSES TWO YEARS IN A ROW IN THE PURPLE BELT DIVISION AND BROWN BELT DIVISION (2003 AND 2004). IN 2008, ANDRE GALVAO JOINED THE WORLD OF MIXED MARTIAL ARTS (MMA), OBTAINING A SUBMISSION VICTORY OVER JEREMIAH METCALF.

THAT SAME YEAR, GALVAO JOINED RAMON LEMOS TO FORM A NEW JIU JITSU TEAM KNOWN AS "ATOS" – MEANING "ACTS." THE TEAM HAS HAD TREMENDOUS SUCCESS IN THE BLACK BELT DIVISIONS WITH SEVERAL COMPETITORS WINNING WORLD CHAMPIONSHIPS, THE PAN AMS, AND THE JIU JITSU PRO CUP IN ABU DHABI.

Q: How long have you been practicing Jiu Jitsu?

A: I have been training in Brazilian Jiu Jitsu for more than 14 years and I can say that those have been the best years of my life, not only for the great success that I have in the sport but also for the great people I have met during this amazing journey. I started to train first with Luiz Carlos Dagmar. Later on, I trained for about eight months in Rio de Janeiro directly with Osvaldo Alves.

Q: When did you begin training with Fernando Terere?

A: When I was a purple belt, my first instructor brought me to training with him. It was really an eye-opening experience for me to see that level of technique and mastery in the art of Jiu Jitsu. Fernando Terere is a very experienced fighter and talented teacher, and you get this when you train with him on a regular basis.

Q: It is true that you were training at judo, too?

A: Yes, I did, and to be honest I think that helped me in progressing in Jiu Jitsu the way I did. Both arts kind of grew on me in a very natural way and the specific skills from one helped me to improve the game in the other. Obviously, I decided to stick with Jiu Jitsu.

> **"Everything is based on hard work. Nothing comes easy or is free. We need to follow our dreams and believe in ourselves."**

Q: Is your Jiu Jitsu game evolving constantly?

A: Absolutely. The art of Jiu Jitsu never stops evolving. The art is a very old Martial Art but there is constant research and evolution on the technical level that makes the sport very challenging: new combinations, new positions, new approaches to old techniques, etc. Jiu Jitsu is an art that is based on you body type and you should learn what really fits you.

Q: What is the most important quality for a new Jiu Jitsu student to have?

A: In my opinion, the new student needs to have dedication and needs to be interested in learning everything he/she can. Later on, the student should understand that the art of Jiu Jitsu has a lot to do with the body type that the student has. Therefore, he or she will have to study what techniques fit better to his/her body type and start working on them. It is a self-discovery process that one has to be fully aware of to be successful in the art.

Q: Is it necessary to fight MMA matches to achieve good self-defense skills?

A: No. MMA is a combat sport and the art of Jiu Jitsu is a Martial Art. You can practice Jiu Jitsu as a sport but it is more than that. I think you just need to train your body for specific situations. If you train for self-defense, you will be able to protect yourself, but if you always train with the sport mentality, that doesn't mean you can face a real self-defense situation successfully. You need to drill the specific techniques to fix them inside your body, in your memory muscles. When you fight in MMA, you face another athlete; in the street, you face an aggressor. These are two different situations. Even if they seem similar because fighting is all those two are about, the truth is that they are two different worlds.

Q: What motivated you to train for so many years?

A: The truth is that I love what I do and I love the art and sport of Jiu Jitsu. I love the training and I enjoy the teaching very much. Jiu Jitsu is pretty much who and what I am and my life evolves around it. Its philosophy doesn't end on the mat but can be used in many other areas of our life. For me, the secret is to keep doing it, to not stop even if you feel tired and get the sense you've reached a plateau. Keep pushing forward ... then all of a sudden, thing click again and you find yourself in a higher level of proficiency.

Q: How do you prepare yourself before a fight?

A: When preparing for a fight, I focus on the task at hand. I train very hard and rest as much as I can. I always allocate six to nine solid weeks for training and I adjust my training according to the time left for the fight. I always try to avoid injuries and calculate the intensity of the training depending on the given week of the preparation cycle. The day before the fight, I like to hang out with my family watching a good movie. The mind needs to relax and get distracted a little ... even if it is just for 24 hours.

Q: Who has been you biggest inspirations?

A: For me, God is my main inspiration, because he is who gave us life and that is what I believe in. On another level, I like to watch films of great athletes like Michael Jordan, Pele, Maradona, etc. They reached their level by pushing themselves beyond their limits and spent a lot of time training hard. Everything is based on hard work. Nothing comes easy or is free. We need to follow our dreams and believe in ourselves. Without dreams to reach for, we are nothing. I know that dedication, discipline, willpower, never giving up in the hard times on the mat and in life, faith, and focus are the keys for success in life and I try to stick to those and make them part of my daily life as much as I can.

Q: Do you think fighters should cross-train or just do Jiu Jitsu?

A: Jiu Jitsu is very complex. You need to know a little bit of the other grappling systems like Judo, Wrestling, Sambo, etc., and this will help you to learn more and be good in any situation regardless of the technical environment. Also, the physical training is really important so you have to select a good trainer who helps you to build a strong conditioning base.

Q: What is you advice for strength and conditioning training?

A: Well, you need to create a solid base for strength and endurance. If you hit the weights, make sure you save time for your Jiu Jitsu, which means that you need to focus on the exercises that really help you. Don't waste time doing a lot of exercises ... focus on power exercises and move on. I see many fighters wasting too much time doing other things in the gym instead of focusing on those that eventually will make them stronger. Find a good strength and conditioning coach who understands about Jiu Jitsu. After all, you wouldn't want a mechanic telling you how to draw blood if you are a nurse, right?

Q: You have developed a personal training system; would you describe it?

A: The main idea is the principle of "drilling." Through proper drilling training, you get to develop the physical attributes that you need to fight or to protect yourself. Obviously, there are different intensity levels in the drills but they are the foundation for everything. I have developed one kind of drill system for before, between, and after the tournaments that enhance the competitor's level substantially.

Just think of all the cognitive skills required to become a world-class Jiu Jitsu champion – hundreds of offensive and defensive techniques – study opponent's games and strategies, etc. Although it is true that the practitioner has to deal with staggering amounts of technical information, the real "key" is not in his/her intelligence to dissect these endless amount of combinations. Scientists have discovered that emotions, which are often

> **"Nobody is talented enough to not have to work hard. Talent comes from intuition to react correctly, and reliable intuition comes from practice."**

dismissed as unreliable, reflect a vast amount of information processing. Our feelings are capable of responding to things we are not even aware of, even noticing details we don't register on a conscious level. You have to rely on your feelings in fighting and not on your analytical intelligence. Expertise requires a lot of effort and repetition. This is because it takes time to train our feelings, to put these useful techniques into the brain. Before we can find the right technique when the opening is there, we need to train many options and technical possibilities. At the end, it looks easy only because we have worked on it very hard. Nobody is talented enough to not have to work hard. Talent comes from intuition to react correctly, and reliable intuition comes from practice. As a teacher, you can teach a student how to pass the guard, but only if he wants to learn it. After all, deliberate practice makes perfect.

Q: What are your plans for the future?

A: I want to grow my association in the U.S., helping my team to get better and successful. I want to show my system to as many people I can. I think I have gathered a substantial amount of Jiu Jitsu knowledge and experience and want to share it in the United States to improve the competitors' level and also to help normal practitioners develop solid confidence in their abilities.

Q: What does Jiu Jitsu mean to you?

A: For me, Jiu Jitsu is the best system in the world ... that is why I keep doing it. It fits me perfectly. I think if you know and understand how the Jiu Jitsu principles of leverage work in combat, you will never stop because you will fall in love with the art. It doesn't matter how old you are, Jiu Jitsu if properly trained, is beneficial for everybody… because you actually use the opponent's energy and body to make the techniques work.